Advance

Teacher's

D0714932

New
Headway

LEARNING RESOU
READING COLLEGE
K

English Course

John and Liz Soars
Mike Sayer

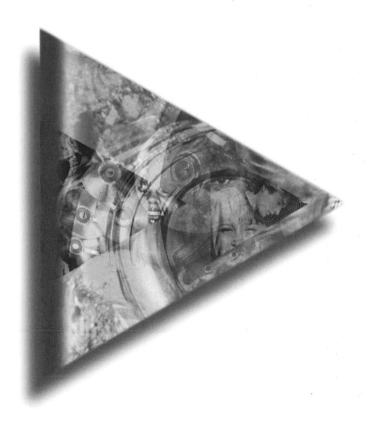

OXFORD
UNIVERSITY PRESS

OXFORD
UNIVERSITY PRESS

Great Clarendon Street, Oxford OX2 6DP

Oxford University Press is a department of the University of Oxford.
It furthers the University's objective of excellence in research, scholarship,
and education by publishing worldwide in

Oxford New York

Auckland Bangkok Buenos Aires Cape Town Chennai
Dar es Salaam Delhi Hong Kong Istanbul Karachi Kolkata
Kuala Lumpur Madrid Melbourne Mexico City Mumbai Nairobi
São Paulo Shanghai Taipei Tokyo Toronto

Oxford and Oxford English are registered trade marks of
Oxford University Press in the UK and in certain other countries

© Oxford University Press 2003

The moral rights of the author have been asserted

Database right Oxford University Press (maker)

First published 2003

ISBN 0 19 436931 5

Printed and bound by Grafiasa S.A. in Portugal

Acknowledgements

**The authors and publisher are grateful to those who have given
permission to reproduce the following extracts and adaptations of
copyright material:**

p119 *Englishman In New York*. Words and Music by Sting © 1987.
Reproduced by permission of G M Sumner/EMI Music Publishing Ltd,
London WC2H 0QY.
p133 *Mary C. Brown And The Hollywood Sign* by D. Previn Universal/MCA
100%. Reproduced by permission of Music Sales Limited.
p135 *When You Are Old And Grey* by Tom Lehrer © 1953 Tom Lehrer.
Reproduced by permission.
p140 *Father and Son* by Cat Stevens. Reproduced by permission of Cat
Music Limited.

Photography by:
Alamy p133 (Hollywood sign)

Photocopiable pages designed by Amanda Hockin

Contents

New Headway Advanced

Introduction

PHOTOCOPIABLE MATERIALS

Photocopiable materials and Extra ideas

Introduction

New Headway Advanced

Description of the course

The aims of *New Headway Advanced* are as follows:

- to encourage students to analyse the systems of language in use
- to extend their range of vocabulary
- to expose them to a variety of challenging and interesting text-types in reading and listening activities
- to stimulate them to give their own opinions and participate in discussions and roleplays
- to develop their writing skills in a variety of genres.

It provides approximately 120 hours' work, that is ten hours per unit. This has to remain a somewhat artificial calculation, as teachers can expand activities and supplement areas with topical material of interest to their particular students. The Workbook is an important component, and it contains not only further practice of the language areas dealt with in the Student's Book, but also extra related grammar and vocabulary exercises. There is also a Teacher's Resource Book, with photocopiable exercises for further grammar, vocabulary, and skills work.

Advanced learners

Students at this level can feel a certain amount of justifiable pride in their achievement. They have probably been studying for many years, and should have benefited from the wisdom of a variety of teachers. They will have had the same grammatical areas explained to them over and over again. They can cope with most text-types, understand films, literature, and newspapers, and should be able to express themselves with an impressive fluency.

However, there can also be a degree of frustration for them, because they know that their abilities are far from those of the native speaker, a goal which very few language learners achieve. At lower levels, progress can be rapid and discernible, but at the advanced level the opposite is the case. For some advanced students, their language production abilities have ossified. They might well acquire new vocabulary, but by and large they manage to avoid grammatical areas they are unsure of. By a process of circumlocution, they can restrict themselves to tried and tested phrases.

In *New Headway Advanced*, students have the knowledge they possess confirmed via all kinds of receptive and productive activities and revision exercises. They are then challenged to explore grammatical areas, some of which they will be studying in more depth than at lower levels, and some of which they might not have encountered before. Examples of the first are modal verbs with their rich subtleties and shades of meaning, the tense system with the dual aspects of perfect and continuous, and the wide variety of linking devices. Examples of the second are ellipsis, discourse markers, and ways of adding emphasis.

Advanced teachers

Many teachers, both native and non-native, are reluctant to teach advanced classes. They can feel that their own knowledge of the grammar is inadequate to deal with students' questions, or that the students will know more than they do themselves. These are both understandable and possible situations. Nothing can make a teacher feel more confident than possessing a profound knowledge of the language. In *New Headway Advanced*, the Grammar Reference section at the back of the book provides essential rules of form and use, and compares and contrasts areas that are easily confused. It is strongly recommended that you read these pages in preparation for the lesson. In addition there are notes on the language input in each unit of the Teacher's Book. For all exercises, answers are provided, and where appropriate there is also an explanation of why this is the answer. Background information is provided on people, places, and events to equip the teacher with ways to answer the students' questions.

Another fear of advanced teachers is that they will run out of material. Advanced students can get through material at an alarming rate, leaving the teacher wondering what to do next. The Teacher's Book contains photocopiable materials with extra ideas and songs, as well as Stop and check revision tests and progress tests. The Workbook contains a comprehensive range of supplementary exercises on grammar and vocabulary and further listening exercises. The Teacher's Resource Book provides photocopiable games and activities to supplement the main course material. There is also a teacher's website with additional materials for teachers: **www.oup.com/elt/teacher/headway**, and a student's site with interactive practice exercises for students: **www.oup.com/elt/headway**.

Don't forget that a lot of your material – articles to read, videos to watch, subjects to debate – will come from topical sources. At all levels, but particularly at advanced level, you need to be aware of your students' interests and bring relevant supplementary material to your lessons.

The organization of the course

Each unit in *New Headway Advanced* has the following components, although not always in the same order.

- **Starter**
  This is to launch the topic of the unit. It can last a short while or longer, depending on the interests of your students.

- **Reading**
  The texts are from a range of sources, all authentic. Some are taken from literature, magazine interviews, tabloid and broadsheet newspapers, and reference books. There is often some vocabulary work that follows on from the text, and some *What do you think?* questions to provoke discussion. If you sense that your class is particularly interested in a certain subject, this is your cue to research some further material.

- **Listening**
  The listening passages include authentic interviews and radio programmes, and an extract from a play. Some of the people are quite famous, some are experts in their own fields.

- **Speaking**
  Speaking activities are threaded throughout the units. There are discussions, roleplays, simulations, and a maze.

- **Language focus**
  This can either be done from the book, as is described in the Student's Book, or you can decide to do the first part with students working in pairs or small groups. The advantage of this second approach is that all students are working, not just one or two who happen to answer the questions. There are suggestions in the Teacher's Book notes on how to organize this.

- **Vocabulary**
  There is work on synonyms and antonyms, phrasal verbs, talking about statistics, homonyms, homophones, homographs, metaphors, and idioms.

- **The last word**
  These activities tend to work on the spoken language, looking for example at accents in English, and word linking. Other examples include exercises on tags and replies, clichés, responding to news, being sarcastic, and softening the message.

- **Writing**
  The writing syllabus is at the back of the book. The writing tasks are linked to the units by theme and language content. They are cued at the end of each Student's Book unit, but can be incorporated at any time to suit you and your students.

The Grammar Reference section

This can be used in a variety of ways.

- If it is not too long, you can refer to it in the lesson as you are doing the Language focus. The advantage is that students are already beginning to think about the area, and they are ready to read a deeper analysis. You can direct their attention to salient points.

- You can ask students to study it at home before they do Workbook exercises for homework. The advantage is that they will give it more time, though you have no way of knowing how much they have understood.

- You can ask students to read the relevant section *before* you deal with it in class. The advantage here is that students will be more prepared for the classroom lesson.

Finally!

New Headway Advanced is, like all similar course books, intended to save you time. At advanced level it can be very difficult, and require a lot of experience, to devise your own syllabus, find all your own material, and make it all cohere. So use the book as you wish. Change the order of activities. Supplement with your own material. Listen to your students' requests. Above all, make sure you control the course book. Try not to let it control you. It is a tool for you to use as much and in whatever way you want to.

1

Avoiding repetition
Describing nationalities
British and American English

Our land is your land!

Introduction to the unit

The theme of this unit is immigration. The main reading texts are about immigrants arriving at Ellis Island in the United States in the early twentieth century, and the main listening text is an interview with two Asian brothers who emigrated to Britain, and became successful businessmen.

Language aims

Avoiding repetition   This unit looks at two grammatical ways of avoiding repetition when speaking. The first one, *Missing words out*, looks at how English abbreviates sentences after the auxiliary or modal verb to avoid repeating information that is known or has just been said. This concept is hardly new to students, as *Are you tired? Yes, I am* is something taught at beginner level, and all languages miss words out to avoid repetition in a comparable way. The problem at higher levels is in getting the form right. The choice of form is dictated by tense or time, and by context.

> **WATCH OUT FOR ...**
> **Form and meaning**
> To work out which auxiliary or modal to use, students must:
> • know their tenses and which auxiliaries go with them: *'I love cheese.' 'So do I.'*
> • reconstruct from the context: *'Take care!' 'I will.'*
> • know the 'one tense back' rule when using hypothesis: *I wish you hadn't.*

To help students as they work out which forms to use in the explanation and practice exercises, use check questions such as *What is the speaker trying to say in this context? What tense is being used? What form do we use after wish, if?*, etc.

The second way of avoiding repetition, *Reduced infinitives*, is easier to grasp and manipulate. The idea of ending a sentence with *to* may be alien to speakers of many other languages, and the key problem with these forms is that students may well avoid using them because of a feeling that they sound wrong.

Grammar Reference 1.1 and 1.2 on SB p147 looks at how auxiliaries are used to avoid repetition, and at reduced infinitives. It is a good idea to read this section carefully before teaching the grammatical section of this unit.

Vocabulary   The *Vocabulary* section looks at words to describe nationalities. There is also work on guessing the meaning of vocabulary in the reading section, and on researching synonyms in context in the *Language Focus* section.

The last word   This section looks at differences in vocabulary between American and British English.

Notes on the unit

STARTER (SB p7)

1   Ask students to work in pairs to discuss what they know about these famous people. You could discuss one as an example to get them started. Conduct a brief whole-class feedback, and find out what students know. Point out that all these people emigrated from their country of birth. (Note: *to emigrate*

means to leave your country of birth, and *to immigrate* means to arrive and live in a new country – so an emigrant leaves, and an immigrant arrives.)

2 Ask students in pairs to match the people to the countries.

Answers
1 Al Capone: born in Italy, died in the United States (there is some dispute as to whether he was born in Brooklyn in the US, as he claimed)
2 Mother Teresa: born in Macedonia, died in India
3 Van Gogh: born in the Netherlands, died in France
4 Karl Marx: born in Germany, died in England
5 Martina Navratilova: born in the Czech Republic (Czechoslovakia at the time), lives in the United States
6 Bob Marley: born in Jamaica, died in the United States
7 Nicole Kidman: born in Hawaii but grew up in Australia, lives in the United States
8 Prince Philip: born in Greece, lives in England

3 In small groups, or as a class if your class is not too large, ask students if they can explain why any of the people emigrated.

Answers
The answers to this question are contained in the biographies below.

BACKGROUND NOTE
Al Capone (1899–1947)
Al Capone was born in 1899 in Italy, though there is some dispute as to whether he was born in Brooklyn, New York. His family were economic migrants to the US. He became notorious as a gangster in Chicago in the 1920s and 1930s.
Mother Teresa (1910–1997)
Agnes Goxha Bojaxhin was born in Skopje, Macedonia. She joined the Sisters of Loreto, an Irish community of nuns, who sent her to a mission in Calcutta in 1928. She spent the rest of her life helping the poor in India. She was awarded the Nobel Peace Prize in 1979.
Vincent Van Gogh (1853–1890)
The artist Vincent Van Gogh was born in the Netherlands, and his early work represented Dutch peasant life in dark, sombre colours. In 1886, he went to live in Paris, to join his brother, Theo, then to Arles in France, where he wanted to form an artist's colony. He shot himself in 1890.
Karl Marx (1818–1883)
Marx was an economist and social philosopher who was born in Germany in 1818. He published the Communist Manifesto with his friend Friedrich Engels in 1848. In 1850, he was expelled from Germany. He spent the rest of his life in London, where he wrote *Das Kapital*. He was buried in Highgate cemetery in London.

Martina Navratilova (1954–)
One of the most successful tennis players ever, Navratilova was born in communist Czechoslovakia. In 1975, she defected to the United States and became a US citizen. She won 13 Grand Slam titles in her career, including seven Wimbledon singles titles.
Bob Marley (1947–1981)
Robert Nesta Marley was born in Jamaica, and grew up in the capital, Kingston. He became the most famous reggae musician of his time. He moved to the US initially to join his mother, and later to escape political violence in Jamaica. He died of cancer in Miami, Florida in 1981.
Nicole Kidman (1967–)
Nicole Kidman was actually born in Hawaii, but she was brought up in Sydney, Australia. Following the success of the film *Dead Calm* in 1989, she moved to the United States to further her film career. She is now a major Hollywood film star.
Prince Philip (1921–)
Consort to the Queen of England, Prince Philip was born in Corfu, Greece. The Prince and his family were evacuated from Greece by a British warship following a change of government. He went to school in Britain, and married the then Princess Elizabeth in 1947.

READING AND SPEAKING (SB p8)

The American dream

The first two exercises of this section are designed to find out what students know about Ellis Island, and to create interest in the topic of immigration.

1 Ask students in pairs to look at the photographs and discuss the significance of what they can identify.

Answers
The Statue of Liberty on Liberty Island: the symbol of the American dream of freedom and opportunity.
Ellis Island: the small island on the left between the Statue of Liberty and the mainland. This used to be the main administrative centre where would-be immigrants to the US were assessed.
The New York skyline: in the background. The Twin Towers of the World Trade Center are noticeable by their absence. They once stood right in the middle of the Manhattan skyscrapers.

2 Ask students to read the introduction and choose the numbers they think are correct. Let them check in pairs, before discussing the questions as a class.

Answers
1 1 12   2 40%   3 5,000

2 Almost all answers are possible, but countries from which many immigrants came include Ireland, Italy, Russia, Germany, Eastern Europe. Many were Jewish.

3 It symbolizes freedom and opportunity. It was the place through which most immigrants entered the United States. On leaving this place and being accepted as immigrants, people must have felt free and full of hope.

3 Note that this extract was written by a British author in the early twentieth century, so the language is literary and rich in style. Let students use a dictionary to check unknown words. Alternatively, in the feedback, ask them to point out examples of literary use, and explain the meaning of these phrases. Key examples you may need to explain are:

It chanced to be = it happened by chance
proved inadequate = turned out to be / was found to be not good enough
It was choked with = it was full of
the long procession files = the long queue of people moves slowly

> **BACKGROUND NOTE**
> **H G Wells (1866–1946)**
> Herbert George Wells was an English author, famous for writing science fiction fantasies such as *The Time Machine*, *The Invisible Man*, and *The Shape of Things to Come*.

Ask students to read the extract and answer the questions. Let them discuss the answers in pairs before checking with the whole class.

Answers
1 A filter is something which a substance has to pass through, for example a coffee filter or an air filter. It holds back solid material or impurities, allowing what the user wants to come through. In the same way, metaphorically, Ellis Island 'filters' people, preventing people they don't want from entering the country.
2 Key phrases and images include: *choked with*, *All day long*, *the long procession files*, *stretch over three miles*, *a cordon of close-marching people round London*, *populate a new Boston.*
He also uses repetition to illustrate the numbers – listing countries, grouping *men, women, children, dirt ... bags* then *bundles, trunks ... boxes*, repeating words such as *long, procession, step, past.*
3 They had to stand in long queues all day long. The place was very crowded. They had to carry all their belongings with them. The people were dirty – there were probably no washing facilities. They were checked by many examiners, as well as clerks and medical officers.
4 **Sample answers:** a highly-populated United States, the 'melting pot', a country made up of people with diverse cultural backgrounds.

4 This is a jigsaw reading. It requires careful management.

If you have a small class, say of 13, think about mixing the students. Point at each student, giving them a letter, ABC, ABC, ABC, ABCA. Then ask them to stand up, and move to sit with students with the same letter. It is a good idea to get students sitting in a circle facing each other. In their new groups, ask them to read about their person and discuss the questions.

If you have a large class, say of 27, divide the students into groups of approximately 4. It doesn't matter if you have odd numbers – with 27, you would have six groups of four, and one of three. Ask three of the groups to read about the Russian girl, two to read about the German boy, and two to read about the Polish baby.

Ask students to discuss the questions in their groups.

Monitor the activity very carefully, and make sure students have all the answers to their questions before moving on to the next activity.

Answers (do not go through these answers until the students have done activity 5)
The Russian girl (text A)
1 William Williams Papers, an Ellis Island commissioner. A commissioner was someone who interviewed and selected new arrivals.
2 The Russian girl has arrived to marry her childhood sweetheart, who already lives in the US. However, he doesn't want to marry her now. She cannot enter the country unless he marries her or she has a job. If she returns to Russia, her family will laugh at her.
3 The commissioners are trying to decide what to do with the girl. They treat her in a detached way, describing her as 'an interesting and puzzling case', but they are keen to help her.
4 She is from a farming family in moderate circumstances (a euphemism for quite poor). She is clean, intelligent-looking, and strong so she was probably brought up well with enough to eat. She has come to America to get married, and going home would bring shame on her, so the morality of the family is that of a simple peasant family of the period.
5 No, but it seems that the commissioner is trying his best to bring about a happy ending.

The German boy (text B)
1 Arnold Weiss, a German Jewish boy of 13 who was an immigrant at Ellis Island.
2 His mother must take a test for reading, and she is illiterate.
3 The commissioners are carrying out the reading test. They treat the immigrants in an officious way.
4 They are German and Jewish. It seems that the boy has come to America with much of his family – two uncles and an aunt are mentioned. One uncle is a pharmacist. His father is not mentioned, so maybe the boy has lost his father. His mother is illiterate. They speak Yiddish.
5 Not sure – but probably.

The Polish baby (text C)
1 Henry Curran, an Ellis Island commissioner. A commissioner was someone who interviewed and selected new arrivals.
2 A Polish woman, returning to America by ship, has given birth to a baby. The woman has permission to enter the country, but the baby doesn't.
3 The commissioners are trying to find a way to admit the baby. They treat the mother with great kindness and have a lot of sympathy for her.
4 The Polish couple were admitted to the United States a year earlier. He works as a coal miner in Pennsylvania. She has had to return to Poland to visit her ill father.
5 Yes. The commissioner rules that the baby is an American citizen.

5 Divide the students into new groups. One way of doing this is to ask students to stand up and find two people who read the other texts and then sit down with them. If you have a large class or odd numbers, you may have to divide the students yourself to avoid chaos! Each group needs to have at least one person from group A, one from group B, and one from group C. However, it doesn't matter if you have, say, two from A, one from B, two from C. Keep the groups small so that all the students have a chance to speak.

Conduct a brief whole-class feedback to check the answers (see exercise 4 above).

Vocabulary work

6 Ask students to find the words and phrases in their text, then explain them to their partners from the other groups. Monitor carefully, and help any students with difficulties. Conduct a brief whole-class feedback to check the answers.

Answers
The Russian girl (text A)
1 clasps and unclasps
2 tears are welling in her eyes
3 her pride was ... wounded
4 everything is at a standstill
5 the tears brimming over
The German boy (text B)
1 called me aside
2 faced
3 certain
4 memorized
5 served the purpose
The Polish baby (text C)
1 trembling
2 that was a blow
3 I had another shot
4 hails from
5 I was stumped

What do you think?

The aim here is to get students talking, and give them an opportunity to express their opinion about the topic of the lesson. Unless you have a very small class, it is best done in small groups, which gives more students the opportunity to speak, and frees up the teacher to monitor, prompt, and note errors.

Divide students into groups of four, five, or six, then give them two or three minutes to read through the questions. Nominate one person in each group to be the discussion leader. It is their job to ask the questions, make sure everybody gets a chance to speak, and to decide when to move on from one question to the next.

Monitor the discussion groups equally, and prompt. You may wish to monitor for errors – walk from group to group, listen carefully, and note any interesting errors made by the students. After the feedback on the discussion, write these errors (anonymously) on the board and discuss them as a class.

Conduct a brief whole-class feedback on what the groups said, just to bring the activity to a close. Don't let this go on too long as there is a danger that students will merely be repeating what they said in the group discussion.

Sample answers
1 It is probably true. However, many other countries have a very diverse variety of immigrants. Brazil for example, has immigrants from Portugal, Spain, and other European countries, as well as from Africa; and Australia has immigrants from the UK and Ireland, as well as more recently from China, Vietnam, Greece, Italy, and former Yugoslavia.
2 *a refugee* = a person forced to leave their country, often because of political or religious persecution
   an illegal immigrant = a person who has come to live in a foreign country without permission
   an immigrant = a person who has come to live permanently in a foreign country
   an asylum seeker = a person who applies to live in a foreign country because they are trying to escape political or religious persecution
Sample reasons for emigrating:
unemployment; natural disasters (e.g. famine, drought); political instability; lack of economic opportunities; moving to a warmer climate; marrying someone from another country

LANGUAGE FOCUS (SB p12)

Avoiding repetition

The *Language Focus* section in each unit aims to get students to think analytically about language. It gives students clear examples of how the language works, then asks them questions or gives them tasks to do to guide them to an understanding of the language. This stage is backed up by controlled written exercises, such as gap-fills, to consolidate understanding, and sometimes by personalized speaking and / or writing activities to help students acquire the language through use.

Here are some suggested approaches to the *Language Focus*. Firstly, rather than teaching from the front of the class, let students work in pairs or threes to read through the initial explanation section. This frees you as a teacher to walk round the classroom, monitor understanding and answer questions. It also allows students to take responsibility for their learning, and to peer teach. Secondly, if the explanation section is divided into smaller sections, let students do one section and do the practice activities later in the unit before moving on to the next section. Thirdly, if you are short of class time, you could ask students to study the explanation section at home before the lesson. That way you can deal briefly with any queries, then devote classroom time to practice.

Don't forget to look at the *Language Aims* section on TB p6, which looks at problems students may have. You should also read the Grammar Reference on SB p147.

LANGUAGE INPUT

1 **Missing words out**
Start by writing on the board: *The girl nods and says 'I am.'* Ask students if they can remember the sentence from the text on p9 about the Russian girl. Ask them to say which words have been omitted and why. They may need to refer back to the text. Ask students in pairs to decide which words have been omitted in the other examples.

> **Answers**
> She told me to tidy up, but I already had (*tidied up*).
> Frank won the match. I didn't think he would (*win the match*).
> A present for me? How kind. You shouldn't have (*got / bought me a present*).

In the feedback, ask students how they worked out the answers. The answer is that they had to think about meaning and time. In other words, it is *had tidied up* because this had already happened before the order was given. *Would win* is necessary because this is future in the past, and *got / bought me a present* reflects the context of the previous comments.

2 **Reduced infinitives**
Ask students in pairs to read the explanation, then decide which words have been omitted.

> **Answers**
> ... She never learnt to (*read*).
> ... So one uncle said, 'Does she have to (*take a test for reading*)?'

In the feedback, check that students understand that the meaning is clear from the context, and that therefore there is no need to repeat the whole phrase.

3 **Synonyms in context**
Ask students in pairs to read the examples, then think of synonyms for the words. Brainstorm suggestions and write them on the board. The students should be able to think of more than one synonym.

> **Sample answers**
> *huge:* enormous, gigantic, vast
> *rich:* wealthy, affluent, prosperous, well-off
> *kill:* murder, assassinate, slaughter, massacre
> *injure:* hurt, harm, maim, wound
> *argument:* row, quarrel, squabble; debate, discussion

Refer students to Grammar Reference 1.1 and 1.2 on SB p147. See TB p6 for suggestions on how to approach this.

Missing words out

1 Read through the example as a class, and ask students why the answer is *couldn't*. Point out that they need to look carefully at the context to work out which word is needed. Ask students to complete the exercise. Let them check in pairs before playing the recording.

T 1.1 Play the recording so that students can check their answers. Note that sometimes there is more than one sample answer to the missing words in the sentence. You may need to debate and accept different answers. Ask students to justify their alternative answer.

Focus attention on the stress and intonation, then ask students to practise the conversations in pairs.

> **Answers and tapescript**
> 2 have / did
> 3 will
> 4 hadn't
> 5 haven't, will / 'm going to
> 6 does
> 7 wasn't / weren't
> 8 hadn't, would have
> 9 would
> 10 am / have
> 11 should / must / ought to
> 12 hadn't
> 13 wouldn't

14 might

15 would ('He *didn't!*' has a particular meaning of mock horror, and isn't appropriate here because the following comments express a lack of surprise.

T 1.1

1 I tried to repair my car, but I couldn't. I didn't have the right tools.

2 'You look awful. Why don't you see a doctor?'
   'I have. He just gave me some pills and told me to take things easy.'

3 'It's a long journey. Take care on the motorway.'
   'Don't worry. We will.'

4 I met your sister last night. She thought we'd met before, but we hadn't.

5 'Have you read this report?'
   'No, I haven't, but I will.'

6 The weather forecast said that it might rain this afternoon. If it does, we'll have to call off the tennis.

7 My car's being mended at the moment. If it wasn't, I'd give you a lift. Sorry.

8 I'm so glad you told Sue exactly what you thought of her, because if you hadn't, I certainly would have!

9 I got that job I applied for, so I was delighted. I really didn't think I would.

10 'Come on, John! It's time you were getting up!'
   'I am! I'll be down in a second.'

11 'I think I'll give Bob a ring.'
   'You should. You haven't been in touch with him for ages.'

12 I went to a party last night, but I wish I hadn't. It was awful.

13 My boyfriend insists on doing all the cooking, but I wish he wouldn't – it's inedible.

14 'Aren't you going to Portugal for your holidays?'
   'Well, we might, but we're still not sure.'

15 'Andy got drunk at Anne's party and started insulting everyone.'
   'He would! That's so typical. He's always doing that.'

2 Ask students in pairs to look at the pictures and prompts, and give them three or four minutes to think of questions to ask. Then give them five minutes to ask as many questions as they can.

3 Ask students to look at the expressions in the *Things in common* box. Check understanding by asking *Which expressions agree with a positive statement?* (the first two), and *Which expressions agree with a negative statement?* (the last three). Then ask them to look at the *Things different* box, and ask what they notice about the use of auxiliary verbs. Point out that we express a difference by using the auxiliary verb in the negative when it disagrees with an affirmative statement, and in the affirmative when it disagrees with a negative statement.

Ask students to prepare to tell the class what they have found out about their partner, using the expressions in

the boxes. Go round the class, and ask different students to make sentences.

Students might think this activity very easy. Insist that they use the full range of short answers, with the correct pronunciation, sentence stress, and intonation.

Reduced infinitives

4 Read through the example as a class, then ask students to complete the exercise. Let them check in pairs before playing the recording.

T 1.2 Play the recording so that students can check their answers. They could practise the conversations, mimicking the stress and intonation of the speakers on the recording. Note that, generally, the intonation rises on the verb, then falls on *to*.

Answers and tapescript

1 A Can you come round for a meal tonight?
   B Thanks very much. I'd love to.
2 A Did you post my letter?
   B Oh, I'm really sorry. I forgot to.
3 A I can't take you to the airport after all. Sorry.
   B But you agreed to!
4 A Was John surprised when he won?
   B He certainly was. He didn't expect to.
5 A Why did you slam the door in my face?
   B It was an accident. I really didn't mean to.
6 A You'll be able to enjoy yourself when the exams finish.
   B Don't worry. I intend to!

Synonyms in context

5 Read through the example as a class, then ask students to complete the exercise. Depending on how much you feel your students need to be stretched, you can either ask for one or two synonyms, or challenge them to find as many as possible. You could monitor and keep a note of which words they have found, and then write the remaining words from the answer key on the board (jumbled up). Students can then work out which sentences these words can be used in. Let them check in pairs or small groups before checking with the whole class.

Answers

1 faith / confidence / belief
2 talented / accomplished / proficient / capable / highly competent
3 convincing / compelling / forceful
4 mislead / delude / trick / deceive / fool
5 strategy / game plan
6 thorough / exhaustive / rigorous
7 irritates / frustrates / exasperates / bugs (informal)
8 essential / vital / crucial
9 risks

10 terrified / petrified / panic-stricken (*frightened and afraid are also synonyms, of course, but because this is a surprising contrast, it is more likely that the speaker will use a stronger adjective than scared to emphasize the contrast.)

6 Ask students in pairs or threes to think of synonyms and write sentences (point out that love, hate, talk and laugh and their synonyms should all be verbs). Alternatively, you could do this exercise as a dictionary and thesaurus group task. Divide students into five groups and provide each group with a dictionary and a thesaurus. Ask each group to research one of the words and find synonyms. After you have checked that their words are suitable synonyms, mix the students so that there is one student from each group in each of the new groups, and ask them to explain their words.

Another way to do this activity, especially if your students find it difficult, is to write some or all of the synonyms from the answer key on the board right at the start of the activity. Using their dictionaries, students must first find which words go with which key word in the coursebook, and then write sentences to illustrate the meaning.

Sample answers
friend
An *acquaintance* is someone you know but not very well.
A *colleague* is someone you work with, and a *classmate* is someone you know at school.
Mate is an informal word for friend, so we talk about my *best mate*, and *mates* that we go out with. We tell secrets to *close friends*, especially our *best friend*.
An *ally* is a friend of your country in war. Someone who is on your side in a personal battle is also an *ally*.
A *companion* is someone who provides you with company, for example on a journey.
love
If you really love something, then you *adore* it. I *adore* walking along beautiful, tropical beaches.
I'm very fond of my students.
I'm keen on football, skiing, diving. They are my hobbies.
If you *think the world of* someone, then you *have a lot of affection for* them. You think they are great.
If you *fancy* someone, you want to start a romantic relationship with them. If it's totally unrealistic, e.g., when a teenager has romantic feelings towards a much older person, then you can say *to have a crush on* someone.
hate
If you really, really hate something, then you *loathe*, or *detest* it. I *loathe* getting up in the morning.
I *can't stand* queuing, and I *can't bear* people who don't listen. Personally, I *have no time for* mobile phones.
Abhor is quite formal, e.g. *The minister said he abhorred all forms of racism.*
When you *despise* someone, you dislike them strongly because you have absolutely no respect for them.

talk
You *chat* or *have a chat with* friends. It's usually pretty informal. You *gossip about* what people are doing. People who like chatting a lot tend to *chatter* endlessly.
More seriously, you *have a conversation with* people.
You *talk things over* with a close friend if you have a problem, and you *have a word with* a colleague or your boss if you need to quickly tell them something important, usually in private.
Politicians *argue about* issues of the day, and academics *discuss* the latest research.
Children *whisper* when they are telling someone a secret that they don't want other people to hear.
Presidents *make speeches* when they want to be elected.
When people *ramble*, they talk about something in a very confused way, for a long time.
You *waffle* when you need to keep talking but don't really know what you're talking about, e.g. *I finished my speech five minutes early, but I managed to keep waffling on until the time was up.*
When you meet someone socially, you often *make small talk*, by discussing unimportant subjects such as the weather and everyday life.
laugh
Little girls *giggle* when they think something is funny, with their hands in front of their mouths.
Little boys *snigger* unpleasantly when they are *laughing at* someone who has done something they think is stupid.
A nice way of laughing is to *chuckle* – Father Christmas chuckles.
You *burst out laughing* when you suddenly laugh very loudly.
When you laugh so much that it starts to hurt, you are *in stitches*.

ADDITIONAL MATERIAL

Workbook Unit 1
These exercises could be done in class to give further practice, for homework, or in a later class as revision.
Exercises 1–3 Avoiding repetition

LISTENING AND SPEAKING (SB p14)

Two brothers from Kenya

This is a long, quite intensive listening activity. The tasks break down the listening into three bite-sized sections. The first two deal with comprehension. The third is very intensive, and asks students to pick out exact words from the recording. The brothers speak fluently and accurately, but with strong Indian accents, which may make understanding difficult for some students.

1 Ask students to look at the photograph and describe what is happening. Then ask them to read the newspaper extract and answer the questions.

2 Ask students to read through the questions in pairs, and discuss what they think the answers might be.

3 **T 1.3** Play the recording while students read the tapescript on SB p132. Ask students to listen for the answers to the questions in 2. The idea of letting students read and listen to part one is to ease them gently into the recording – to give them a chance to get used to Vijay's and Bhikhu's accent.

BACKGROUND NOTE
Features of the brothers' accent
The brothers speak fluent, accurate English. However, they have a strong Indian English accent. This is a result of a tenser articulation than British English, with vowels produced further forward, and of a variation in the way voiceless consonants such as /p/ and /t/, and alveolar consonants, /t/ and /d/, are pronounced. The intonation pattern is also different, notably the rise in pitch used to express emphasis.
You may wish to point out that English (with Indian English pronunciation) is spoken as a first language by many people of Indian origin, on the Indian subcontinent, in Britain, in the United States, and in Indian communities in east and south Africa.

---

4 Ask students to read the statements. Check that they understand the difference between *complement* (suit, combine well with), and *compliment* (praise). They are pronounced the same with stress on the first syllable.

   T 1.4 Play part two of the recording. This time students listen only. Ask students to decide whether the statements are true or false. Let them check in pairs and correct the false statements before checking with the whole class.

5 Ask students to read the sentences and guess what the missing words might be.

   T 1.5 Play part three of the recording and ask students to listen carefully for the words, but not to write yet. After playing the recording, ask students to fill in any words they can and check with a partner. Play the recording again, pausing after each sentence with missing words. Play and pause as many times as necessary until most if not all of the class have got the answers.

What do you think?

See TB p9 for suggestions on how to approach this.

- Asians make up about 4% of the British population. Of these, about one million are of Indian origin, half a million are Pakistani, and 200, 000 Bangladeshi.
The major reason why there is a large Asian minority in Britain is that the Indian subcontinent was, until 1946, part of the British Empire, so there are strong historical and cultural links between Britain and the subcontinent. In the 1950s and 1960s, people from the subcontinent were encouraged to come and live in Britain because of the labour shortage in the UK.
- Many British Asians are now third, fourth, or fifth generation British, and young Asians born and brought up in the UK often speak with the same accent or dialect as white British citizens. A reason why the brothers have retained their accent may be that they have strong family ties, and lived until their teenage years within a British Asian community abroad, where exposure to non-Asian British accents was less common.

VOCABULARY AND SPEAKING (SB p15)

Describing nationalities

1   Ask students in pairs to complete the chart. Encourage them to use a dictionary, and make sure they add their own country if it is not already in the table. If they use a dictionary, ask them to mark the stress on each word they write in the table. It is a good idea to copy the answers table onto an OHT or large sheet of A3 paper.

Answers
See table overleaf

2   **T 1.6**   Play the recording. Ask students to guess where the speakers are from and note what they say about their country and nationality. Let students check in pairs before checking with the whole class. You may need to play the recording twice. Note that even for advanced students, being able to recognize an accent is very difficult, so it is the clues in what the people say that will probably allow them to guess where the people come from.

Answers
1   **Eric – Canadian**: big, frozen, ice, up north, eskimos, red-coated policeman – but this is just a stereotype. Bilingual, 40% French-speaking, dispersed population with 90% living within 90 kilometres of the US border. US domination of culture – TV, sport. Inferiority complex relative to US. Europeans think they are American.
2   **Mary – Scottish** (Glaswegian): stereotype is miserable, mean, dour, unhappy with lot, proud, nationalistic, esp. in sport, anti-English. In truth, people have a generous spirit, but they can be pessimistic.

3   **Julia – Spanish**: stereotype is loud (which she thinks is because they all talk at the same time), disorganized (also well-deserved according to her), and lazy (which she doesn't think is true, as Spanish people now follow European timetables). Also sociable and outgoing (which she says is because they rarely do things on their own, and there are so many places to go out to, until late).
4   **Zoltan – Hungarian**: stereotype is that food is spicy, and that Hungary is all horses and plains. In truth, they use paprika but the food is not that hot, and one in five people live in Budapest, and of the rest, most live in towns.
5   **Rosemary – American**: seen by the British as loud and arrogant, but she thinks this is because the Americans rebelled against the British in the past. She says that while some Americans are narrow and arrogant, there are many who are aware of what goes on in the world.
6   **Tristan – English**: stereotype is cold, uptight, hypocritical and two-faced; nowadays also seen as yobbish, heavy drinkers, potentially violent.

T 1.6   See SB Tapescripts p133

3–4   Divide students into groups of three or four. Read through the example, then ask them to choose a few nationalities and describe them to each other. Ask students to describe their own nationality stereotype.

USEFUL PHRASES
They are supposed to be / have …
They come across as being …
They have a reputation for …
They give the impression of being …
I'd always thought of them as being …
Actually, I have found that …
It's just a myth because …
Judging from the (people) I've met, …
If the (people) I've met are anything to go by, …

ADDITIONAL MATERIAL

Workbook Unit 1
Exercise 4 Listening – Home from home?
Exercise 6 Vocabulary – Immigration and politics

Answers (Describing nationalities from p14)

Country	Adjective	Person	Nation	Language(s)
'Britain	'British	a 'Briton	the 'British	'English, Welsh, 'Gaelic
'Scotland	'Scottish (Scotch is only used for whisky)	a Scot	the 'Scottish	'English, 'Gaelic
France	French	a 'Frenchman / woman	the French	French, 'Breton, Basque
'Belgium	'Belgian	a 'Belgian	the 'Belgians	'Flemish, French
The 'Netherlands/ 'Holland	Dutch	a 'Dutchman / woman	the Dutch	Dutch
'Denmark	'Danish	a Dane	the 'Danish	'Danish
'Sweden	'Swedish	a Swede	the 'Swedes	'Swedish
'Poland	'Polish	a Pole	the Poles	'Polish
'Turkey	'Turkish	a Turk	the Turks	'Turkish
Spain	'Spanish	a 'Spaniard	the 'Spanish, 'Spaniards	'Spanish, Basque, Cata'lonian, Ca'stilian, Ga'lician
'Switzerland	Swiss	a Swiss	the Swiss	'German, French, I'talian, Ro'mansch
Argen'tina	Argen'tinian	an Argen'tinian	the Argen'tinians / the 'Argentines	'Spanish
Pe'ru	Pe'ruvian	a Pe'ruvian	the Pe'ruvians	'Spanish
'Iceland	Ice'landic	an 'Icelander	the Icelanders	Ice'landic
New 'Zealand	New 'Zealand	a New 'Zealander	the New 'Zealanders	'English
Afghani'stan	Af'ghani	an 'Afghan	the 'Afghans	'Farsi, 'Pashto

The list of languages spoken in these countries is not necessarily comprehensive. Many countries have other, less widely-spoken, languages and dialects in daily use ('living' languages) – in Afghanistan, for example, there are 45 living languages, and in Peru there are 92!

British and American English

1 **T 1.7** Ask students in pairs to listen and compare the two conversations.

Answers
The first conversation is British English. The differences are:

British	American
flat	apartment
block of flats	apartment building
the centre of town	downtown
Have you got	Do you have
a garden	a yard
No, we haven't	No, we don't
a car park	a parking lot
at the back	in the back

2 **T 1.8** Play the recording. Ask students in pairs to write the conversations in British English. You could do the first as a class to get them started.

3 **T 1.9** Play the recording. Ask students to compare their ideas. In the feedback, discuss how students' conversations were different from those on the recording. Ask different pairs to act out their conversations with British accents.

Answers and tapescript
1 A Have you got the time?
  B Yeah, it's five to four.
  A Did you say five past?
  B No, five *to* four.
2 A What are you going to do at the weekend?
  B The usual. Play football with my kids, and do a bit of gardening.
3 A Did you enjoy the match?
  B Yeah, it was great, but we had to queue for half an hour to get tickets.
4 A Did you have a good holiday?
  B Yeah, really good.
  A How long were you away?
  B Five days altogether. From Monday to Friday.
5 A Can you post this letter and parcel for me?
  B Of course.
  A And can you call at the off-licence and buy a six-pack of Stella and some crisps?
  B Is that all?

6 **A** Did you watch *The Birds* on telly last night?
  B I did, even though I've seen it twice before.
  A My third time. Isn't it just a terrific film?
  B It certainly is. One of my favourites.
7 **A** Have they brought the bill yet?
  B Yeah, they just have. But I can't read a thing. The lighting is so bad in here.
8 **A** Do we need to stop for petrol?
  B Yes, why not. I need to go to the loo anyway.

4 Ask students in pairs to use their dictionaries to find the British English equivalent of the words. Do they know any more American English words or expressions?

Answers

American English	British English
cellphone	mobile phone
garbage	rubbish
bathrobe	dressing gown
cookie	biscuit
drugstore	chemist's
closet	cupboard
truck	lorry
sidewalk	pavement
fall	autumn
elevator	lift
windshield	windscreen
pants	trousers

Other words and expressions

stove	cooker
eggplant	aubergine
candy	sweets
hood	bonnet (on car)
trunk	boot (on car)
vacation	holiday
subway	underground
movie theater	cinema
mean (of mood)	angry
cheap	mean (with money)

ADDITIONAL MATERIAL

Workbook Unit 1
Exercise 8 American versus British English – prepositions

DON'T FORGET!

Writing Unit 1
Formal and informal letters (SB p117)

Workbook Unit 1
Exercise 5 Pronunciation – Losing a syllable
Exercise 7 Verb + Preposition

Song
An Englishman in New York (TB p119)

2

Phrasal verbs
Tense review
Sounds and spelling

Never lost for words!

Introduction to the unit

The theme of this unit is literature and literary people. The main reading text is a newspaper article about a meeting with Iris Murdoch, the famous Anglo-Irish novelist. It deals with her loving relationship with her husband, and the fact that at the time of the interview she was losing her powers as a writer because she was in the early stages of Alzheimer's disease. The main listening text is an extract from *The Importance of being Earnest* by Oscar Wilde. There is an opportunity for students to act out a scene from the play.

Note that the life of Iris Murdoch has been made into a recent British film, called *Iris* (2001), and that a new film version of *The Importance of Being Earnest* was released in 2002. If your students are interested, and you have access to a good video library or shop, it might be worth seeking these films out.

Language aims

Tense review This unit features a tense review. The assumption is that students know forms and basic rules (though these are revised in the unit), but sometimes have real problems knowing how to choose the correct tense to use. Consequently, the emphasis is on contrasting different tenses and getting students to think about the difference in meaning between them. To this end, students are asked to consider time, aspect, meaning, the nature of the action, and the speaker's intention when speaking. These areas are explored in detail in the Grammar Reference on SB p148.

> **WATCH OUT FOR ...**
> **Aspect**
> To work out which tense to use, students must think about time and aspect.
> - Simple: completed and permanent
> - Continuous: in progress and temporary
> - Perfect: an action with a result relevant to a later time

Simple and continuous The simple aspect describes completed whole actions, whereas the continuous aspect describes activities that are in progress. Simple is about completion and permanence, whereas continuous is about duration and temporariness.

Problems students will have here arise from their first language being different. Present Simple forms are used in many Latin languages to express the future where English uses the Present Continuous. Present and past forms are often used in other languages to express the idea of the Present Perfect in English.

Try to avoid L1 interference problems by getting students to apply the aspect rules across tenses. Ask check questions such as *Is it completed or in progress? Is it temporary or permanent? Does it have a sense of duration?*

Perfect and non-perfect The perfect aspect expresses the idea that an action is completed some time before a later time, and produces a result relevant to that later time.

Many languages express the Present Perfect with a present tense: **I live here for ten years* or a past tense: **I never went to Paris.*

Getting students to think about how the perfect aspect changes meaning is a good way to help students to see its purpose. Again, ask check questions such as *Did it happen in the past? Do we know when? What's the result now?*

Active and passive Passive forms move the focus of attention from the subject of an active sentence to the object. Problems may arise because the passive is often used in English where the active, reflexive, or an impersonal construction might be used in other languages. English tends to avoid reflexives and impersonal constructions beginning with 'one'.

The Grammar Reference on SB p148 looks at time, aspect, and how to choose the correct tense. It is a good idea to read this carefully before teaching the grammatical section of this unit.

Vocabulary   The *Vocabulary* section looks at phrasal verbs. In particular, it explores the literal and metaphorical meanings of a number of phrasal verbs, and looks at whether they are separable or not. There is an explanation of the grammar of phrasal verbs in the Grammar Reference on SB p147.

The last word   This section looks at how English spelling is often not phonetic, and how the same spelling can be pronounced in different ways. There is an exercise on homophones.

Notes on the unit

STARTER (SB p17)

1   Check that students know the types of book. You may need to explain *Chick Lit* in more detail. *Chick* is an informal word for an attractive young woman. *Chick Lit* is usually written by a young woman about the lives of young women, in particular their relationships, and is often written in a trendy, vernacular style. It is now often conflated as *ChickLit* or *Chicklit*.

Ask students in pairs to match the extracts, covers, and types of book. You could do the first as an example to get them started. In the feedback, find out which were easiest and which most difficult to identify. Ask students if they have read any of the books, and which ones appeal to them.

Answers
The Lost Continent by Bill Bryson – a travel story
Hamlet by William Shakespeare – a classical drama
Fair Game by Elizabeth Young – a modern romance (Chick Lit)
A Time to Kill by John Grisham – a thriller
The Lord of the Rings by J. R. R. Tolkien – a fantasy
Cider with Rosie by Laurie Lee – an autobiography

2   Ask students to discuss the questions in pairs or threes. In the feedback, ask a few students to summarize briefly for the class what their partner has told them about their reading habits.

3   Ask which students have read books in English. Ask them to tell the class briefly what the book was about. Build up a list of reasons on the board why reading in English is a good idea.

Sample answers
Pleasurable: a lot of major fiction is written in English, and it is good to read it first-hand rather than through translation.
Improves your reading skills: a great way to build your passive vocabulary, and to revise words you have half-forgotten.
Motivating: it reminds you why you are learning English in the first place, helps develop a feel for how English speakers express themselves, opens a window onto the culture of English-speaking people

EXTENSION ACTIVITY
Reading for pleasure is a great way for advanced students to build their passive vocabulary. It can also be very motivating, as being able to read a 'real' book is proof that they are getting pretty good at English. So encourage your students to read. Here are some ideas.

Bring in four or five books that you like and think your students might like reading. They don't have to be 'heavy' – novels that are modern and not too long or literary are probably best to read in terms of building vocabulary. Tell the class briefly what they are about, and answer any questions. Then encourage students to go out and buy or borrow the book they liked best from your recommendations.

If your class are staying together for some time, you could choose one of your recommended books to read as a class. Ask everyone to buy the book. Set chapters to read for homework, and devote some class time each week to a discussion in which one student has to summarize the chapter, and you discuss the plot and themes as a class, and predict what will happen next.

Ask students to bring in a book in English which they know, summarize it, and recommend it for the class. You could do this as an occasional warmer before lessons. Encourage the class to recommend and lend each other books.

Ask students to write reviews or summaries of books they have read, which you can pin on the wall for other students to read.

READING AND SPEAKING (SB p18)

Losing her words

Lead in to set the scene and create interest by finding out what students know about Iris Murdoch. Bring in a couple of her novels, if you have any in the school library. Write *Iris Murdoch* on the board and ask if anyone can tell you anything about her. This may well be the case if someone has seen the recent film of her life. If they have never heard of her, tell them she was a famous English novelist, who died recently. Ask students what they would like to find out about her. You could build up some questions on the board, such as, *When was she born? What was her most successful novel? What did she write about?*

1   Divide students into AB pairs. Ask Students A to look at the biodata on SB p18, and Students B to look at a photocopy of the biodata on TB p120. Give them a few minutes to read their information, and to think of how to ask the necessary questions to complete their text. Then ask students in pairs to take it in turns to ask and answer questions to complete the missing information in their biodata.

Answers
1   Dublin
2   classics
3   a UN refugee camp
4   1954
5   the Booker Prize
6   'the unique strangeness of human beings'
7   English Literature
8   long, happy, if unusual
9   Alzheimer's Disease
10 Judi Dench and Kate Winslet

2   Read the introduction as a class, then ask students to look at the headings and answer the questions. Let them discuss in pairs, before discussing with the whole class.

> **BACKGROUND NOTE**
> *Alzheimer's* /ˈæltshaɪməz/ *disease* is one of several disorders that cause the gradual loss of brain cells, resulting in progressive mental deterioration. The disease was first described in 1906 by German physician Dr Alois Alzheimer. Although the disease was once considered rare, research has shown that it is the leading cause of dementia.

Answers
The first heading suggests that the house is occupied by writers or academics who are very disorganized. The second suggests that the occupants are comfortable in each other's company, and have probably lived together for a long time, and the third that work is not very productive at the moment. *Writer's block* is when a writer cannot find the will or inspiration to write.

3   Ask students to read the first part of the article and answer the questions. Let them discuss the answers in pairs before checking with the whole class. They will need dictionaries to check the vocabulary.

Answers
1   By a sign telling her to 'knock vigorously' and by John Bayley's cheery face at the window.
2   *chaotic, eccentric, dark*
3   Likeable. They are friendly in a cheery, eccentric way.

4 a *cheery* = lively, cheerful, friendly. The journalist sees this big, smiling face of a friendly old man, his jaw moving up and down with a mouthful of baked beans.
  b Here *heaving* means so full they are about to burst. If somebody cuts you open, you *spill your guts*. In other words, your intestines fall out. It is a very dramatic metaphor, and means that the over-full carrier bags have split open (like a body) and their insides (the paper) have fallen out.
  c *spirals* means she goes round in a circular motion. In other words, rather than just walking into the room, Iris enters quickly, perhaps going round in a circle as she does so, like a ballet dancer.
  e *abandoned* means left alone because of being unwanted or unsuccessful. It is usually used for children, animals, ships, or houses, so it is an overly-dramatic image for a glass of wine. *Tucked away* means hidden, but we usually use it to describe, for example, something hidden at the bottom of a drawer to keep it safe. It contrasts oddly with *abandoned* because it implies that the wine glass has been purposefully hidden for later.

4   Ask students to read the second part of the article and answer the questions. Let them discuss the answers in pairs before checking with the whole class.

Answers
1   Because there are rumours she has given up writing.
2   Because Iris may think she is rude if she asks her why she has stopped writing.
3   John explains it as writer's block, something that has happened before, and he seems optimistic that it will pass. His explanation is practical, but also wishful thinking. Iris tries to explain the mental process that she is experiencing and says she is in a bad, quiet place. She feels gloomy, and has the impression that she's falling. She tries hard to be optimistic but is not as convinced as John that she will get better.
4   Having a philosophical mind, she worked out the whole novel in advance in careful detail.
5   She doesn't finish sentences. She says things in an absent way. She describes what she is experiencing in terms of darkness and falling.

5–6 Ask students to read the third part of the article and answer the questions. Let them discuss their answers in pairs before checking with the whole class.

Answers
1   It is touching, fresh and young. They are at ease with each other. The journalist is saying that this level of comfort and support is the result of a long and happy marriage.
2   He says that Iris has never been interested in being a mum, and says that is typical of great women writers. He doesn't seem bitter.

3 He quotes the doctors as saying that the brain can find its way round a block after a while.

7 Ask students to answer the questions on the whole article. It is a good idea to change pairs or put students in threes to discuss this task, which is more interpretative than the previous two.

Check that students understand the words in 4. They may not know *bewildered*, which means very confused, *distracted*, which means not concentrating on what's happening, and *dispirited*, which means losing hope.

Answers
1 Like its occupants, the house is disorganized, full of books (intellectual), homely, eccentric, and dark (like Iris' mind).
2 In part two he talks of her philosophical mind and the way she worked everything out in advance in meticulous detail when writing a novel. In part three he compares her to great women novelists such as Jane Austen and George Eliot.
3 He is cheerful and joky with her, making silly jokes such as the pun on *pour*, encourages her to see her problems as temporary, and praises her talent. He is being very supportive because actually she is quite depressed. He seems to do all the jobs about the house, opening the door, making the coffee, and generally looking after her. His optimism is also a sign that he loves her so much that he is afraid of losing her.
4 **John**: loving, supportive, cheerful, encouraging, considerate
Iris: bewildered, distracted, dispirited
Both: unconventional, loveable, childlike, gentle

Vocabulary work

8 Ask students to find the words in the text, then match them to the definitions. Let them check in pairs before checking with the whole class. Make sure that students have a guess at the meaning in the context of the article before looking in dictionaries.

Answers
1 d 2 c 3 g 4 h 5 j 6 a 7 b 8 e 9 i 10 f

What do you think?

See TB p9 for suggestions on how to approach this.

Sample answers
• She might have said it because he's always been faithful and supportive. John is clearly very much in love with her. He is very proud of her.
• Before, it was a more equal relationship. After, he has become more of a nurse.
• Because she was a great novelist and intellectual, reliant on her mind for her work.

Phrasal verbs

This section looks at the way many common phrasal verbs have a variety of meanings, some literal and others metaphorical. The Language Input box asks students to analyse form and meaning by looking at some contextualized examples, and also brings up the question of whether a phrasal verb is separable or not. Exercise 1 revises and extends students' knowledge of literal and metaphorical phrasal verbs with gap-fill activities. Exercises 2 and 3 look at the particular meaning of certain particles. Exercise 4 is a speaking activity to consolidate students' ability to use some of this language.

LANGUAGE INPUT

1 Ask students in pairs to look at the examples and answer the questions.

Answers
Take in is used literally in sentences 1 and 2.
It is separable

2 Ask students to look at the article about Iris Murdoch on SB pp19–20 and complete the sentences with the correct phrasal verbs.

Answers
1 There's a glass tucked *away* under each armchair.
2 There are rumours she has given *up* writing.
3 In the past you've *worked* the novel out in advance.
4 He heads *off* to the kitchen to make coffee.
5 I may get better. I expect something will *turn up*.
6 (The brain) can come *up against* a block.

Refer students to Grammar Reference 2.1–4 on SB p147. See TB p5 for suggestions on how to approach this.

1 Ask students in pairs to complete the sentences.

Answers

1 give up	11 has ... put up
2 're giving away	12 putting ... down
3 gave ... away	13 're getting up to
4 gave ... up	14 did ... get up to
5 work out	15 do ... get on with
6 has worked/is working ... up	16 did ... get on with
7 work up	17 go in for
8 working out	18 'm going down with
9 put ... up	19 went down ... with
10 put ... down	20 goes in for

2 Ask students in pairs to compare the sentences and discuss the effect of the particles.

3 Ask students in pairs to complete the sentences.

4 **T 2.1** Play the recording and ask students to listen and respond to the lines of conversation. (For tapescript, see **T 2.2** .)

T 2.2 Play the recording so that students can compare their answers. If they didn't do too well the first time, you could let them practise the exchanges again in pairs, trying to remember what the people said on the recording.

LISTENING AND SPEAKING (SB p22)

I have nothing to declare but my genius!

This listening is a short extract from *The Importance of Being Earnest*, a comedy play written by Oscar Wilde in 1895 for the London stage. Students may be familiar with the recent film version (2002). The level of vocabulary is high – Wilde's characters express themselves in a formal way, using latinate words to show their class and education. However, this should not be too much of a problem, especially if your students happen to be speakers of Latin languages. To get the most out of the extract, students need to be tuned in to the comically formal situation of the interview, and to the way Wilde's humour is based on clever and witty sayings. In the lead-in, there are exercises which look at Wilde's humorous epigrams. The listening task is quite straightforward, asking questions to check students' comprehension of the basic storyline. The students then read the extract in detail to find vocabulary and examples of comic effect. You will need to photocopy the scene (on TB p121) before the lesson.

1 Ask students to read the quotations and discuss their impressions with a partner.

You may wish to point out that the secret to the wit here is the careful balance of each sentence. For example, *well-written or badly-written, being talked about, and ... not being talked about, anything but temptation.*

> **EXTENSION ACTIVITY**
>
> You could write the first part of some other epigrams by Oscar Wilde on the board, and ask students in pairs to try and complete them:
>
> In examinations the foolish ask questions that ... (*the wise cannot answer.*)
>
> Everyone who is incapable of learning has ... (*taken up teaching.*)
>
> I never put off until tomorrow what I can do ... (*the day after.*)
>
> The play was a great success, but the audience ... (*was a disaster.*)
>
> Let students share their suggestions in class, and then you can provide the actual answers.

2 Ask students in pairs to decide whether the statements are true or false. Monitor to see how much they know, but don't give answers yet.

3 Ask students to read the biodata to check their answers to the statements in 2 and to answer the questions. You may need to explain *shrewd* (here clever, in the sense of well-observed and well-judged), *sparkling* (here full of wit, energy, and fun in an exciting way), and *masterpiece* (best work).

5 False. He was imprisoned for homosexual practices. *The Importance of being Earnest* is considered to be his masterpiece. *Earnest* means very serious. *Ernest* is a man's name – common in the late nineteenth century, but unfashionable now. The two words are homophones and are pronounced the same – /'ɜːnɪst/. The joke is that Ernest takes himself too seriously.

4 **T 2.3** Take a little time to set the scene. It's 1895. Lady Bracknell is interviewing young Jack Worthing. Ask students *What do you think Lady Bracknell will be like? Why do you think she's interviewing Jack?* Ask students to listen to the recording and answer the first question, *Why is Jack being interviewed?* Feedback on the answer, then ask students in pairs to discuss questions 2 to 7. You will probably need to check the vocabulary in 7 (see answers below). You may need to play the recording a second time.

GLOSSARY

Words marked (–) have a negative connotation.

reserved	quiet, shy, unexpressive
aristocratic	coming from (or behaving like) an upper-class family
snobbish (–)	looking down on people from lower class
overbearing (–)	dominating others through force of personality
timid (–)	pathetically shy and weak
witty	clever and funny with words
prejudiced (–)	having a negative and biased view of someone, often based on class, race, or sex
earnest	too serious
inarticulate (–)	unable to express yourself clearly or well
arrogant (–)	feeling superior to other people
courteous	very polite and helpful
haughty (–)	snobbish and arrogant
patronizing (–)	talking down to people, treating them as if they are stupid or inferior

Answers

1 To find out whether he is suitable to marry Lady Bracknell's only daughter.
2 He doesn't have one. His money comes from investments, so he doesn't earn it.
3 Gwendolen is Lady Bracknell's daughter.
4 Lady Bracknell is pleased that Jack smokes; that he knows nothing; that he has investments.
   She is displeased that he owns a house on the unfashionable side of Belgrave Square; that he has lost both his parents; that he was found in a handbag in a cloakroom.

5 His real parents appear to have abandoned him as a baby, leaving him in a handbag in a railway station. A *handbag* here means some sort of hand luggage, like a modern-day hold-all. He was adopted by the late (i.e. now dead) Thomas Cardew. He has no known relatives.
6 No
7 To find some relations, and at least one parent.
8 *Aristocratic, snobbish, overbearing, witty* (but not always intentionally), *prejudiced, arrogant, haughty, patronising.* Arguably, *earnest.*
   T 2.6 See SB Tapescripts p133 and TB p121

5 Give students photocopies of the scene (TB p121) and ask them to read and listen to it again and answer the questions.

Answers

1 Her direct, personal questions, and insensitive comments (e.g., suggesting that losing his parents was careless, that being born in a handbag was an indiscretion, and that he should find some relations) are all examples of being *patronizing, haughty,* and *overbearing.* She also dismisses him at the end.
   She wants to know about his income, address, and family, and comments that living off investments is satisfactory. She declares that 149 Belgrave Square is unfashionable, and insists that not knowing your family or place of birth cannot result in having a recognized position in society. These are all examples of being *aristocratic, snobbish, arrogant,* and *prejudiced.*
   She is unconsciously *witty* in many of the things she says, but of course she is merely a vehicle for Wilde's criticisms of the upper classes. For example, *Ignorance is like an exotic fruit; touch it and the bloom is gone.* This is a witty thing to say, but to actually believe it is stupid. Lady Bracknell may say witty things, but the joke is on her.
2 'Worthing' is the name of a seaside resort. The man who found Jack as a baby happened to have a railway ticket for Worthing in his pocket at the time.
3 They were often idle, ignorant, and snobbish.
   The most important things to them were coming from a good family, having a position in society, being brought up properly, and having inherited wealth from land or investments. Their attitude to marriage was that the husband should be able to provide for his wife in terms of money, and provide the benefits of a good family and position in society. Parental permission was required. Twenty-nine appears to have been a good age for men to get married. They had an income from land or investments, but didn't work. They had a country house and a town house, hopefully in a fashionable area of London.
4 Oscar Wilde makes this scene funny by:
   The mock formality of the scene. Lady Bracknell has a pencil and notebook, asks very direct and personal

questions, makes notes, and shakes her head. Even in the nineteenth century, a prospective son-in-law would not have been interviewed as if he were applying for a job.

The silliness of the story of Jack's adoption. Jack tells his story very seriously, with lots of irrelevant details such as the fact that the handbag had handles and was left on the Brighton line. Lady Bracknell responds with horror and insensitivity.

Lady Bracknell's aphorisms. Of course, the character is being serious, but it is a way for Wilde to show his brilliance at making witty comments. For example, the comment *To lose one parent ... careless* is funny because to suggest that losing a parent is like losing a purse is a subtle play on the meaning of *lose*, and a gloriously insensitive thing for Lady Bracknell to say.

Some of Wilde's witty comments are clever criticisms of upper class people in 1895, and many people in his first audiences would have felt themselves the victim of his humour. For example, suggesting that smoking is a good occupation for the upper classes, and that living at 149 Belgrave Square was unfashionable.

Vocabulary work

6 Ask students in pairs to find synonyms in the extract for the words in italics. Do the first one as an example.

Answers
1 idle
2 tampers
3 make out, poachers ... make anything out of it
4 unspoiled ... reside
5 late ... of ... charitable and kindly disposition
6 In what locality ... come across
7 immaterial
8 confess ... bewildered
9 bred ... display a contempt
10 brought up

What do you think?

The aim here is to get students talking, and give them an opportunity to speculate about what happens in the play. If your students enjoy performing, it is an opportunity to act out the scene, which is not only fun but can be good for confidence and pronunciation, as students mimic how the actors speak their lines.

Ask students to discuss the questions in pairs, then have a brief class discussion to find out who thinks what. Give students the summary of the plot from the bottom of the photocopy (TB p121) and find out whose ideas were closest.

If you feel your students would enjoy acting – it's a good idea to ask them if they are keen to do it! – give each pair a few minutes to prepare the scene. Monitor, and encourage them to enjoy the very exaggerated intonation that

charcterizes Lady Bracknell. You could model this yourself with short examples such as *Found!* and *A handbag!* When they are ready, ask some of the pairs to come up and act out the scene. (It would be useful to have photocopies of the extract, as this will make it easier for students to read whilst performing.) Limit it to three or four, otherwise it gets a bit too repetitive. Less confident students could read the extract aloud whilst remaining in their seats. It's a good idea to ask those students who you know will do this activity particularly well to perform last, so that others don't have a hard act to follow. Monitor the performances carefully, and at the end give plenty of praise, but feed back on students' pronunciation as well.

LANGUAGE FOCUS (SB p24)

Tense review

See TB p10 for suggestions on how to approach this.

Don't forget to look at the *Language Aims* section on TB p17, which looks at problems students may have. You should also read the Grammar Reference on SB p148.

1 Ask students in pairs to complete the charts with the verb forms in italics. Ask them to think of their own examples to complete the blank spaces in the charts. Note that in the Answers table below, suggested answers to complete the blanks are in italics.

Answers
ACTIVE

	Simple	Continuous
Present	have	are being
Past	didn't recognize	*was living*
Future	will be	*will be doing*
Present Perfect	have seen	have ... been doing
Past Perfect	had realized	had been lying
Future Perfect	*will have lived*	will have been living

PASSIVE

	Simple	Continuous
Present	*is used*	is being used
Past	was found	was being cleaned
Future	*will be found*	
Present Perfect	have been silenced	
Past Perfect	had been rebuilt	
Future Perfect	*will have been rebuilt*	

Refer students to the Grammar Reference on SB p148. See TB p5 for suggestions on how to approach this.

Simple and continuous

2 Ask students in pairs to decide which sentences can be both simple and continuous. Go round monitoring and helping. Hold a question and answer session in which students share their knowledge. At advanced level, one student can often answer another's query very clearly (which saves you having to do it!).

> **Answers**
> In each sentence both the simple and continuous can be used, with two exceptions. The continuous forms, *I'm not knowing why* in 1 and *I've been cutting my finger* in 3, are not possible.

1 *Everyone's very nice to me. / Everyone's being very nice to me.*

The continuous form describes something happening now. Ask students if it's common to use the verb *to be* in the continuous form. They may have learnt that as a state verb it should always be used in the simple form. In fact it can be used in the continuous form to signify a temporary (and often deliberate) mode of behaviour that is different from the norm (e.g., in the example in exercise 1, *You're being very quiet*). Here, the speaker is clearly puzzled by this abnormal experience and wonders *why* everyone is being very nice, when they're not usually. Perhaps they are deliberately preparing the speaker for some bad news, or a difficult request.

The simple form describes something that is generally true. People are nice, not just now, but all the time. A good context is a patient in a hospital describing the nurses – they are not only nice now, but every day, all the time.

*I don't know why. / *I'm not knowing why* cannot be used.

Know is a state verb that can only be used in the simple form.

2 *I'll see Luis later. / I'll be seeing Luis later.*

The Future Simple form is used to express an intention made at the moment of speaking. Here, the speaker is making a decision. Depending on context, it could be a promise or a threat, e.g. *'We've had some very negative feedback on the proposal. You need to talk to Rob and Luis about it as soon as possible.' 'OK. Ask Rob to come in now. I'll see Luis later.'* The Future Continuous form, depending on the context, could be either describing something in progress at a particular time in the future, *What will you be doing at 8 tomorrow morning? I'll be seeing Luis*, or something that will happen in the future in the normal course of events, *It is Tuesday, so I'll be seeing Luis later – it's what always happens on Tuesday.* This latter use has no element of intention or volition. As such, it is very reassuring – describing something that is a perfectly normal routine occurrence. That is why this form is always used in announcements by airline pilots,

e.g. *We will be landing at Heathrow airport in just over 20 minutes.*

3 *I've cut my finger. / *I've been cutting my finger* cannot be used.

In this context, *I've cut my finger* is in the Present Perfect Simple form, used to describe the present result of a past action – one action, completed before now, with a result now, which is that it is cut and it hurts. The Present Perfect Continuous is highly unlikely because the continuous aspect of cutting implies that the action is repetitive and has duration. Only the self-destructive would engage in such an activity. You can point out that *I've been cutting wood for the fire* is however acceptable.

It really hurts. / It's really hurting.

Both can be used, with little change in meaning. Similar verbs are *feel* and *ache*.

4 *always gives / is always giving*

Using the Present Simple Form expresses a habitual action and it is neutral in tone. Using the Present Continuous expresses a habitual action, but also conveys the speaker's attitude. It depends on the context. It could be expressing an annoying habit – the speaker is annoyed that David spends all his money on Pam.

5 *What do you do? / What are you doing?*

The question in the Present Simple form asks about something that is always true. The most common context for this question is to ask someone what their permanent job is: *What do you do? I'm a doctor.* The question in the Present Continuous form asks about something that is happening now. It is temporary and has duration. The question *What are you doing?* often expresses puzzlement or annoyance, and you can emphasize how bizarre this sounds when it is mistakenly used in the wrong context, e.g., at a party, when the speaker is intending to ask about someone's job. You can ask someone, *What are you doing these days?* to ask what work or activities are in progress in their lives at the moment: *What are you doing these days? Oh, nothing much. I'm working part-time in a temporary teaching job.*

6 *He fired a gun. / He was firing a gun.*

We use the Past Simple to describe finished past actions. *He fired a gun* describes a single event – it happened once. We use the Past Continuous to describe something in progress at a time in the past – *At that moment he was firing a gun* means that he was in the middle of the action of firing. However, with such a short action (firing a gun), it is unlikely that something could happen in the middle of it, unless it is repeated. So, *He was firing a gun when I saw him* probably means he was in the process of repeatedly firing the gun.

7 *She died. / She was dying.*

We use the Past Simple to describe a finished past action. We use the Past Continuous to describe something in progress at a time in the past. *She was dying* means she was in the process of dying – not dead yet.

8 *I've checked my emails / I've been checking my emails*

Both forms refer to a past event with a present result. If the Present Perfect Simple is used it means the action is completed, and the main result that is emphasized is a logical result of this completion – the emails are now checked, so I can do something else. If the continuous form is used, it does not say whether all the emails have been checked or not. The emphasis will therefore be on an *incidental* result of the activity: *I've been checking my emails. That's why I'm late*, or *That's why the computer is on.*

9 *The train leaves in five minutes. / The train is leaving in five minutes.*

We use the Present Simple to talk about an impersonal, timetable future. We use the Present Continuous to refer to a personal, diary future. So, the Present Simple might be used in a train announcement, whereas the harassed parent shouting at his / her kids might say: *Come on, kids! The train is leaving in five minutes.*

10 *That room is used as a study. / That room is being used as a study.*

The first sentence is the Present Simple passive. We use the Present Simple to describe something that is always true – the room is permanently a study. The second sentence is the Present Continuous passive. We use the Present Continuous to describe something happening now – the room is temporarily a study.

Perfect and non-perfect

3 Ask students to discuss the differences. Go round monitoring and helping. Again, you could hold a question and answer session in which students share their knowledge.

Answers

1 *They've been married for thirty years.*
It started in the past and continues up to now.
They were married for thirty years.
It started and finished in the past. It is a completed past event so they are now either divorced or dead.
2 *I come from Scotland.*
A state that is always true. I am Scottish.
I've come from Scotland.
A present result of a past action. Scotland is where I was before I came here.

3 *When I've talked to him, I'll tell you.*
I'll tell you after I finish talking to him.
When I talk to him, I'll tell him.
I'll tell him at the time I am talking to him.
4 *The arrangements will be finalized on Friday.*
A statement of future fact. This will take place on Friday.
The arrangements will have been finalized by Friday.
This will take place some time between now and before Friday.
5 *Did you ever meet my grandfather?*
In the past – now he is dead.
Have you ever met my grandfather?
At any time up to now. He's still alive and you still have the chance to meet him.
6 *I wish I knew the way.*
But I don't. A regret about now – wishing something was different in the present. Because it is hypothetical, we use the past form knew to refer to an unreal present.
I wish I'd known the way.
But I didn't. A regret about the past. Because it is hypothetical, we use the Past Perfect to refer to an unreal past.

4 See if anyone can explain the joke. The two different uses of the Present Perfect that the joke rests on are *recent past time*, and *life experience*. We often say *I've had a lovely evening* to compliment our host as we leave. It expresses the present result (a feeling of pleasure) of a recent past action (having a lovely evening). But Groucho shows that he is using the Present Perfect to describe an experience *sometime in his life*, not a recent one.

Active and passive

5 Ask students in pairs to correct the sentences. Do the first as an example to get them started.

Answers

1 ... Jack *is being interviewed* by Lady Bracknell.
2 His money *is invested* in stocks and shares.
3 Gwendolen can't *be expected* to live in the country.
4 Jack *was given* the name Worthing.
5 The bag *had been found* at Victoria Station.
6 Oscar Wilde *was imprisoned* for two years.

Tenses and verb forms

6 **T 2.4** Ask students to close their books and listen to the recording. The opening lines are from book extract 3 on SB p17. Ask students in pairs to answer the questions.

Answers
Harriet is single, and is unfortunately not looking very good when she meets her friend, Nina, who has a new boyfriend with her. Harriet is very attracted to this man. Nina is a very stylish, elegant woman, who always looks like a fashion model, and is usually seen with a boyfriend.

7 **T 2.4** Ask students to read the extract and choose the correct verb forms. Play the recording again so that students can check their answers. Ask students to speculate about what happens next in the story.

Answers and tapescript
I never (1) **set out** to pinch anyone's bloke, let alone Nina's. The day it all (2) **started**, picking up a bloke was the last thing on my mind. Even I (3) **don't go out** on the pull in manky old combats and a sweater that (4) **'s seen** better days. All I (5) **was thinking** of, on that drizzly afternoon was (6) **finding** a cab home. (7) **Having started off** in mist-like fashion, the drizzle (8) **had moved up** a gear, as if it (9) **were thinking** about (10) **turning into** proper rain. At this point I was just up the road from Covent Garden with drizzled-on hair and a jumper starting (11) **to smell** of a wet Shetland sheep. That was when I saw Nina, (12) **coming** out of a smart little restaurant, with a bloke on her arm.

If I can misquote Jane Austen here, it is a truth universally (13) **acknowledged** that if you are fated (14) **to bump into** someone like Nina when you (15) **haven't seen** her for four years, you (16) **will be looking** like a pig's breakfast. While she (17) **will be looking** like a Sunday Times fashion shoot in silk and cashmere. Only about six paces away, she (18) **was talking and laughing** in her silver-tinkle way to the bloke, who (19) **was holding** her umbrella up to stop her (20) **getting** wet. The last time I (21) **'d seen** her (at a wedding four years back) she (22) **'d had** some tall, dark specimen in tow. Although everything about him was theoretically perfect I (23) **hadn't been** particularly impressed, to me he (24) **'d seemed** just a bit *plastic*, somehow. I (25) **don't** quite **know** what it was with this one – he wasn't classically good-looking, exactly, but the spark (26) **hit** me at once!

Summary of what happens next
Nina leaves, and her boyfriend starts a conversation with Harriet, who borrows some money from him for a taxi. She gets in touch with him in order to pay him back. They become friends, and eventually a relationship develops between them ...

ADDITIONAL MATERIAL

Workbook Unit 2

Exercises 1–3 Tense review
Exercise 10 The grammar of phrasal verbs

THE LAST WORD (SB p26)

Sounds and spelling

1 Ask students in pairs to write down all the English words they know containing the letters *ough*. In the feedback, insist on good pronunciation.

Answers
From the poem: tough /tʌf/, bought /bɔːt/, cough /kɒf/, dough /dəʊ/, thorough /'θʌrə/, plough /plaʊ/, enough /ɪ'nʌf/ and through /θruː/.
Others: brought /brɔːt/, thought /θɔːt/, fought /fɔːt/, nought /nɔːt/, sought /sɔːt/, bough /baʊ/, rough /rʌf/, drought /draʊt/, although /ɔː'ðəʊ/.

2 Ask students to read the poem and decide on the pronunciation of the words in italics. Point out that the poem has a two-line rhyming structure, which will help them to get the pronunciation of the words in italics at the end of a line. Let them check in pairs. It is a good idea to do this as a dictionary task. Make sure students can recognize the phonetic symbols used. Refer them to the phonetics symbols chart on the inside back cover of the Student's Book.

3 **T 2.5** Play the recording so that students can check their pronunciation. Then ask students in pairs to practise reading the poem aloud, taking it in turns to read a verse each.

4 Ask students in pairs to write words from the poem in column A, next to their phonetic transcription.

T 2.6 Play the recording. Students listen and complete column B with words with the same sound as those in column A.

Answers and tapescript

		A	B
1	/θruː/	through	threw
2	/hɜːd/	heard	herd
3	/miːt/	meat	meet
4	/swiːt/	suite	sweet
5	/hɪə/	here	hear
6	/dɪə/	dear	deer
7	/beə/	bear	bare
8	/peə/	pear	pair
9	/rəʊz/	rose	rows
10	/tʃuːz/	choose	chews

T 2.6
1 She threw the ring into the bin with the rubbish.
2 Sorry we're late, we got behind a farmer with a herd of cattle in the lane.
3 We'll meet you outside the cinema at six o'clock.
4 Oh, how sweet of you to remember my birthday!
5 Speak up! I can't hear a word you're saying.

6 We saw some deer when we were walking in the mountains.
7 The cupboards are bare. We'll have to go shopping.
8 Those two are a right pair of troublemakers.
9 The children sat in orderly rows in the school hall.
10 Uncle Bill chews every mouthful of food twenty times.

5 Ask students in pairs to practise saying the words in phonetic script. Ask them to write the homophones in the columns.

Answers

		A	B
1	/pɔː/	pour	paw
2	/biːn/	been	bean
3	/wɪtʃ/	which	witch
4	/weə/	where	wear
5	/wɔː/	wore	war
6	/θrəʊn/	throne	thrown
7	/kɔːt/	court	caught
8	/ˈflaʊə/	flower	flour
9	/piːs/	peace	piece

BACKGROUND NOTE
English has very irregular spelling because its spelling system developed from a Germanic and French root, and English has absorbed a huge number of words from other languages. This has resulted in many words where the spelling has little connection with the present pronunciation. But students should also be reassured that there *are* regularities in English spelling!

DON'T FORGET!

Writing Unit 2 Story telling (SB pp118–119)

Workbook Unit 2
Exercise 4 Listening – A book I enjoyed
Exercise 5 A poem
Exercises 6–7 Adjectives to describe people
Exercise 8 Common spelling errors
Exercise 9 Synonyms – Verbs with a similar meaning to *speak*

3

Describing trends
Comparing statistics
Adverbs 1 • Word linking

Big business

Introduction to the unit

The theme of this unit is big business. In particular, it deals with globalization and the way big business impacts on ecology, the developing world, and the way we live our lives. The main reading text is an article about the global economy, which argues that consumerism is having a negative effect on our quality of life, and results in the exploitation of markets and workers in developing countries. The main listening text is an interview with business entrepreneur Anita Roddick, founder of The Body Shop. She talks about how immigrants make good entrepreneurs because they are innovative, and how multinational corporations should be resisted as they begin to dominate the global economy. Naturally, the theme will be of particular interest to your students if they have a business background. However, as it looks at the relationship between business and general topics such as globalization, ecology, and the developing world, it will also appeal to students who have an interest in global developments in general.

Language aims

Adverbs This is the first of four units that deal with adverbs. Unit 4 looks at comment adverbs or discourse markers such as *anyway*, Unit 10 looks at intensifying adverbs such as *absolutely*, and Unit 12 looks at linking adverbs such as *however*. This unit looks at adverb collocations, the way some adverbs have two forms, and a common adverb with many meanings, *just*. There are three key areas to consider with adverbs: meaning, collocation with adjectives and verbs, and the position they take in the sentence. Grammar Reference 3.1–6 on SB p150 explores these areas in detail.

> **WATCH OUT FOR …**
> **Collocation and form**
> Students need to think about the meaning, collocation, and form of adverbs.
> - Adverbs often collocate with verbs and adjectives when there is a semantic link, e.g. *deeply affected*.
> - Some adverbs have two forms: *hard* / *hardly*.
> - *Just* has many meanings depending on context.

Adverb collocations Adverbs modify verbs and adjectives. Often, usage has resulted in some adverbs collocating specifically with certain verbs and adjectives. For example, we say *deeply worried* not *sorely worried*. This is because there is a semantic link between the adverb and the verb/adjective. Emotions can be deep, so we say *deeply affected, deeply regret*. Similarly, there are semantic links with collocations such as *freely admit, desperately anxious, highly recommend*.

Adverbs with two forms This looks at an area which causes confusion for students. The fact that, for example, English can use both *hard* and *hardly* as adverbs with different meanings is difficult to remember. Exercise 3 deals with the meaning and sentence position of some of the more common adverbs that have two forms.

Sentence position At intermediate level, a common error students make is to get the sentence position of adverbs wrong: ~~I like very much ice-cream~~, ~~I read often magazines~~. The rules for position of adverbs are dealt with in detail in Grammar Reference 3.1–3 on SB p150. Advanced students should be able to self-correct such errors. However, make sure you listen out for any mistakes regarding the position of the adverb.

just *Just* has many meanings depending on context, and is also sometimes used as a filler, when it has very little meaning. The aim in this unit is to make students aware of this, provide some examples of use, and get them to work out meaning from context. Encourage students to note down ways that *just* is used as they continue to experience spoken English in and out of the classroom.

Grammar Reference 3.1–6 on SB p150 looks at adverbs in detail. It is a good idea to read this carefully before teaching the grammatical section of this unit.

Vocabulary The *Vocabulary* section looks at describing trends. In particular, it looks at synonyms of *fall* and *increase*, adverbs and adjectives that collocate with words such as *fall* and *increase*, and also looks at some comparative forms. The students must use this language to give a presentation.

The last word This section looks at word linking and the intrusive sounds /j/, /w/, and /r/.

Notes on the unit

STARTER (SB p27)

1 Introduce the topic by finding a well-known logo in a magazine and pinning it to the board. Ask what the name of the company is, and what it produces. Check that students know what a logo is. You could extend the vocabulary area here by eliciting: *brand, make, label, product, designer goods*.

Ask students in pairs to look at the logos and discuss the questions.

Answers
1 McDonalds: fast food
2 Nike: trainers/sportswear
3 Vodaphone: mobile phone packages
4 Toyota: cars/motorbikes/musical instruments
5 Shell: oil
6 Apple: computers and digital accessories
7 The Body Shop: cosmetics
8 Mercedes: cars / trucks
9 Quantas: flights

2 Ask students to discuss the questions in pairs or threes. Have a brief class feedback, and find out which students are particularly conscious of branding when they shop.

Sample answers
Brands are used to advertise a product in order to achieve brand recognition. They are also used to establish customer loyalty.

READING AND SPEAKING (SB p28)

The global economy

1 Ask students in pairs to define globalization and consumerism. Elicit a list of pros and cons and write them on the board.

Answers
Globalization: the idea that the world is developing a single economy and culture as a result of improved technology and communications and the influence of large multinational companies. It is sometimes used derogatively by anti-globalization campaigners to refer to the way American multinationals dominate and exploit the economies of less powerful nations.
Consumerism: the capitalist economic belief that it is good for a country if people purchase and use many goods and services – supply and demand. Again, it is a term often used critically by detractors.
Pros: free markets across the world; multinationals create jobs in developing countries; people in poorer and developing countries want to be able to purchase first world products; breaking down cultural barriers.
Cons: multinationals exploit developing markets and third world workforces – sell their products (e.g. cigarettes), to consumers who can't really afford them, and employ workers at much lower salaries than in developed countries; growing third world debt; the destruction of industries and products in developing countries; destroying culture of non-American countries; the disappearance of the cultural diversity of nations, also often referred to as Coca-colonization.

2 Read through the sentences as a class, and decide whether they are facts or opinions. Ask students to take two or three minutes to consider their reaction to the facts and opinions, then have a brief class discussion.

Answers
1, 3, and 6 are facts. The rest are opinions.

3 Ask students to look at the title of the article, and see if they can explain it. It is a cynical, darkly humorous way of describing the shallowness of life in a consumer society – we live to consume, which covers both eating and buying. The rest of the time we sleep, and this makes the fact that we die at the end of it all seem particularly grotesque.

Ask students to read the article and find out which of the topics in 2 are mentioned.

Answers
Topics 1, 4, 7, and 8 are mentioned.

4 Ask students to read the article again and decide which statements are true, and which false. Let students check in pairs before conducting whole-class feedback.

Answers
1 True
2 False: *the majority of us are deeply worried*
3 False: *More spending doesn't mean that life is getting better. We all know it often means the opposite.*
4 True

5 False: *We don't need the things that the economy produces as much as the economy needs our sense of need for these things.*

6 False: *We buy clothes that are manufactured in sweat shops by virtual slaves in poor parts of the world.*

7 True

8 True

5 Ask students in pairs to discuss what they understand by the statements highlighted in the text.

Answers

1 *men in suits*: businessmen and anyone working in the world of high finance.

2 *drained and stressed*: exhausted and under a lot of pressure.

3 *ironic ... devices in our lives*: it's a joke that we have no free time when there are so many machines in the house, such as dishwashers, which are supposed to save us time.

4 *hassling for ... gadgets*: the children are always demanding the most modern electronic products, which they have perhaps seen advertised.

5 *goes into stalemate*: the system stops working.

6 *Need is the miracle ...*: need is the 'magic solution' to the problem of keeping the economy in a state of constant growth.

7 *hunger that cannot be satiated*: metaphorically, this feeling of needing to buy goods is a feeling that cannot be satisfied. We go on buying even though we don't need to buy anything.

8 *this ecstasy of consumption*: this wonderful feeling of spending and spending. The writer is being ironic.

9 *break the cycle*: put an end to this self-perpetuating system, which keeps the rich countries rich and the poor countries poor.

10 *oblivious to the impact ...*: unaware of the influence our behaviour has on the world.

What do you think?

See TB p9 for suggestions on how to approach this.

Sample answers

1 **Jonathan Rowe mentions:** an American company manufactures both high fat food and diet products. You can buy luxury foods from poor countries that can't feed their own people.

Other examples: luxury products such as computers are often exported to be assembled in poorer countries, then reimported back to rich countries.

Call centres are often located in poor countries, where salaries are low, so when someone rings their 'local' electricity company, they are actually ringing someone on the other side of the world.

Developing countries are often prevented from manufacturing their own raw materials by strict import tariffs in developed countries.

2 Students' own ideas.

3 Jonathan Rowe has a negative attitude towards multinational corporations, which hypocritically produce both high-fat food and diet products. He thinks supermarkets produce too many versions of the same product. He thinks economists are wrong – we don't need to keep circulating money. He thinks Western banks and companies who use cheap labour are exploitative. He criticizes cars and congestion, so presumably is in favour of public transport. His argument is basically anti-globalist, anti-pollution.

EXTENSION ACTIVITY

You could have a class debate. Write a motion on the board: *We believe that consumerism and economic growth is essential to global prosperity.*

Divide the class into a group or groups to argue for the motion, and a group or groups to argue against. Have equal numbers of groups, so, if you have a class of eight, have two groups of four, and, if you have a class of twenty, have four groups of five.

Give each group a few minutes to brainstorm arguments in favour of their standpoint, then ask one person from each group to stand up and present their arguments to the class. The class can challenge their arguments and any member of the group can try to answer their challenges.

At the end, you could have a vote to see whose argument is the most persuasive.

Some suggested arguments

In favour

Spending creates wealth and jobs.

Without consumerism there would be a smaller range of products.

Without the stimulus of consumerism there would be less invention and innovation of new products.

Consumerism in the developed world creates jobs in the developing world.

Against

Over-consumption causes pollution and the exploitation of natural resources.

People feel drained, stressed and under pressure because of the need to earn to consume.

It creates a gap between haves and have-nots.

Manufacturers exploit people by creating false needs for products they don't need.

Large companies exploit producers in the developing world.

VOCABULARY AND SPEAKING (SB p30)

This section looks at the language required to describe trends and compare statistics. There is some revision of the way adjectives, adverbs, and comparatives are used. The aim is that by the end of this section students can give a presentation using this area of language. Point out that students do not need to be business specialists to find this language useful. In all areas of life we are increasingly required to give presentations that rely on this kind of language.

Describing trends

You could lead in by previewing students' ability to describe trends. Write on the board: *house prices, inflation, the price of computer software/cars/clothes, the cost of going out, the cost of living*. Ask students in pairs to tell each other whether these things are going up or down. Ask them to use as many different phrases for expressing these ideas as they can. Conduct a brief whole-class feedback.

1 Ask students in pairs to look at the headlines and answer the question. In the feedback, elicit the verbs and write them on the board under two headings, *going up* and *going down*, to check their meanings.

> **Answers**
> **Going up:** soars, shoot up, leap, picks up slightly
> **Going down:** tumbles, slump, plunge, plummet

Ask which of these can be both verb and noun (*leap, tumble, slump, plunge*).

2 Check the meaning and pronunciation of the adjectives and adverbs in the boxes. Note that the rate of rise or fall ranges from a small amount (slight) to a large amount (substantial). Point out that the stress in *dram'atic(ally)* and *sub'stantial(ly)* is on the second syllable. Ask students in pairs to practise using the words in exercises 1 and 2 to describe the company's profits. Monitor and check.

T 3.1 Play the recording so that students can compare their answers.

> **Answer and tapescript**
> Halico enjoyed a steady rise in profits in January. Unfortunately they fell dramatically in February, then picked up in March and April when they went up gradually. May saw profits shooting up, but then the company suffered a substantial decrease in June. In July and August profits increased slightly, then went up steadily in the early autumn months of September and October, before tumbling sharply in November. They then evened out in December.

3 Check that students understand *peak*, (reach the highest point) and *level out*, (stop going up or down). Ask students to describe the company's overheads using words from the lesson. In the feedback, ask one or two pairs to briefly summarize the information in the graph.

4 **T 3.2** Play the recording. Ask students to listen and complete the graph.

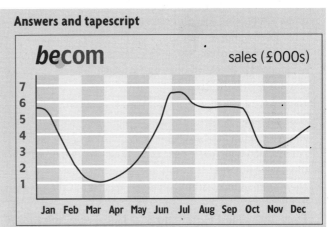

T 3.2

Becom's sales began the year healthily, with January figures in the mid five thousand units a month. They dropped dramatically in February and March, plummeting to one thousand. Sales picked up slightly in April, then shot up in the early summer months of May and June, at the end of which period sales were peaking at six thousand five hundred a month. There was a bit of a downturn in July, when sales dropped by eight hundred, but then they remained stable in August and September. October saw a substantial decrease, down to three thousand, before sales picked up in the build-up to Christmas, rising steadily to end the year at four thousand five hundred.

Comparing statistics

5 Read through the charts and the example sentences with the class. Ask two or three students to make a sentence using the information. Then put students in pairs to make further sentences. You may wish to point out stress and pronunciation features in these sentences, for example stress on key information:

David spends twice as much on accommodation as John does.

6 Divide the class into small groups of three or four. Photocopy and hand out one of the sets of statistics on TB p123 to each group. Ask the groups to prepare a presentation using vocabulary from the lesson. Monitor and check. When they are ready, ask each group to nominate one person to read out their presentation to another group. Put pairs or groups together to read out their presentations. You could also choose two groups to read out their presentation to the class.

> **Sample answers**
> There was a slight rise in interest rates between January and February.
> Interest rates fell slightly between February and March.
> There was a dramatic decrease in interest rates between March and April. / Interest rates plunged/tumbled.
> Interest rates levelled out between April and May.

Interest rates rose sharply between May and June. / Interest rates soared/shot up.
There were approximately twice as many street thefts and muggings this year as (there were) last year.
Shoplifting fell slightly.
There were a few more burglaries this year in comparison with last year.
There was a dramatic decrease in the number of car thefts.
There weren't anywhere near as many car thefts this year as there were last year.
There were as many armed robberies this year as there were last year.
There were almost twice as many violent assaults this year as there were last year.
The number of violent assaults rose substantially.

EXTENSION ACTIVITY

Photocopy enough copies of the company profile sheet on TB p124 for all the students in your class. Hand them out to the students. Ask students to research and complete their company profile, and prepare a presentation. You could do the presentations in small groups, or, if you have a small class, as a whole class activity.

Obviously this will work best if you have a mature class of business-minded students with a range of jobs. However, you could still do this activity with students of school or college age. Write out the names of well-known companies on pieces of paper (*Coca-Cola*, *McDonalds*, *Microsoft*, etc.) and hand them out to students. Then ask students to imagine they work for this company and complete the company profile sheet and prepare a presentation.

You can give them a copy of the *How to make a presentation* sheet on TB p141.

LANGUAGE FOCUS (SB p32)

See TB p10 for suggestions on how to approach this.

Don't forget to look at the *Language Aims* section on TB p28, which looks at problems students may have. You should also read Grammar Reference 3.1–6 on SB p150.

Adverb collocations

ALTERNATIVE LEAD-IN

If you prefer to start your lesson board-focused rather than going straight into the exercises, try this as a lead-in: write a jumbled list of verb + adverb and adverb + adjective collocations on the board, and ask students in pairs to match them, for example:

sleep	heavily
live	soundly
fall	dangerously
happily	dressed
badly	devoted
hopelessly	married

Answers

sleep soundly	happily married
live dangerously	badly dressed
fall heavily	hopelessly devoted

Ask students what rules they know for the use and form of adverbs.

Answer

Adverbs of manner often end with -*ly*; adverbs of manner often go after verbs but before adjectives.

LANGUAGE INPUT

Ask students to read through the adverb collocations from the text. Ask them if they can think of any other common verb + adverb or adverb + adjective collocations.

Refer students to Grammar Reference 3.4 on SB p150. See TB p5 for suggestions on how to approach this.

1 Ask students in pairs to complete the sentences with adverbs from the box.

Answers

1 desperately	7 sorely
2 eagerly	8 distinctly
3 highly	9 conscientiously
4 virtually	10 deeply
5 severely	11 fatally
6 interminably	12 perfectly

2 Ask students in pairs to match verbs and adverbs from the box. Do the first as an example. Ask students to make sentences using the adverb collocations.

Answers

scream hysterically	break something deliberately
gaze longingly	work conscientiously
love passionately	apologize profusely

Adverbs with two forms

LANGUAGE INPUT

Ask students to look at the examples of adverbs with two forms. Ask them if they can think of any other examples.

Refer students to Grammar Reference 3.5 on SB p150. See TB p5 for suggestions on how to approach this.

3 Ask students to complete the sentences with the correct form of the adverb. In the feedback, discuss which examples have significantly different meanings.

Answers
1 We all work extremely hard. *(with a lot of effort)*
   Some countries can hardly feed their own people. *(almost not)*
2 Manchester won the match easily. *(with no difficulty)*
   Relax! Take it easy! *(in a relaxed way)*
3 I hate it when people arrive late. *(not on time)*
   What have you been doing lately? *(recently)*
4 'Can you lend me some money?' 'Sure.' *(of course)*
   Surely you can see that your plan just wouldn't work? *(tell me I'm right)*
5 He was wrongly accused of being a spy. *(incorrectly)*
   At first everything was great, but then it all went wrong. *(badly)*
6 He talked freely about his criminal past. *(without constraint)*
   The prisoner walked free after twenty years in jail. *(at liberty)*
7 What do you like most about me? *(more than anything else)*
   She worked wherever she could, mostly in restaurants. *(principally)*
8 She has travelled widely in Europe and Asia. *(extensively)*
   When I got home, the door was wide open. *(completely)*

just

4 Ask students in pairs to discuss the meaning of *just* in each sentence.

Answers
1 exactly
2 only
3 equally/no less than
4 at this very moment/ right now
5 almost not
6 simply
7 simply
8 nearly/almost
9 emphasizes what you're saying
10 simply

Refer students to Grammar Reference 3.6 on SB p150. See TB p5 for suggestions on how to approach this.

Note that adverbs are also dealt with in Units 10 and 11.

5 Ask students in pairs to add *just* to the sentences and match them to the definitions in the Grammar Reference on SB p150.

Answers
1 ... *Just* listening to you ... *(simply)*
2 I've *just* read ... *(a short time before)*
3 ... I'm *just* going to the loo. *(right now)*
4 ... which was *just* what I needed. *(exactly)*
5 ... is *just* as hopeless ... *(equally)*
6 ... and *just* managed to ... *(nearly not possible)*
7 Do *just* what I say. *(exactly)*
   Just do what I say. *(simply)*
8 We're *just* about ten minutes ... *(almost)*

6 **T 3.3** Play the recording. Ask students to listen and answer the focus question.

Answer and tapescript
The latest crisis is that Members of Parliament have voted themselves a 50% pay rise, while other public sector workers such as nurses and teachers are being offered very small rises.

T 3.3 See SB Tapescripts p134

Ask students in pairs to see if they can remember any uses of *just* on the recording. Conduct a brief whole-class feedback. Write the phrases they can remember on the board, and discuss the meanings of *just*.

Answers
May I just say straight away that ... *(simply)*
... has offered nurses just 2.6% ... *(only)*
... which are just as heavy. *(equally)*
If I can just finish ... *(simply)*
... fair and just settlements ... (here, *just* is an adjective which means *fair*)

7 **T 3.3** Ask students to read through the lines, and correct any differences they can remember. Then play the recording again. If students have problems, you could play and pause the recording so that students can note the differences. Refer students to the tapescript on SB p134 so that they can check their answers.

Answers
1 We've been hearing endlessly in the media ...
2 Polls distinctly show that ...
3 My government fully deserves every penny ...
4 I greatly respect our public sector workers, they work hard ...
5 Your ministers have repeatedly urged workers to ...
6 It seems perfectly plain to me ...
7 The effectiveness of the nation's MPs is being severely hampered by lack of funds.
8 Their salaries are pathetically low compared to those people working in industry.
9 My own salary is being reviewed separately *and* it will be reviewed fairly.
10 I believe passionately in fair and just settlements ...

More adverbs: straight away, strongly, hardly, hard, conscientiously, regularly, highly, lately, mainly

ADDITIONAL MATERIAL

Workbook Unit 3
Exercise 1 Adverb collocations
Exercise 2 Adverbs with two forms
Exercise 3 *just*
Exercise 6 Describing trends

An interview with Anita Roddick

This listening is an interview with business entrepreneur Anita Roddick. It is quite long, and has been divided into three parts. Anita Roddick speaks clearly, with a standard British English accent. The only problem with comprehension the students may have is that she often fails to finish sentences or interrupts herself as she strives to explain her point of view. The tasks are designed to help with this. In the lead-in, the students predict Anita Roddick's views, then, as they listen, comprehension questions guide them through her argument.

1 Ask students what they know about The Body Shop and Anita Roddick.

BACKGROUND NOTE

Anita Roddick, chairman of The Body Shop, was born in 1942 and raised in the south-east of England, near Brighton. Her Italian immigrant mother and American father ran a café.

Anita travelled widely, and formed strong opinions about injustice in the world. She was, for example, expelled from South Africa after going to a jazz club on black night, violating apartheid laws. When she returned to England, she met Gordon Roddick and the two were married in 1971.

She started The Body Shop by concocting cosmetics from ingredients that she had stored in her garage. She opened her first shop in Brighton with just 15 products, which she packaged in five sizes so it looked as if she had at least 100. It was so successful that other people wanted to open Body Shops, so the Roddicks set up a system of franchises, which have spread all over the world.

The Body Shop has developed a reputation for supporting social and environmental causes. Roddick has a net worth estimated at more than $200 million, making her one of England's wealthiest women.

---

2 Ask students in pairs to read through the views and briefly predict which they think Anita Roddick will hold.

T 3.4 Play the recording. Ask students to listen to all three parts of the interview, and decide which of the views are expressed. Let them discuss in pairs before checking with the whole class.

Answers
She thinks that:
1 Business school kills creativity.
2 Successful business people are compassionate, or should be.
3 Money is just a means to an end.

4 It is vital to protect the environment.
5 Think locally.
6 Amass wealth and give it away.

T 3.4 See SB Tapescripts p134

3 **T 3.4** Allow students a little time to read through the questions about part one, then play the recording and let them check in pairs before conducting whole-class feedback. Follow the same procedure for part two and part three. With a small class, you could ask one of the students to control the cassette or CD player. The other students can ask them to pause and replay parts of the recording until they have got all the answers.

Answers
Part one
1 You can learn about financial science, market, product development and finance. Business school can polish you. But you can't learn how to be entrepreneurial or innovative.
2 Immigrants are outsiders, not part of the system, which makes them braver and different. Entrepreneurs are manic traders, buyers and sellers, full of ideas. They are not interested in money and are bad at managing.
3 It *oils the wheels* – in other words, it allows you to follow through your entrepreneurial idea and further develop your business ambitions.
4 She doesn't want to be the biggest retailer in the world. She wants to be the most idiosyncratic, wildest, and bravest.
Part two
5 Everything. Our lives, the world, government and political thinking, our health, our safety, what we eat, what we think.
6 Because they ignore local and national laws, and people who stand up for environmental or human rights issues.
7 Support local communities, local economic iniatives, local farming. Trade with the grassroots in an honourable way – pay living wages, respect human rights.
Part three
8 They don't want to talk about it because it would mean their mother was dead; they feel they already have good homes and jobs so they don't need her money.
9 Leaving her money to supporting humanitarian issues, such as building schools in Africa and eliminating sweat shops and child or slave labour.
10 You can be generous.

Language work

Ask students in pairs to discuss what they think the extracts from the recording mean. Do the first as an example. You could allow students to look at the phrases in the context of the tapescript on SB p134.

What do you think?

SPEAKING (SB p35)

An advertising campaign

This is an extended roleplay. If you take time to prepare roles and ideas, it should last between thirty and sixty minutes, and, of course, the more time the students have to prepare, the better their presentations will be.

A quick lead-in is to bring in a well-known product – a chocolate bar or drink, for example – and tell the students it is time to relaunch it because sales are falling. Elicit suggestions from the students of how they could relaunch it: *change the name; change the packaging; change the advertising to target a different age group; drop/raise the price.*

1   As far as possible, divide the students into groups of six (if necessary, two students can share the role of either B, C, D, E, or F). Then read through the introduction as a class. Ask students to look at the chart, which shows them how to structure their answer. Then nominate roles or ask the students to decide who is going to take which role. You could ask one student in each group to be secretary – it is their job to copy the model chart and complete it with ideas from their discussion.

Ask students to look at their role cards (TB p122), then plan the campaign. Give the students adequate time, say 15–20 minutes, though be prepared to extend this if the students are really getting into it. Monitor the discussion

groups equally, and prompt. You may wish to monitor for error – walk from group to group, listen carefully, and note any interesting errors made by the students. After the feedback to the presentations, write these errors (anonymously) on the board and discuss them with the class.

2   Ask one person from each group to present their group's proposals.

What do you think?

See TB p9 for suggestions on how to approach this.

THE LAST WORD (SB p36)

Word linking and intrusive sounds

1   Start by writing *English is an international language* on the board. Ask students to tell you which words link, and why. Mark the links. Point out that the consonant sound at the end of each of the first three words joins with the vowel sound of the next word. In natural speech, the linking makes it sounds as if you are saying, /ʃɪzənɪn/ to join the first four words. Some students may point out that there is linking between *international* and *language* – only one /l/ sound is pronounced.

Ask students in pairs to mark the links, and practise saying the sentences to each other.

T 3.5 Play the recording so that the students can check their answers.

Point out that it is this use of word linking that often causes comprehension problems when students are exposed to natural spoken English. An amusing example of possible misunderstanding is the sentence '*You have to get a potato clock tomorrow!*' Write this on the board and ask students if they can work out what the native speaker really said ('*You have to get up at eight o'clock tomorrow!*')

2 Read through the examples, and discuss the rules as a class. If you prefer to work from the board, copy the phrases onto the board, and elicit the intrusive sounds from the students.

T 3.6 Play the recording so that the students can hear the intrusive sounds.

> **Answers**
> We add /w/ when a rounded vowel sound (e.g. /uː/ at the end of a word is linked to the following word.
> We add /j/ when a spread vowel sound (e.g. /iː/) at the end of a word is linked to the following word.
> We can also add /r/ between two vowels, usually schwa sounds. The use of the intrusive 'r' has traditionally been considered bad pronunciation, although it is in fact very common in standard English.

3 Ask students to look at the examples.

T 3.7 Play the recording. Point out that there is a lot of linking and intrusion because letters are often just a vowel sound, or a vowel + consonant or consonant + vowel sound, so, when said at speed, they need to be linked by other consonant sounds.

Ask students in pairs to spell out their names to each other. What features of linking and intrusion do they notice?

4 **T 3.8** Read the introduction as a class, then play the recording. Students write down the names they hear. Let them check in pairs before writing the names up on the board in feedback.

> **Answers and tapescript**
> Marc De Weck
> Pilar Asajani
> Ginny Dummet
>
> **T 3.8**
> **1**
> **A** Could I have your first name, please?
> **B** It's Marc. That's M – A – R, and then C for Charlie, not K for Kilo.
> **A** And the surname?
> **B** De Weck.
> **A** Could you spell that for me?
> **B** Yes. It's two words. First D - . . .
> **A** Is that T for Tango?

> **B** No, D for Delta, and E for Echo. And then a separate word, WECK.
> **A** Is that with a V for Victor?
> **B** No, it's W for Whisky – E – C – K.
> **2**
> **C** And your name, please?
> **D** It's Pilar Asajani.
> **C** Could you spell the first name for me?
> **D** It's P - . . .
> **C** B for Bravo?
> **D** No, P for Papa – I for India – L – A - R.
> **C** OK . . . Pilar. And your surname, please?
> **D** Asajani. That's A – S . . .
> **C** Was that F for Freddie?
> **D** No, it's A – S for Sierra – A, then J for Juliet – A – N for November, and I for India.
> **3**
> **E** . . . And could I have the name of the other person who'll be driving the car?
> **F** Yes, it's Ginny Dummet.
> **E** Jimmy. You mean, J for Juliet – I - . . .
> **F** No, it's G for Golf – I – double N - . . .
> **E** Double M for Mike?
> **F** No, double N for November, and Y.
> **E** Was that I for India or Y for Yankee?
> **F** Y for Yankee. And the surname is Dummet . . . D – . . .
> **E** D for Delta?
> **F** That's right. D for Delta – U – double M for Mike – E – T.

5 Do this as a mingling activity. Copy the name and job cards on TB p123, and hand out one to each student. Give students a minute or two to think about how they are going to spell out their name and company. Ask them to stand up, walk round the class, and spell out their name and company to as many other people as they can. Monitor and correct any errors with pronunciation, linking, or intrusion.

Don't forget!

Writing Unit 3 Writing a business report (SB pp120–121)

Workbook Exercise 4 Listening – Anita Roddick on the working environment
Exercise 5 Pronunciation – Multi-syllable homographs
Exercise 7 Prepositions
Exercise 8 Idioms

Stop and check 1 (TB pp143–144)

4

Synonyms and antonyms 1
Discourse markers
Tags and replies

Celebrity

Introduction to the unit

The theme of this unit is celebrity. The main reading text is an article about the cult of celebrity, how we are obsessed with the lives of famous people. The main listening text is an interview with the famous Hollywood star, Liza Minnelli, who talks about her life and work. The speaking is a maze activity in which students must plan their career as an A-list celebrity.

Language aims

Discourse markers   This unit looks at discourse markers – words and expressions that show how a piece of discourse is constructed. They are used to connect what is being said now to what has been said or is about to be said, and to show the speaker's attitude. They also perform tasks such as clarifying, emphasizing points, getting back to the main point, etc.

> **WATCH OUT FOR ...**
> **Function and meaning**
> Discourse markers are difficult to use accurately because:
> • they lack a concrete meaning – they express attitudes and perform tasks
> • they often differ from discourse markers used in the students' L1
> • it's difficult to remember where they go in a sentence

This is a very difficult area for students to use accurately in natural speech. This is because there are a lot of them, they rarely equate to discourse markers in the learner's L1, and rather than having a concrete meaning, they express what the speaker is thinking. If you and your students all share the same first language, it is worth considering which phrases translate easily, and which don't. Discourse markers are a great source of false friends, for example in German *also* and *natürlich* are used differently from *also* and *naturally* in English. Similarly, the Italian *almeno* is not used in exactly the same way as the English *at least.*

The position of the discourse marker in the sentence can also be a problem. As with adverbs, students must learn whether discourse markers can go at the start, end or in the middle of a statement.

Grammar Reference 4.1 on SB p151 has a list of many discourse markers, showing their position in the sentence, and what they are expressing. It is a good idea for you to read this carefully before teaching the grammatical section of this unit.

Vocabulary   The *Vocabulary* section looks at synonyms and antonyms. It asks students to research synonyms and antonyms in the main reading text.

The last word   This section looks at tags and replies. Using tag questions appropriately is very difficult for language learners. First of all, it is difficult to 'feel' when it is appropriate to use them. For example, a learner is likely to choose *Have you seen my keys?* rather than *You haven't seen my keys, have you?* because the latter is rather subtly expressing an idea along the lines of *I know you probably haven't, and I'm only asking just in case, but do you know where my keys are?* Secondly, the form is tricky to grasp – it involves manipulating auxiliary verbs, which must agree with the tense of the main statement, and, depending on what you are trying to say, may be negative where the main statement is positive, or may be the same as the main statement. Thirdly, stress and intonation are very important with tag questions. A rising intonation on the tag means you are asking a real question to check something, whereas a falling intonation means you are not really checking – you are just asking for agreement or simply trying to engage the listener in conversation. Consequently, this is an area where students need to listen to and practise intonation.

Students will of course be familiar with standard question tags (which doesn't mean they use them appropriately). However, same-way tags and reinforcement tags could well be new.

Notes on the unit

STARTER (SB p37)

1–2 Ask students in pairs to match the lines to make quotations.

T 4.1 Play the recording so that students can check their answers and discuss how far they agree with the quotations. Ask students if they can come up with their own recipe for success.

> ### Answers and tapescript
> 1 A celebrity is a person who works hard all his life to become well known, and then wears dark glasses to avoid being recognized. (Fred Allen)
> 2 I don't want to achieve immortality through my work. I want to achieve it through not dying. (Woody Allen)
> 3 There is only one thing worse than being talked about, and that is not being talked about. (Oscar Wilde)
> 4 What goes up, must come down. (Anonymous)
> 5 Winning isn't everything, but it sure as hell beats losing. (Charlie Brown)
> 6 Whenever a friend succeeds, a little something in me dies. (Gore Vidal)
> 7 Genius is one per cent inspiration, ninety-nine per cent perspiration. (Thomas Edison)
> 8 If at first you don't succeed, try, try again. (Robert Bruce)
> 9 Nothing succeeds like succcess. (Proverb)
> 10 Let me tell you about the rich. They are different from you and me. (F Scott Fitzgerald)

> ### BACKGROUND NOTE
> **Fred Allen (1894–1956)**
> American stage and radio comedian.
>
> **Woody Allen (1935–)**
> American writer-director-comedian, famous for the neurotic character he plays in many of his films. His most famous films are *Annie Hall, Manhattan,* and *Hannah and Her Sisters.*
>
> **Oscar Wilde** (See Listening and Speaking Unit 2 SB p22)

> **Charlie Brown**
> Cartoon character in the comic strip *Peanuts* by Charles Schultz, which began in 1950 and ran until 2000. *Peanuts* is famous for the philosophical thoughts of Charlie Brown and his dog Snoopy.
>
> **Gore Vidal (1925–)**
> American novelist, playwright, and essayist.
>
> **Thomas Edison (1847–1931)**
> American inventor, most famous for inventing electric light.
>
> **Robert the Bruce (1274–1329)**
> Scottish hero in the battles against England for the control of Scotland. Legend has it that after one terrible defeat, Robert the Bruce was hiding in a cave, where he watched a spider attempting to place a web across a wide space. Each time it failed, it climbed up and tried again. Robert took a lesson from the spider and continued to fight against the English.
>
> **F Scott Fitzgerald (1853–1948)**
> Stylish American author, famous for his novel *The Great Gatsby*, published in 1925.

READING AND SPEAKING (SB p38)

The cult of celebrity

Bring in magazine pictures of people who are in the news at the moment, pin the pictures to the board, and ask one or two questions about them to get students started: *Why are they famous? Why are they in the news? What's the gossip?* Alternatively, bring in one or two magazines like *Hello!* and ask students what sort of things such magazines tell us about the lives of celebrities.

1 Discuss the questions as a class, or, if your class is large, in groups of four or five with a brief whole-class feedback at the end.

> **Answers**
> The term *the cult of celebrity* refers to the way ordinary people are so fascinated by the lives of celebrities that they love to watch them, read about their private lives, follow their careers, in a way that is almost worshipful.

2 Ask students in pairs to discuss and check that they know the words and phrases. You could do this as a dictionary research task.

Answers

an icon	a famous person who people admire and see as a symbol of a particular idea or way of life
a sitcom	a situation comedy – a TV comedy which is set in a typical situation, for example, in a family home
confessional TV	TV programme where people reveal secrets about their personal lives. Most famously, *Oprah* in the US.
the afterlife	life after death; heaven
to ogle sth / sb	to stare at rudely, usually with a strong sexual interest
fair game for criticism	If you are *fair game* you are an acceptable target and it is not unfair to criticize you.
to scrutinize sth / sb	to look at it / them in detail / critically
to bestow fame on sb	to make them famous – usually, bestow means give, in the sense of give an honour / a title
a fly-on-the-wall documentary	where a secret or intrusive camera follows the real lives of people in the documentary
like a lamb to the slaughter	going to meet your fate naively / without resistance

3   Ask students to read the text quite quickly for gist. Set a gist question, for example *Does the writer think our relationship with the famous is a healthy one?*

Then ask students to complete the text with the missing phrases. Let students check their answers in pairs before checking with the whole class.

Answers
1 g   2 d   3 b   4 f   5 i   6 j   7 a   8 c   9 e   10 h

4   Ask students to do this task in pairs. Ask them to look at each viewpoint and skim through the text until they find evidence to show agreement or disagreement. Ask students to underline or note the evidence then discuss it with their partner. In feedback, elicit evidence from different pairs, and discuss whether the students' views differ.

Answers
Most fame is undeserved – he'd agree:
... many modern celebrities are no more special than the rest of us ... (para 2)
... possible for people who are living ordinary private lives to become famous ... through the media ... (para 4)
... totally talentless people ... are simply famous for being famous. (para 7)

It is possible to survive fame intact – he'd disagree:
... you become public property, and everybody wants to claim a bit of you. (para 1)
... object of envy ... fair game for criticism ... spite (para 1)
... unable to tell where their real selves end and the PR-manufactured images begin. (para 2)
The public is consistent in the way it treats celebrities – he'd disagree:
We treat the famous with a mixture of reverence and brutality. (para 2)
We adore them, praise them, scrutinize them, and destroy them. (para 2)
We build them up and knock them down. (para 2)
Newspapers used to be more respectful – he'd agree:
... it was deemed contemptible for journalists to delve into the private lives of famous people ... (para 3)
Television subjects ordinary people to humiliation – he'd agree:
The readiness of people to let programme-makers into their homes, to answer the most intimate questions about their lives, and to allow themselves to be filmed in the most undignified and unflattering situations ...' (para 4)
Most people want to be famous – he'd agree:
The readiness of people to let programme-makers into their homes ... (para 4)
... a large proportion of (10-year-olds) will say that they would like to be famous. (para 5)
... perfectly normal people think nothing of confessing ... on daytime television ... (para 5)
... celebrity is the nearest (we) get to immortality ... (para 6)
The cult of celebrity should make us feel ashamed – he'd agree:
I fear as a nation we're losing our sense of shame in this regard. (para 8)

5   Ask students in pairs or threes to discuss the questions. Depending on the interest of the students, this could develop into a long open discussion in feedback.

Answers
1   Students' own suggestions.
2   In an age without religion or belief in an afterlife, celebrity is the nearest we get to immortality. The mass media has created an insatiable need for celebrity stories.
3   Because he is guilty of being as obsessed with celebrity as everybody else.
4   The *viciousness of voyeurism* is a dramatic way of saying that constantly reading about and being interested in celebrities is a cruel invasion of privacy, equivalent to spying on people in a voyeuristic way. The *myths we too readily absorb* are the invented stories which surround famous people.

What do you think?

1 Ask students to discuss the questions.

> **Sample answers**
> - We like to hear bad news about famous people because it helps to compensate for our envy of them and the idea we have that they live perfect lives. Celebrities are unreal in the sense that they become icons, and we no longer attribute to them the qualities of ordinary people.
> - *Reality TV* is the *Big Brother*-type of TV show, where the cameras constantly monitor a group of people over a period of time, so that we can observe the dynamics between them in a particular situation.
> - *Stalkers* are obsessive people who become fixated on someone and try endlessly to make contact with them. When the object of their obsession does not co-operate, and reveals a personality that does not correspond to the fantasy of the stalker, killing them is a way of removing this unbearable reality.

2 Ask students to read what the celebrities say, then in groups of four or five discuss the meaning of the quotations and whether they agree with them. Conduct a brief whole-class feedback.

3 Ask the class if they can think of examples of the different types of celebrity mentioned.

VOCABULARY (SB p41)

The aim here is to extend students' passive vocabulary by looking at synonyms and antonyms of words in the article on SB p39. Encourage students in pairs or groups to research the words in the article, to make guesses from context, and to teach each other. Encourage the use of dictionaries.

Synonyms

1 Ask students in pairs to find words in the article that are synonymous with words in the task.

> **Answers**
> **Paragraph 1**
> | forced | *thrust (upon)* |
> | fame | *celebrity* |
> | respect (noun) | *admiration* |
>
> **Paragraph 2**
> | great respect and admiration | *reverence* |
> | cruelty | *brutality* |
> | worship (verb) | *adore* |
> | examine | *scrutinize* |
> | ruin (verb) | *destroy* |
> | compassion, sympathy | *mercy* |

guilt	*shame*
suppose	*assume*
exactly	*precisely*

Paragraph 3
result (noun)	*consequence*
mainly	*largely*
considered	*deemed*

Paragraph 4
belief	*faith*
killers	*murderers*
killed	*assassinated*

2 Ask students to complete the sentences with synonyms. They can research the answers by referring back to the article on SB p39. Let them check their answers in pairs before checking with the whole class.

> **Answers**
> 1 achievement
> 2 criticizes
> 3 confession
> 4 amazed
> 5 curb

Antonyms

3 Ask students to complete the sentences with antonyms. Let them check their answers in pairs before checking with the whole class.

> **Answers**
> 1 manufactured / invented / fabricated
> 2 contempt
> 3 loathe / hate / detest
> 4 disaster / failure
> 5 fake
> 6 stress
> 7 familiar
> 8 bends / curves
> 9 wild
> 10 deliberate / on purpose

Discourse markers

Discourse markers are largely features of spoken English, so they are introduced here in a spoken context. Students compare an extract of spoken English with discourse markers to the same extract without. The practice activities aim to develop students' ability to recognize what the expressions mean in context.

Don't forget to look at the *Language Aims* section on TB p37, which looks at problems students may have. You should also read Grammar Reference 4.1 on SB p151.

1 **T 4.2** Set the gist question, then play the recording. Students complete the task in pairs.

You may need to explain the following expressions:
to have a field day = to have a great opportunity to do something you enjoy
to fall over each other to do sth = to compete very hard to be the first to do something
to top it off = to complete something successfully with one final action.

Answers and tapescript
The woman is talking about attending the premiere of a new film, at which a number of major stars were present.
1 Seeing famous stars.
2 They were expensive and had designer labels.
3 They were falling over each other to interview the stars.
4 The film.
5 The premiere of a new film.

T 4.2
All the A list stars were there. That model, Angeline, I think it was Angeline, was there with her new boyfriend. They've been secretly going out for months. Oh, it was a glittering occasion. Stars everywhere and the crowds outside simply begging for autographs. I couldn't believe my eyes. And the dresses! I don't know how much they would have cost, a fortune, I imagine. All designer labels. The photographers were having a field day, and there were reporters everywhere, falling over each other to interview the biggest names. We didn't have the best seats, we were in the back row. We could still see everything. I was so busy star spotting that I didn't take in the plot. You'd have been the same. I'm not too keen on thrillers but it must have been good because at the end the whole audience rose to its feet and clapped. I'm not terribly sure what the story was about, but you really must go to see it when it's on general release. It was an amazing evening and to top it off we went to Quaglino's for supper afterwards and Sarah Jane Fox and Brad Brat were at the next table. How cool is that? Sarah Jane Fox has awful skin problems. Who cares about that when you've got that much money?

2 **T 4.3** Tell students they are going to listen to the extract again, but that this time something has been added. Ask them to listen, and find out what. In the feedback, see if they can remember any expressions that have been added.

Answers
The difference is the addition of discourse markers: *at least, apparently, anyway, quite honestly, I mean, naturally, obviously, admittedly, as a matter of fact, mind you, actually, no doubt, to tell you the truth, as I was saying, all in all, though, guess what, by the way.*

LANGUAGE INPUT

Read though the examples as a class. Ask students if they can remember any examples of expressions which give the speaker's attitude, and expressions that structure discourse, from the recording.

Refer students to Grammar Reference 4.1 on SB p151.

3 Ask students to complete the monologue with expressions from the box. Let them discuss the answers in pairs before checking with the whole class. Of course, a number of the expressions could be used in more than one place, so be prepared to consider and accept alternative answers in the feedback.

T 4.3 Play the recording so that students can check their answers.

Answers and tapescript
1 at least
2 Apparently
3 Anyway / Naturally / Obviously
4 Quite honestly / Anyway / To tell you the truth
5 I mean / Quite honestly
6 naturally / of course
7 obviously / naturally
8 of course / naturally
9 so to speak
10 Admittedly / Mind you, / To tell you the truth,
11 as a matter of fact
12 Mind you,
13 Actually / To tell you the truth
14 No doubt
15 To tell you the truth / As a matter of fact / Quite honestly / Actually
16 As I was saying
17 All in all, though / Anyway,
18 guess what?
19 By the way / Mind you, / To tell you the truth
20 Still / Mind you

T 4.3

All the A-list stars were there. That model, Angeline, at least I think it was Angeline, was there with her new boyfriend. Apparently they've been secretly going out for months. Anyway, it was a glittering occasion. Stars everywhere and the crowds outside simply begging for autographs. Quite honestly I couldn't believe my eyes. And the dresses! I mean, I don't know how much they would have cost – a fortune, I imagine. All designer labels, naturally. The photographers were obviously having a field day, and of course there were reporters everywhere, falling over each other so to speak, to interview the biggest names.

Admittedly we didn't have the best seats – as a matter of fact we were in the back row. Mind you, we could still see everything. Actually, I was so busy star spotting that I didn't take in the plot. No doubt you'd have been the same. To tell you the truth, I'm not too keen on thrillers but it must have been good because at the end the whole audience rose to its feet and clapped. As I was saying, I'm not terribly sure what the story was about, but you really must go and see it when it's on general release.

All in all, though, it was an amazing evening and to top it off we went to Quaglino's for supper afterwards and guess what? Sarah Jane Fox and Brad Brat were at the next table. How cool is that? By the way, Sarah Jane Fox has awful skin problems. Still, who cares about that when you've got that much money!

4 Ask students to complete the conversation with discourse markers or other appropriate words. Let them check their answers in pairs before checking with the whole class.

T 4.4 Play the recording so that students can compare their answers.

Sample answers and tapescript
A = Anna   B = Ben

A Have you heard that Jan is thinking of marrying Paul?
B (1) **Really?** I don't know what she sees in him.
A I know what you mean. Mind you, (2) **he is a millionaire.**
B Yes, I suppose having all that money does help.
A Where did he get his money from?
B Apparently, (3) **he made a fortune in IT.**
A He's been married three times before. Did you know that?
B (4) **Actually**, it's just the once, I think.
A I suppose they'll have a big wedding.
B Of course (5) **they will. It'll be massive.**
A Oh, well. Good luck to them.
B Absolutely. (6) **By the way**, did you hear that Sara and Jeff had a car accident?
A Oh no! What happened?
B It wasn't serious. They skidded into a tree, but (7) **fortunately** they weren't going fast. The car's a write-off, but (8) **at least** no one was injured.

A Thank goodness for that. I should get in touch with them, but I don't have their address.
B As a matter of fact, (9) **it's in my diary**. I'll give it to you.
A Great. Thanks a lot. (10) **Anyway**, I must be going. I'm meeting Jan for lunch.
B Right. Nice to talk to you. Bye.

5 Ask students to complete the sentences with their own ideas. Do the first as an example. Let students check their answers in pairs before checking with the whole class.

Sample answers
1 Actually, we have. We met at a conference last year. / Actually, I don't think we have.
2 Basically, I have worked very hard and been very lucky.
3 Surely he doesn't need so much money. / Surely he knows it is a very unpopular decision.
4 Apparently, they're going to get married / get divorced / have a baby / move house.
5 I mean, they're too young / they have very little in common / I don't know what they see in each other.
6 Mind you, there are drawbacks like having your name all over the newspapers.
7 To tell you the truth, I thought it was really boring.
8 By the way, do you have that £5 you owe me?
9 After all, he has my telephone number.
10 Anyway, there isn't much I can do about it.

ADDITIONAL MATERIAL

Workbook Unit 4
Exercise 1 Discourse markers

SPEAKING (SB p44)

How to become an A-list celebrity

This is a reading maze, similar to the sort of activity often used in business training to develop team-building and decision-making skills. A maze can be an excellent activity to provoke much animated discussion in class, and students often have lots of fun doing it.

AIMS AND PREPARATION
Before class, you will need to photocopy and cut out the situation cards on TB pp125–132. You need one complete set of cards for each group of about four students. It's a good idea to stick the cards onto different-coloured stiff cardboard. That way, the cards will last a lot longer, and you can easily put the sets of cards back together in different-coloured sets.
The task consists of an initial situation with a menu of choices as to what to do next. Students work in small groups to decide what is best to do. Think about how best to group your students whilst preparing this lesson. You need to avoid grouping quiet students together –

the talkative ones need to be distributed. Four per group is a nice number – it is small enough for everyone to participate, and large enough for there to be a variety of opinions. Hopefully, they will rarely agree on the best course of action, so will need to persuade the others in their group. When a decision has finally been made, they tell you which number they want to go to.

Often the groups take a very long over their first three or four decisions, then they make subsequent decisions with less argument. They will come to an end of the maze after about eight or nine decisions. Obviously, you have no way of knowing just how long this activity will take, but you can expect the actual maze to last a minimum of about 30 minutes.

There are 26 different endings to the maze, 13 of them successful, and 13 ending in failure.

1 Lead in briefly by pinning up a picture of someone students will recognize as an A-list celebrity on the board. Explain that an A-list celebrity is somebody famous enough to be invited to all the best parties and premières. Ask *What could you do to become an A-list celebrity?*

Divide students into their groups of four or five and read the introduction to the activity as a class.

2 Ask students to read Situation 1 in the Student's Book. Meanwhile arrange the piles of role cards carefully, one for each group.

As the groups decide which situation they want to move to, find their appropriate card and give it to them. Encourage students to take it in turns to read out each card to their group, and tell them to discuss their options fully before asking for the next card. Point out that the aim is not to finish quickly, but to become famous. Go round monitoring and helping as necessary.

3 The process continues until the various groups come to the end of the maze. If one group finishes very early, you can ask them to go back and try again, making different decisions.

Inevitably, groups will finish at different times. Ask groups to consider their performance. Where did they go wrong? What should they have done? This will prepare them for some of the *What do you think?* questions which follow.

GLOSSARY

to come clean = to admit to something
destitute = without money and other basics of life
devious = behaving in a dishonest way
dish the dirt = reveal harmful information about someone
extortionate = outrageously expensive
futile = having no chance of success

geek = a boring person, usually obsessed with technical subjects
to get wind of = to hear about
mingle = to mix with
mocked = ridiculed
nerd = an embarrassingly stupid and unstylish person
obscene = offensive
to pluck up = to find (the courage)
press clippings = pieces cut from newspapers
pseudonym = a name used instead of your real name
to scour = to examine in detail
siblings = brothers and sisters
sordid = immoral or dishonest
streak = to run naked in a public place
tarnish = to spoil
wannabee = a person who wants to be famous
wrecked = ruined

What do you think?

In the feedback, find out which groups achieved celebrity status, and which didn't. Give groups a few minutes to discuss their decisions, then ask one student from each group to tell the class where they made right or wrong decisions. Discuss the way in which the group made their decisions, explaining that activities such as these are used in management training because they practise the process of decision-making and groups cooperating together. It is important that everyone has their say, and that they all listen to each other. It is no good if one person dominates.

Sample answers
A good leader is:
• decisive
• strong-minded / determined
• able to listen to other people
• able to lead without alienating people with different opinions
• not afraid to make tough decisions and get it wrong

LISTENING (SB p44)

An interview with a Hollywood star

This is a long listening activity divided into three short, bite-sized sections. The interview is punctuated by short bursts of songs from Liza Minnelli's shows. The tasks to each section involve prediction, comprehension questions, completing and answering questions, and inferring how Liza feels from what she says. Liza Minnelli speaks clearly, but in a lively and enthusiastic way.

1 You need to lead in to this topic by finding out what students know about Liza Minnelli. Ask students in pairs to look at the picture and decide whether the statements

are true or false. Don't give the answers at this stage. Elicit anything else any students know about Liza Minnelli.

BACKGROUND NOTE

A brief biography of Liza Minnelli

Born in 1946, Liza Minnelli is the archetypal Hollywood child. Her mother was Judy Garland (famous for playing Dorothy in *The Wizard of Oz*), and her father was Vincente Minnelli, the director, who made films such as *Father of the Bride* and *The Bad and the Beautiful*. Liza is a singer and actor. Her most successful roles have been in musicals. She won an Oscar for *Cabaret* in 1972. Other successful films include *New York, New York* and *Arthur*.

---

2 **T 4.5** Play the first part of the recording. Ask students to listen and correct the false statements in exercise1, then in pairs to discuss questions 1 to 6. You may need to play the recording a second time.

Answers
Exercise 1
1 False. She has been married four times.
2 False. There were *a few close friends* (said ironically as they were very famous guests).
3 True
4 True, but alcohol and drugs rather than natural health problems
5 False (but she went to school in England)

Exercise 2
1 The languages are English, French, and German. A cabaret is an entertainment, especially involving singing and dancing, provided in a restaurant or night-club while the customers are eating or drinking. The cabaret in the musical film from which this song comes was set in Berlin in the 1930s.
2 London feels like a second home because she spent part of her childhood at school in London. London audiences are the best in the world because they are responsive.
3 They respond, presumably by cheering or clapping, in a way that feels very interactive. The more they appreciate her singing, the better she wants to sing for them.
4 She puts on an English accent.
5 Sparkling and glittering like the inside of a diamond.
6 Marriage.

T 4.5 See SB Tapescripts p136

3 Ask students to read through the gapped questions in pairs, and discuss what they think the whole question might be.

T 4.6 Play the second part of the recording. Ask students to listen and complete the interviewer's questions. Let them check in pairs and listen again if necessary. Then ask students to answer the questions in their pairs.

Answers
1 Did it manage to still feel like a personal affair to you? *Yes, because the people that were invited are the people who are our friends.*
2 I think yours was a bit more glamorous though, wasn't it? *Don't know. We had a good time.*
3 How did you cope with all of that? *It didn't bother us.*
4 So you haven't fallen out with him over it? *No. I know his sense of humour.*

All the guests were famous because all her friends are famous. If she worked in shipping, her friends would be 'shipping' people.
Elton John said David was gay (homosexual).

T 4.6 See SB Tapescripts p136

4 **T 4.7** Play the third part of the recording. Ask students to think about how Liza feels when talking about the different situations. Let students discuss in pairs before discussing with the whole class.

Answers
1 She is proud of her independence: *made my mark; never took another cent from my family*.
2 She feels affectionate and says that they were supportive, funny, loving, and proud of her. She denies rumours that her upbringing was in any way harder than most people's.
3 She apologizes and sympathizes with her rebelliousness: *hope you enjoyed it*.
4 She has fond memories of it.
5 She feels close to her. She is a dear friend she has known all her life and still keeps in touch with.

T 4.7 See SB Tapescripts p136

Language work

Ask students in pairs to complete the sentences then check their answers with the tapescript on SB p136.

Answers
1 plagued
2 forward to performing
3 of a diamond ... sparkles ... glitters
4 kidding around (joking)
5 follow in your mother's footsteps
6 relish the performance in front of (*relish* = thoroughly enjoy)

What do you think?

EXTENSION ACTIVITY

Photocopy enough copies of the questionnaire on TB p134 for all the students in your class. Hand them out to the students. Tell students that they should choose a celebrity who they like and research the answers to the questions on the questionnaire at home. They could use the Internet, books, magazines, or their own general knowledge. In class, divide students into pairs, and ask them to take it in turns to be interviewers and celebrities by going through the questions on the questionnaire.

THE LAST WORD (SB p46)

You did, did you?

Using tag questions appropriately is very difficult for language learners. The aim of this section is to expose students to the different ways tags and replies work and to raise awareness. This is done by listening to conversations and by studying rules in the Grammar Reference. Practice is very controlled, and it is not expected that students will be able to go away and manipulate this area straightaway. As with the focus on auxiliaries in Unit 1, this section has a more general aim of further exposing students to the way auxiliaries are a key to the mastery of spoken English.

1 Ask students to look at the example of a tag question. What kind of tag is it, and what does it express?

Answer
It is a same way tag. It rises and is used after an affirmative statement. Liza is expressing surprise and pleasure in reaction to the interviewer's comment.

2 **T 4.8** Ask students to underline the tags and replies in the conversation. Play the recording, and ask them to draw an arrow above each tag or reply to show whether they rise or fall. Let students check their answers in pairs before checking with the whole class. You may need to play the recording more than once, or play and pause, as some students may find it difficult to hear the intonation pattern.

Refer students to Grammar Reference 4.2–3 on SB p151.

Answers and tapescript

A Liza Minnelli is just fantastic. Her concert was amazing.

B It was, wasn't it? And she puts so much energy into her songs, doesn't she?

A Yes, she does. Who wrote that song about marriage, and the way it changes the world?

B She did. It's one of the few songs she ever wrote, actually.

A So she can write as well as sing, can she? What a talent! Did you like her costumes?

B Yes, I did. I thought they were fantastic. I've seen most of them before.

A Have you? I haven't. She's playing again tomorrow, isn't she?

B Yes, I think so. Let's go again, shall we?

A All right. She's one of the all time greats, Liza Minelli is.

3 Ask students in pairs to add tags and replies to the conversations. This is quite difficult, so make students aware that there is often more than one possible answer, and that you just want them to have a go at thinking about how tags and replies might add to the conversations. It is a good idea to write the first conversation on the board, and work through it with the class as an example first.

T 4.9 Play the recording so that students can check their answers. Then ask students in pairs to practise the conversations. Make sure they are really trying to copy the intonation.

Sample answers and tapescript

1 A You haven't seen my car keys, have you?

 B No, I haven't. You had them this morning, didn't you?

 A Yes, I did. If I can't find them, I'll be late for work, won't I?

 B Panic over. Here they are!

 A Well done. You're a star, you are!

2 A You didn't like that meal, did you? You were pushing it around the plate.

 B No, I didn't. Well, it hadn't been cooked properly, had it? Your steak was all right, was it?

 A Yes. It was fine. Let's get the bill and go home, shall we?

 B OK. We won't be coming back here in a hurry, will we?

3 A You've forgotten the map, haven't you?

 B Oh, dear. Yes, I have.

A But I put it next to the car keys.

B Well, I didn't see it, did I?

A You're blind, you are.

B Oh, and you're perfect, are you?

4   The aim here is to provide some very controlled practice of tags and replies. Model the example with exaggerated stress and intonation. Then give students time to read through the statements and think about what they might say – don't let them write anything down. Ask students in pairs to take it in turns to say and respond to the statements in different ways.

T 4.10 Play the recording so that students can compare their ideas.

Sample answers and tapescript

1   *Jeremy earns an absolute fortune!*
He does, doesn't he?
Does he? I had no idea. How much?
So he's rich, is he? Well, well, well.
He's a rich man, Jeremy is.

2   *Peter's new German girlfriend, Anna, is very beautiful.*
Yes, she is.
Is she? She's not my type, actually.
So she's German, is she?
He's a lucky man, Peter is.

3   *Jane and John are going to Florida on holiday. They're so lucky.*
They are, aren't they?
Are they? I wish I was going.
So they're going to Florida, are they?
They're lucky, Jane and John are.

4   *Zidane played really well in the match on Sunday, didn't he?*
He did, didn't he?
Did he? I didn't think so.
He's a great player, Zidane is.

5   *Harrods is a great shop. You can buy everything there.*
You can, can't you?
Can you? I bet you can't buy a camel.
It's a wonderful shop, Harrods is.

6   *I think our teacher is the best.*
She is, isn't she?
Is she? I don't think she's as good as the one we had last year.
So you like her, do you?
She's a great teacher, Sylvia is.

7   *Simon's a very experienced traveller. He's been everywhere.*
He has, hasn't he?
Has he? I didn't realize.
He has, has he? I must ask him about it some time.
He's certainly been around, Simon has.

DON'T FORGET!

Writing Unit 4 Expressing a personal opinion (SB p122)

Workbook Unit 4
Exercise 2 Tags and replies
Exercise 3 Intonation in question tags
Exercise 4 Listening – Would you like to be famous?
Exercise 5 Fame and media vocabulary
Exercises 6–7 Synonyms and antonyms
Exercise 8 Phrasal verbs with a particle and preposition

Song
Mary C. Brown and the Hollywood sign (TB p134)

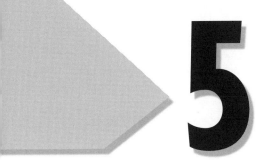

5

Ways of adding emphasis
Proverbs and poetry
Getting emotional

Love is ... ?

Introduction to the unit

The theme of this unit is love. The main reading texts are about unusual ways of meeting partners, and the main listening text is an interview with a 102-year-old lady who describes how she met her husband. The unit also includes a romantic Shakespearean sonnet on love.

Language aims

Ways of adding emphasis This unit looks at different ways of adding emphasis to a sentence. It introduces students to various examples of cleft or divided sentences.

> **WATCH OUT FOR ...**
> **Form, stress, and intonation**
> We add emphasis to a sentence in the following ways:
> * by emphasizing different parts of the sentence: ***What** she **did** was ...*
> * by emphasizing the whole sentence: ***What happened was that** she ...*
> * by using negative inversion: ***Never** have I ...*
> * by stressing the emphasized part of the sentence, and using an expressive tone range

The problem is in getting the form right. The various forms are very complex, so students will need lots of written accuracy practice, transforming base sentences to cleft sentences. However, once mastered, these forms are grammatically regular, so students should also be expected to be able to manipulate them to some extent in personalized fluency activities.

Students often work though activities such as this, following form rules, without thinking about why certain words might be emphasized in the first place.

So, get students to contrast these three sentences from the Grammar Reference:

> *Lucy moved to London.*
> *What Lucy did was move to London.*
> *Where Lucy moved to was London.*

In the second sentence, the word *was* comes before *move to London*, and so emphasizes that particular phrase as the answer to the question *What?* In the third sentence, *was* comes before *London* and so emphasizes *London* as the answer to the question *Where?* When students grasp this, the logic of structures such as *It was Lucy who moved to London, Why Lucy moved to London was because she got a job*, or *Who Lucy moved to London with was John*, should become apparent.

A further problem with these structures occurs with stress and intonation. The main stress is of course on the part of the sentence which is being emphasized. Students need to start their voice high and strongly stress key information as they produce the sentence. There are recognition and production activities in the practice exercises.

Grammar Reference 5.1–4 on SB p152 looks at the ways of adding emphasis discussed above. It also looks at shifting stress and emphatic *do, does,* and *did*. It is a good idea for you to read this carefully before teaching the grammatical section of this unit.

Vocabulary The *Vocabulary* section looks at proverbs. There is also work on guessing the meaning of vocabulary in the *Reading* section.

The last word This section looks at expressing emotion through tone and stress.

Notes on the unit

STARTER (SB p47)

1–3 Ask students in pairs to look at the pictures and discuss the questions. In the feedback, with a mature class, encourage students to discuss their experiences. If you have a teenage class, you may wish to avoid questions 2 and 3.

Sample answers

The types of love portrayed in the pictures are:
Line 1 – love of self / narcissistic love, love of pets, romantic / married love
Line 2 – parental love, religious love, teenage love
Line 3 – sibling love, hero worship, love in old age
A *soul mate* is a person you have a special relationship with because you share feelings and beliefs.

READING AND SPEAKING (SB p48)

Fateful attraction

1 Ask students to tell the class where their parents met.

ALTERNATIVE LEAD-IN

Write the following on the board: *a dating agency, the Internet, a windswept railway station, at the photocopier at work, at a disco, on a beach, at a conference, on a plane, at the gym*. Ask students in pairs or threes to discuss which of these places are the most common places to meet people, which are the most romantic, and, if they haven't met their perfect partner yet, what is the most romantic place they can think of to meet that person.

---

2 This is a jigsaw reading. Divide students into A and B groups. There should be about four students in each group, so, in a class of 16, you should have two A groups of four and two B groups of four. Ask Groups A to read article A, and Groups B to read article B. When they are ready, ask each group to discuss the questions.

Answers

Article A

1 Tina sent Andrew a random text message, and he replied.
2 For the first few months it was just fun, texting each other. Then they met in Somerset, and Andrew started driving over regularly on his motorbike at weekends. Then it got serious, and Andrew moved in. Then they got married.
3 They were originally attracted by personality and the fact that they had things in common. Tina didn't think much of Andrew's photo. However, when they met, Tina thought Andrew was better looking than in his photo, and Andrew thought Tina was stunning.
4 Tina feels that Andrew was out there waiting for her. Andrew says he never believed in fate but that 'when something like this happens, you realize that the odds are billions to one', which implies that he now believes they were fated to meet.

Article B

1 Emma cycled into Ross on her bike.
2 Ross sent Emma flowers. Emma went to thank Ross. A few weeks later Ross asked Emma out for dinner. They have been married for 11 years.
3 Emma was blown away, though she doesn't say if this was because Ross was *tall and blonde*. Ross thought Emma was gorgeous, particularly with her red hair, which struck him immediately.
4 Emma believes in fate, but thinks you have to act to 'build' your own destiny.

---

3 Rearrange students into AB pairs and ask them to compare the stories, using their answers to exercise 2.

Answers

Students' own ideas. But since Ross and Emma lived in the same town, had seen each other before, and Emma was very striking, perhaps their meeting was less dependent on fate than that between Tina and Andrew.

Vocabulary work

4 Ask students individually to find the phrases in their article. Make sure that they try to guess meaning from context before checking in their dictionary.

Answers

Article A

spur of the moment = spontaneously; without thinking about it or planning it
messaging back and forth = sending texts on the mobile phone from one person to the other and back
not overly impressed = not very or particularly impressed (often used ironically)
in the flesh = in real life (not in a photo or on TV)

---

make a serious commitment = decide to make a relationship serious, by, for example, getting engaged, married, or moving in together
knock sth on the head = end sth; here, end a relationship

Article B
burst out laughing = suddenly start laughing
scrambled to my feet = got up quickly but ungracefully
tore off along the path = went off very fast along the path
blown away = impressed in a way that is overwhelming. You can be blown away by someone's beauty, charm, or personality, so here it implies that the girl was so impressed by the boy's good looks and charm that she was very attracted to him.
mane of red hair = long, thick red hair. Usually, *mane* is used to describe the hair of a horse or lion.
catapulted into a garden = sent flying through the air into a garden (as if fired from a catapult)

5   Ask students in pairs to match the synonyms.

Answers

bizarre = weird	*blush = go red*
random = haphazard	*mates = pals*
stunning = striking	*alleyway = narrow path*
guts = courage	*between buildings*
bashfully = shyly	*retrieve = fetch (back)*
dumbstruck = lost for words	

6   **T 5.1** Play the recording and set a focus question: *How did Martine and Jaap* (pronounced /ja:p/) *meet?* (Martine is French and Jaap is Dutch. Both speak very good English.)

Answer
Jaap knocked on the door of a house at the summit of a mountain during a walking holiday. Martine opened the door.

T 5.1   See SB Tapescripts p137

Ask students to tell Martine and Jaap's story in their own words. This passage is exploited more intensively in Unit 5 exercise 5 of the Workbook (WB p32), so there is no need to go into detailed comprehension and vocabulary work at this stage.

What do you think?

Have a brief whole-class discussion about fate and relationships, using the questions in the Student's Book.

Sample answers
• Martine and Jaap's is probably the most romantic meeting.
• Tina and Andrew's is probably the most dependent on fate.
• Alternatives to fate: dating agency, Internet dating, a contact ad in a newspaper, an arranged marriage.

Ways of adding emphasis

Don't forget to look at the *Language Aims* section on TB p47, which looks at problems students may have. You should also read Grammar Reference 5.1–4 on SB p152.

1   Start by writing on the board: *I loved Tina's personality.* Elicit from students different ways of rephrasing this simple sentence in order to emphasize it. Suggestions include:

What I loved about Tina was her personality.
The thing I loved about Tina was her personality.
Tina's personality was what I loved (about her).
It was Tina's personality that I loved.

Put students in pairs or groups, making sure that each pair or group have read the same article. Ask them to write in the sentences which use emphatic phrases. Go round monitoring and helping as necessary.

Ask students to compare the two versions of the sentences and discuss the effect that the differences have. Rearrange students so that they can compare their answers with someone who read the other article.

Answers
Article A
Holding him for the first time is something I'll never forget.
The thing I loved about Tina was her personality.
What we do is either make a serious commitment or knock it on the head.
There was nothing I wanted more.

Article B
What I think is that you have to build your own destiny.
What I remember is seeing this very striking girl.
What I did was go straight to the local florist.
Finally, I did find the courage to ask her out.

The effect of the differences is to add emphasis.

LANGUAGE INPUT

Work through points 1–4 as a class. Points 1–3 look at how to form emphatic sentences, while point 4 looks at stress and pronunciation. You may wish to copy the example sentences on to the board or an OHT, so that you can underline and point out key aspects of form and stress.

1   Discuss **a** and **b** as a class, or in pairs followed by a whole-class discussion. Point out that these are cleft sentences, and that the purpose of adding certain structures to base sentences is to add emphasis to what you really want to say, for example, ***What I love about Tina is …*** means *I'm going to tell you **the thing that** I really love about her.*

Point out the form by underlining the structures that have been added:

What I love **about** Tina **is** her personality.
It's Tina's personality **that** I love.
What he **does is** criticize me ...

2 Point out that the negative expression goes at the start of the sentence, and there is inversion between subject and auxiliary verb.
I'll never ... ⇨ Never will I ...

3 Point out that the action of the verb is emphasized by stressing the auxiliary verb. Doing this with the Present Simple or Past Simple involves changing the form (*find ⇨ do find; found ⇨ did find*).

4 Model and drill some of the sentences from 1, 2, and 3. Then put students in pairs or threes to practise. Remind them to stress more strongly than usual. Note the following main stresses in these phrases:
*The **thing** I **love** about Tina is her perso**nal**ity.*
*It's Tina's perso**nal**ity that I **like**.*
*What he **does** is **crit**icize me con**stant**ly.*
***Never** will I forget **hold**ing him for the **first** time.*
*Finally, I **did** find the courage to ask her out.*

Refer students to Grammar Reference 5.1–4 on SB p152.

The accuracy practice exercises which follow practise form and pronunciation, and involve recognition, production, and personalized practice.

2 **T 5.2** Ask students to listen and identify ways of adding emphasis.

Answers and tapescript
1 I *do* do my homework immediately after class.
2 What it was, was love at first sight.
3 The thing most couples don't realise is how difficult married life can be.
4 It's the parents I blame for badly-behaved kids.
5 Not only are the values of society at risk but also the very survival of our nation is threatened.
6 Only then did I understand what she meant.
7 It was Sam that broke the blue vase!
8 I won't marry *anybody*.

3 The aim of this exercise is to practise shifting stress and intonation. Ask students in pairs to make the sentence emphatic in six different ways.

T 5.3 Play the recording, then ask students in pairs to practise the conversations. A good way to do this is to play each question and response, pause the recording, and ask students what line prompted each particular response.
Students can also look at the tapescript on SB p137.

Answers and tapescript
T 5.3

Question	Response
What's your favourite holiday?	We like walking in Scotland.
1 We like going skiing in Austria.	What *we* like is walking in Scotland.
2 What do you like doing on holiday?	*One* thing we *like* is *walking in Scotland*.
3 You like walking in Wales, don't you?	*Scotland* is where we like walking.
4 You like driving in Scotland, don't you?	It's *walking* in Scotland we like.
5 Dont you just hate walking in Scotland?	Walking in Scotland is something we *like*.
6 What do you like more than walking in Scotland?	There's *nothing* we like more than walking in Scotland.

4 Ask students in pairs to rephrase the sentences. There will be several possible variations for each one. You could set this exercise and the next one for homework.

Sample answers
1 What love does is change the course of your life.
2 Something she does is repeatedly contradict me.
3 What you have to do first is decide your priorities.
4 Bill's courage is what I admire.
5 What you should do is go to Spain for your holiday.
6 **B** I did tell him – honestly!
7 Never have I been so humiliated in my life.
8 Only occasionally do we eat out.

5 Ask students to use their own ideas to complete the sentences. Ask them to read sentences to the class, paying attention to stress and intonation.

T 5.4 Play the recording so that students can compare their answers.

Sample answers and tapescript
1 What I can't *stand* about the Royal Family is that they're like a soap opera.
2 What surprises me *every* time the Queen speaks is the way she pronounces her vowels.
3 The thing that annoys me *most* about politicians is that they don't keep their promises.
4 What we did after class yesterday was race home to watch the football match on TV.
5 It's our *teacher* who knows all the answers.
6 Something I've *never* told you is that I've been married before.
7 What the *government* should do is come up with a better transport policy.
8 *Never* in my *life* have I heard such a ridiculous story!

Ask students to prepare a presentation on *The thing I love the most*. It could be anything they feel passionate about: their job, car, clothes, food, a hobby such as skiing or gardening, or an area of study such as philosophy or history. Give them a copy of the *How to make a presentation* sheet on p141, and ask them to use ways of adding emphasis in their presentation (e.g. *What I really like about … is …*). You could ask them to bring in pictures or objects to illustrate the presentation. As these presentations will be of interest to all the students, you could ask one student to give a presentation at the start of each lesson. After the presentation, you could give each speaker feedback on the key errors they made, either orally or in writing.

ADDITIONAL MATERIAL

Workbook Unit 5
Exercise 1–4 Emphasis
Exercise 5 Listening – Martine and Jaap

VOCABULARY AND SPEAKING (SB p52)

Proverbs and poetry

Lead in to the first part of the lesson by writing on the board: *The way to a man's heart is … .* Ask students how they think this well-known proverb could end. Elicit amusing as well as likely endings.

1 Ask students to match the lines and make proverbs. In the feedback, find out whether they have similar proverbs in their own language. Let them check their answers in pairs before checking with the whole class.

Answers
1 Love is blind.
2 The course of true love never did run smooth.
3 All the world loves a lover.
4 Cold hands, warm heart.
5 All's fair in love and war.
6 Hell hath no fury like a woman scorned.
7 The way to a man's heart is through his stomach.
8 Marry in haste, repent at leisure.
9 Better to have loved and lost than never to have loved at all.
10 A little of what you fancy does you good.
11 Absence makes the heart grow fonder.
12 Familiarity breeds contempt.

2 Ask students in pairs to complete the replies with proverbs from exercise 1.

T 5.5 Play the recording so that students can check their answers. Ask students in their pairs to make similar lines of conversation using the other proverbs. Pairs then act out a conversation with another pair, who have to

respond with an appropriate proverb. Ask some students to act out their conversations for the class.

Answers and tapescript
1 A D'you know, when he left her, she threw all of his belongings out onto the street!
  B You know what they say – hell hath no fury like a woman scorned.
2 A They're back together again but their relationship's had a bumpy ride.
  B You know what they say – the course of true love never did run smooth.
3 A Go on then. I'll have one more. But that's the last one.
  B You know what they say – a little of what you fancy does you good.
4 A Good heavens! You? Going to cookery classes? You *must* be in love!
  B You know what they say – the way to a man's heart is through his stomach.
5 A But I don't want you to go off to Borneo for six months. How'll I survive?
  B You know what they say – absence makes the heart grow fonder.
6 A Oooh! Take your hands off my back! They're freezing!
  B You know what they say – cold hands, warm heart.

3 Ask students if they know which two proverbs come from Shakespeare.

Answers
Love is blind. (*The Merchant of Venice*)
The course of true love never did run smooth. (*A Midsummer Night's Dream*)
Though they sound Shakespearean, the following two belong to other major English writers:
Better to have loved and lost than never to have loved at all. (Tennyson)
Hell hath no fury like a woman scorned. (Congreve)

4 **T 5.6** Set the focus task, and play the recording.

Answer (tapescript follows exercise 5)
Summer.

5 Ask students in pairs to choose the correct word to complete each line. Do the first as an example. You may want to point out that the strict form of a sonnet provides some clues as to which word may be missing: A sonnet has fourteen lines, there are ten syllables to a line, and a Shakespearean sonnet has a fixed rhyming scheme, (ABAB, CDCD, EFEF, GG).

T 5.6 Play the recording again so that students can check their answers.

Answers and tapescript
SONNET NUMBER XVIII by William Shakespeare
Shall I compare thee to a **summer's** day?
Thou art more **lovely** and more temperate:
Rough winds do shake the darling buds of May,
And summer's lease hath **all** too short a date:
Sometime too hot the eye of heaven **shines**,
And often is his gold **complexion** dimmed,
And every fair from fair sometime declines,
By chance, or nature's changing course untrimmed:
But thy eternal summer shall not **fade**,
Nor lose possession of that fair thou ow'st,
Nor shall death **brag** thou wander'st in his shade,
When in eternal lines to time thou **grow'st**,
So long as men can **breathe**, or eyes can see,
So long lives this, and this gives life to thee.

Your students may enjoy reading the poem aloud. Put them in groups and ask them to take turns reading the poem to each other.

Alternatively, you could prepare students for this exercise by asking them to listen to the recording again, underlining strong stresses and marking clear pauses with an oblique:
Shall I compare thee / to a summer's day? /
That way, when they read out the poem, their stress and rhythm should be better.

6   Ask students in pairs to match the modern renditions to the line in the poem which they paraphrase. Point out that many of the words and phrases here are archaic and poetic, so there is not much point in students learning them.

Answers
1 a / b	5 i / j
2 d	6 k / l
3 e / f	7 m / n
4 g / h	

7   Discuss this as a class.

Sample answer
You could compare a loved one to jewellery, flowers, sweet food such as honey, the sea, the stars, the moon, the sun.

LISTENING AND SPEAKING (SB p53)

When love lasts forever

1   Lead in by asking whether your students celebrate St Valentine's Day. Ask some follow-up questions: *What do people typically do on St Valentine's Day? Is it usually men who send cards and buy flowers, or usually women, or both? Do you think it is a good thing to celebrate or just an excuse for florists and stationers to make money?*

ALTERNATIVE LEAD-IN
You could lead in to the specific topic of the listening by asking students how dating now and dating eighty years ago is different. Eighty years ago, how did people of the opposite sex in their country meet, get to know each other, get engaged, get married?
Here's a vocabulary exercise that you could do. Write the following words on the board: *court* (someone), *pop the question, go on a date with* (someone), *courtship, ask for someone's hand in marriage, dating.*
Ask students to pair words which have the same meaning, and to decide which word in each pair refers to relationships now, and which one refers to relationships eighty years ago.

Answers
court = go on a date with
pop the question = ask for someone's hand in marriage
courtship = dating
Court, ask for someone's hand, and *courtship* are old-fashioned.

2   **T 5.7**   Read the introduction and ask students to read through the lines and questions. Then play the recording and ask students to answer the questions.

Answers and tapescript
1   Her husband recently died.
2   Her husband Fred came through (survived) the First World War.
3   He walked past her and raised his hat in an attempt to get her attention.
4   He was clearly desperate to speak to her. By starting the conversation Olive stopped him feeling so awkward and embarrassed as he desperately tried to think of some way of speaking to her.
5   Getting married.
6   Their love for each other. Later in life.
7   The fact that she loved him.

T 5.7   See SB Tapescripts p137

3   Ask students in pairs to discuss and answer the questions. You may need to play the recording again.

Answers
1   He walked past her six times while she was watching a band in the park. Eventually, she spoke to him.
2   He came round and took her for a walk regularly. One evening, he asked her to marry him, but told her he had no money. She agreed to marry him, but not in a hurry.
3   Loving each other and making each other happy.
4   Fred was always asking Olive if she loved him, and she was always reassuring him that she did.
5   He says: *Oh ... what can you say?*

What do you think?

Conduct a brief whole-class discussion. Encourage students to talk about any relationships in their family that have lasted a long time.

ADDITIONAL MATERIAL

Workbook Unit 5
Exercise 12 Phrasal verbs – Relationships

THE LAST WORD (SB p54)

Getting emotional

1   **T 5.8** Ask students to read and listen to the recording. After each line, ask students in pairs to discuss who could be speaking and what the situation might be. Conduct a whole-class feedback.

> **Sample answers**
> 1 Angry father telling his son / daughter to move their old car.
> 2 Lover. On a special day such as an anniversary or a wedding day.
> 3 Mother trying to get a child to admit to doing something.
> 4 Student looking at a painting by an art teacher.
> 5 A party animal on being asked if they are free one evening.
> 6 A nosy person, trying to get a secret out of someone.
> 7 A wife on the way home after her husband has criticized her in front of friends.
> 8 Husband on seeing his wife walk in, late.
> 9 Mother telling people about her child's exam performance.
> 10 Parent encouraging child who has come third in a race.
> 11 Parent encouraging a child who has fallen over not to cry.
> 12 Hero on being praised for doing something brave.
> 13 Student thanking host family before leaving.
> 14 Someone finding themselves in a night club with a lot of violent people.
> 15 Friend amazed to be told that a mutual friend got married in green wellington boots.
> 16 Husband reacting to being criticized for being lazy and unfit.

2   Ask students in pairs to match the emotions to the lines in exercise 1. You may need to play the recording again.

> **Answers**
> | | | | |
> |---|---|---|---|
> | 1 | fury | 9 | pride |
> | 2 | adoration | 10 | encouragement |
> | 3 | suspicion / sarcasm | 11 | reassurance |
> | 4 | admiration | 12 | modesty |
> | 5 | boastfulness | 13 | gratitude |
> | 6 | curiosity | 14 | fear |
> | 7 | irritation | 15 | astonishment / amusement |
> | 8 | relief / anxiety | 16 | indignation |

3   **T 5.8** Ask students in pairs to practise saying the lines. Encourage students to compare their stress and intonation to that on the recording.

4   **T 5.9** Play the recording, pausing it to give students time to speculate on the emotion expressed in each example. Ask students to discuss their answers in pairs, then conduct a whole-class feedback. Students may disagree with the answers and suggest alternatives, and this should provoke some discussion using the words for the different emotions.

> **Answers**
> 1 indignation / fury
> 2 curiosity / suspicion
> 3 amusement
> 4 irritation
> 5 adoration
> 6 astonishment

DON'T FORGET!

Writing Unit 5 Discussing pros and cons (SB p123)

Workbook Unit 5
Exercise 6 Pronunciation – Sentence stress
Exercises 7–10 Vocabulary
Exercise 11 Synonyms – Verbs to describe different sounds
Exercise 12 Phrasal verbs – Relationships
Endquotes on love

Song
When you are old and grey (TB p135)

Distancing the facts
Nouns formed from phrasal verbs
Responding to news

Introduction to the unit

The theme of this unit is newspapers and journalism. The main reading texts are two newspaper articles on the same subject, a royal scandal story about how Prince Harry, youngest son of Prince Charles, has been caught underage drinking. This section of the unit contrasts the way the story is told in a tabloid newspaper (*The Sun*), and how it is told in a quality broadsheet, (*The Independent on Sunday*). The main listening text is an interview with a foreign correspondent, who talks about his career and how reporting foreign news has changed.

Language aims

Distancing the facts This unit looks at two different passive constructions, and two constructions using the verbs *seem* and *appear*, all of which are typically used in newspaper articles to give information without stating categorically that it is true. They are all ways in which the writer puts distance between him or herself and the facts.

> **WATCH OUT FOR …**
> **Form and context**
> When using passive constructions to distance the facts, students need to think about:
> • the written context in which these constructions are used
> • learning the fixed forms used to express this idea

The context in which this sort of language is usually used is quite restricted. These structures are generally used in written language rather than spoken. Here the language is introduced and practised in the context of newspaper reporting.

The form of these structures is complex yet predictable. There is plenty of practice within the unit in written transformation exercises to help students become familiar with them. The basic forms introduced are:

1   *It* + passive verb + (*that*) + clause
    It is said that he works in the City.

2   Subject + passive verb + *to* infinitive
    He is said to work in the City.

3   *It* + (*would*) *seem(s)* / *appear(s)* + (*that*) + clause
    It would seem that he works in the City.

4   Subject + (*would*) *seem(s)* / *appear(s)* + *to* infinitive
    He appears to work in the City.

Grammar Reference 6.1–3 on SB pp152–153 looks at passive constructions, as well as *seem* and *appear*. It is a good idea for you to read this carefully before teaching the grammatical section of this unit.

Vocabulary The *Vocabulary* section looks at nouns formed from phrasal verbs, by combining verb + preposition, (*cutback*), or preposition + verb, (*update*). There is also work on formal words and informal words, idioms in the *Reading* section, and some passive vocabulary extension in the *Listening* section.

The last word This section generally looks at common expressions used to respond to news, and at how to sound sarcastic.

Notes on the unit

STARTER (SB p55)

If you have access to English-language newspapers, find a typical tabloid headline about something currently in the news. Photocopy the headline and put it on the board, and ask students about it. *What current news story is it describing? Is it from a sensationalist tabloid or serious broadsheet?*

1 Ask students to say why the words are typical of headlines, then ask them in pairs to complete the headlines.

GLOSSARY

axe = cut, get rid of
ban = prohibition
bank raid = bank robbery
bid to break even = attempt to stop making losses
Bogus vicar cons widow = a man impersonating a vicar tricks a widow
cops = police
crack = very addictive form of cocaine
deal blow = seriously undermine
drug haul = seizure of large amount of drugs
dumps = leaves
fury = anger
gay = homosexual
hubby and missus = husband and wife
measly = pathetically small
orgy = group sex
PC = police constable
probe = investigation
row = angry argument
swoop = sudden raid
spells havoc for hols = means chaos for holidays
sword maniac = dangerously mad person armed with a sword

Answers
They are short and dramatic to grab the attention of the reader, and to fit into the banner style of headline typical of tabloids.
 1 Neighbours' **row** over hedge ends in court
 2 BA to **axe** 5,000 jobs in **bid** to break even
 3 OAPs' **fury** at measly 1.5% rise in pensions
 4 £50 million hubby puts bank **ban** on missus
 5 Sword maniac shot by **cops**
 6 New **probe** into murders reveals fresh clues
 7 Wife **dumps** husband in sex **orgy**
 8 Police **swoop** on crack factory – huge drug **haul**
 9 PC shot in bank **raid** dies
 10 New inflation figures deal **blow** to recovery hopes
 11 Bogus vicar **cons** widow of life savings
 12 Air traffic control strike threat spells **havoc** for hols

2 **T 6.1** Play the recording. Ask students to listen and answer the focus questions. If you have access to the newspapers mentioned by the speakers, bring in copies of each, and briefly introduce them to students before they listen.

Answers and tapescript
1 *The Guardian*: well-written, no predictable political bias, crossword
2 *The Independent / Observer* on Sundays: trusts them, no obvious political affiliations, impartial, interesting, particularly features, good coverage of the arts
3 The *Mail* (the *Daily Mail*): light-weight, readable, not too wordy, articles on health, fashion, film stars, diets. But very right-wing – anti-Europe, xenophobic, homophobic
4 *The Sun*, *The Mirror*, *The Times*, the *Financial Times*: a broad spectrum
The Sun: news about celebrities
The Mirror: left-wing conscience
The Times: good features
the *FT*: helps with investments
5 The *International Herald Tribune*: good viewpoint of foreign affairs around the world, keep in touch with the USA, baseball coverage

T 6.1
1 I must confess I don't buy a newspaper every day. When I do buy one, it tends to be *The Guardian*. It's well written, and it doesn't have a predictable political bias. It also has a crossword that is exactly the right level of difficulty for me.
2 I get *The Independent* every day, and *The Observer* on Sundays. They're the only newspapers I trust. They don't have the obvious political affiliations of some of the other dailies, they seem relatively impartial. They have interesting sections. I listen to the news all day long, so I tend to like the feature sections of newspapers rather than the news reporting. *The Independent* has good coverage of the arts - exhibitions, shows, concerts, reviews.
3 I get the *Mail*. It's pretty light-weight and readable. I find the broadsheets a bit too wordy for me. The *Mail* has articles on health, fashion, film stars, diets. I don't like its politics, however. It's a real right-wing rag. Anti-Europe, xenophobic, homophobic. I sometimes wonder why I buy it.
4 I'm a bit of a newspaper junkie. I read *The Sun*, *The Mirror*, *The Times*, and the *Financial Times*. I like to get a broad spectrum. The Sun tells me what's happening to celebs. *The Mirror* presents the left-wing conscience. *The Times* has some good features. And the *Financial Times* helps me with my investment portfolio.
5 I get the *International Herald Tribune*. It provides a good viewpoint of foreign affairs around the world. And it keeps me in touch with the States. I also get to find out what's happening in Major League Baseball, and see how my team the Yankees are faring.

3 In a multinational class, ask students to discuss the questions in small groups. Ask one student to lead the discussion, asking the questions, and making sure everyone has a chance to speak. Ask another student to make notes, then briefly feedback on what was said to the rest of the class.

BACKGROUND NOTE

Low-brow daily tabloid newspapers
The Sun, The Mirror, The Star. They all cover sport, gossip, scandalous stories about the Royal family and celebrities, and contain lots of competitions, free gifts, and pictures of topless girls. *The Mirror* is traditionally more left-wing. *The Sun* is the biggest-selling British daily.

Middlebrow daily tabloids
The *Daily Mail*, the *Daily Express*. Both are right of centre, and aim for middle class, middle-aged, middle brow England. They feature sport and gossip, but also plenty of commentary on politics and current issues.

Highbrow daily broadsheets
The Times, The Daily Telegraph, The Guardian, The Independent, The Scotsman (in Scotland). *The Daily Telegraph* is politically to the right, *The Guardian* to the left, *The Times* slightly right of centre, and *The Independent* claims to be impartial. Intensive coverage of news and politics. However, they all also provide extensive sports coverage, lots of features, and *The Times*, in particular, is not afraid to publish a bit of celebrity gossip.

Sunday newspapers
All the above newspapers above have Sunday equivalents, with the exception of *The Sun* and *The Guardian*, whose approximate equivalents would be *The News of the World* and *The Observer*. Sunday newspapers in Britain are huge, and filled with lots of supplements: magazines, separate sports and arts sections, etc.

READING AND SPEAKING (SB p56)

Tabloid and broadsheet newspapers

These are two authentic newspaper articles, reporting a 'scandal' story about the British Royal Family. As such, they are typical of the way British newspapers report on the Royal soap opera. Prince Harry is the second and youngest son of the heir to the throne, Prince Charles, the Prince of Wales. His mother was Princess Diana, who died in 1997, and his older brother is Prince William, next in line to the throne after Prince Charles.

1 Ask students in pairs to look at the front pages of the two newspapers and discuss their impressions.

Answers
tabloid: *The Sun*
broadsheet: *The Independent on Sunday*
The headline in *The Sun* is much bigger and more dramatic, more informal, (*Harry* not *Prince Harry*), and it uses shorter, dramatic words.
The photograph in *The Sun* is a paparazzi photograph compared to *The Independent on Sunday*'s portrait photograph.
The layout in *The Sun* makes this story fill the entire front page, whereas *The Independent on Sunday* front page features other stories.
The Sun uses the word *exclusive* because it has had exclusive interviews with some sources.
The text on the front page of *The Sun* is very short, in order to make space for the large headline.

2 Ask students to read the articles, summarize the stories, and answer the questions.

Sample summaries
The Sun
Prince Harry has admitted smoking cannabis and drinking in a local pub. His school, Eton College, has warned Harry that his behaviour will be under scrutiny. Harry's father, Prince Charles, ordered his son to visit a drugs rehabilitation unit to frighten him into turning his back on drugs.
The Independent on Sunday
Last June and July, Prince Charles sent his two sons, Harry and William, to visit Featherstone Lodge Rehabilitation Centre to learn about the danger of drugs. This followed the discovery that 16-year-old Prince Harry had taken drugs and drunk alcohol. Many young aristocrats and politicians' children have recently succumbed to drink and drugs.
Answers
The Independent on Sunday is more factual and objective.
The Sun is more sensational.
The Independent on Sunday has longer, more complex sentences.
The Sun uses more informal, idiomatic, conversational language.
The Independent on Sunday uses more formal, controlled, concise language.

3–6 Ask students in pairs to do the tasks. Go round monitoring and helping as necessary. Allow pairs to check their answers with another pair before checking with the whole class.

Answers
Exercise 3
The Sun obtained information from unnamed sources, senior sources at Eton, Eton insiders, and an unnamed pupil who was expelled from Eton for cannabis use.

The Independent on Sunday obtained information from unnamed sources (reports said ...), Bill Puddicome, chief executive of Phoenix House, a spokesman for St James' Palace, and the *Mail on Sunday*.

The Independent on Sunday attributes its sources more because, as a quality newspaper, it wishes to show that it has investigated thoroughly. Long-winded references to sources would spoil the dramatic flow of the tabloid's style.

Exercise 4

Harry sent to drug rehabilitation unit ⇨ When this happened ⇨ Why this happened ⇨ What Harry did there ⇨ Other famous children guilty of drink and drugs behaviour ⇨ A reported drinking incident involving Harry ⇨ An underage drinking episode involving the Prince's father

Exercise 5

The Sun: Harry, Prince Harry, teenager, youngster, the Prince, his (Charles') son, Eton pupil

The Independent on Sunday: Prince Harry, Harry, the Prince

Exercise 6

from *The Sun*:

John Lewis is headmaster of Eton.

Highgrove is where Prince Charles lives. It's Harry's home.

The News of the World is a Sunday tabloid.

The Berkshire college refers to Eton.

from *The Independent on Sunday*:

Featherstone Lodge is the drug rehabilitation centre that Prince Harry was sent to visit.

The Rattlebone Inn is a pub where Prince Harry was seen drinking.

St James's Palace is Prince Charles' official London residence, where his offices are.

David Baker was landlord of the Rattlebone Inn at the time of the incident.

Language work

7 Ask students in pairs to make questions.

Answers

2 How did Prince Charles find out that his son had been taking drugs?

3 Why did Prince Charles insist on him visiting a drug rehabilitation centre?

4 Was the visit instructive?

5 What is the potential danger of using cannabis?

6 What is Eton's policy on drugs?

7 What was Harry said to have done at the Rattlebone Inn?

8 How did William react when he was offered a joint? (*a joint* = a cannabis cigarette)

8 Ask students in pairs to find the words and idioms in the texts, and match them to the words in the boxes. Monitor this activity carefully, and help any students with difficulties. Rather than going through all the words

in the feedback, ask students if there any words that they were not sure about and would like to have explained in more detail.

Answers

The Sun	*The Independent*
pot	emerged
has had the yellow card	alerted
booze	harrowing
a handful	consequences
going off the rails	widespread
nipped in the bud	succumbed
all eyes will be on ...	premises

EXTENSION ACTIVITY

Find and photocopy a major international news story from a British or American newspaper, and hand it out to the students. Ask them to read the headline and tell you what the story is about. As homework, ask the students to find the same news story in a publication in their own language (in a newspaper or on the Internet) and answer these questions:

1 What facts are different in the two publications?

2 What difference in tone or emphasis do you notice? Why do you think this is?

3 How would you compare the style of reporting in English with that in your own language?

In class, ask students to discuss their findings (they could do it in groups if you have a large class).

LANGUAGE FOCUS (SB p59)

Distancing the facts

Don't forget to look at the *Language Aims* section on TB p55, which looks at problems students may have. You should also read Grammar Reference 6.1–3 on SB pp152–153.

LANGUAGE INPUT

Read through the sentences with the students. Check the form of the phrases in bold. Point out that these are commonly-used language constructions in newspaper articles because it allows the writer to give information without stating it to be categorically true. It also allows the writer to put distance between him or herself and the facts. In other words, the writer is saying, this is not my opinion, it is what other people have said, reported, or believe to be true.

1 **Passive constructions**

Ask students in pairs to read through the active sentences and note the way they have changed to passive sentences in 1 and 2.

> *It* is followed by the passive verb + (*that*) + clause.
> *He* is followed by the passive verb + *to* infinitive.
>
> 2 **seem** and **appear**
> Ask students in pairs to read through the examples.
> There are two forms:
> Subject + *seem(s)* / *appear(s)* + *to* + infinitive
> *He seems to have learned …*
> *It* + *seems* / *appears* + (*that*) + clause
> *It appears that the Prince took …*
>
> Refer students to Grammar Reference 6.1–3 on SB pp152–153.

Passive constructions

1 Ask students to rewrite the sentences. Do the first as an example. Let students check their answers in pairs before checking with the whole class.

Answers
1 The international criminal Jimmy Rosendale is reported to be living in Ireland.
2 He is believed to be the head of a gang of bank robbers.
3 The gang is known to have carried out a series of robberies.
4 They are supposed to have escaped with over €1 million.
5 They are thought to be targeting banks in small provincial towns.
6 Jimmy Rosendale is said to be wanted for questioning by police in five countries.
7 He is understood to have escaped from police custody by bribing a warder.
8 He is assumed to have been involved in criminal activities all his life.
9 He is presumed to have learnt his trade from his father.
10 His father is alleged to be / have been the mastermind behind the 2001 gold bullion robbery.

seem and *appear*

2 Ask students to change the sentences. Do the first as an example. Let students check their answers in pairs before checking with the whole class.

Answers
1 The weather seems to be changing.
2 We appear to have missed the train.
3 It appears / would appear that Peter has been attacked by a bull. / It appeared that Peter had been attacked by a bull.
4 It seems / would seem that he has survived the ordeal. / It seemed that he had survived the ordeal.
5 The Government would seem to have changed its policy.
6 They appear to be worried about losing the next election.

Reporting the news

3 Divide students into small groups of three or four to write a short article. Ask them first to decide which headline to choose, then to brainstorm ideas and vocabulary that they could use to write the article. Finally, nominate one person in each group to write the article while others contribute. Monitor and prompt students to use passive constructions. Pin the articles on the classroom walls for all students to read.

You could ask students to write a further article based on a different headline individually for homework.

> **GLOSSARY**
> *PM* = Prime Minister
> *TV soap star* = a star of a television soap opera
> *to wed* = to get married
> *embezzle* = use money in your care for illegal, personal gain
> *wins place at Oxford* = gets a place to study at Oxford University

4 **T 6.2** Let the students choose someone to write on the board, or choose one of the students yourself. This student will write the dictation on the board while the rest of the class helps. You will need to start, stop, and rewind the recording frequently and quickly. This can be a very challenging exercise, with new vocabulary for which the students need to work out the spelling, lots of contracted forms, and complex sentences with many subordinate clauses.

> **Tapescript**
> Here is the news at eight o'clock.
>
> News is coming in of an earthquake in southern China. Five hundred people are believed to have died, with over two thousand injured. International rescue teams have arrived in the area, and a huge humanitarian operation is underway. The earthquake is reported to have been 6.4 on the Richter scale.
>
> A Monet painting has been stolen from the Louvre museum in Paris. Thieves are thought to have hidden themselves while the museum was closing, then escaped through a skylight. The painting is said to be worth $50 million.
>
> The crisis over rising house prices seems to be settling down. Interest rates fell a further half a per cent last month. Government sources said that it is hoped that prices will level out to an overall rise of five per cent over the last twelve months.

ADDITIONAL MATERIAL

Workbook Unit 6
Exercises 1–3 Passives
Exercise 4 Listening – Can it be true?
Exercise 5 Pronunciation – Reading the news

Nouns formed from phrasal verbs

LANGUAGE INPUT

1–2 Ask students to read through the rules. The stress is on the first syllable of the compound nouns, (**up**date). Note that compound verbs are usually stressed on the second syllable, (up**date**).

1 Ask students in pairs to complete the sentences. Let students research the answers in their dictionaries.

Answers

2	outfit	9	downloads
3	outlook	10	breakthroughs
4	outlets	11	breakdown
5	takeaway	12	break-up
6	takeovers	13	backup
7	downfall	14	shake-up
8	downpour	15	set-up

2 Ask students in pairs to choose five or six words from the box that they don't know or are not sure about. Ask them to write definitions and sample sentences with gaps to check these words, in the same way that the words were checked in exercise 1. When students are ready, ask one pair to change their work with another pair, then try to complete the sentences.

GLOSSARY

lookout = place from which someone watches for an intruder, enemy, etc.
setback = a problem that delays or stops progress
outbreak = sudden start of a disease or an episode of violence
backlash = extreme reaction to an event
upkeep = maintenance
slip-up = a careless mistake
offshoot = a company, group or organization that has developed from a larger one
comeback = a return to success and fame
showdown = a big meeting, argument or fight that finally settles a disagreement, or proves who is best
upturn = improvement
write-off = a car that is too badly damaged to be repaired (the insurance company writes it off their books)
drawback = disadvantage
hold-up = a delay / an armed robbery
outburst = a sudden expression of strong feeling
knock-out = a hit that knocks you down and leaves you unable to get up again

A foreign correspondent

This interview with a foreign correspondent is an intensive listening activity. The tasks, which deal with comprehension and interpretation, break down the listening into two bite-sized sections. Simon Winchester speaks at length, with a certain amount of rephrasing and a high level of vocabulary.

1 Ask students to look at the photograph and describe what is happening. This is an opportunity to elicit some interesting vocabulary: *journalist, correspondent, cover a news story.* (Note that a correspondent is a journalist who deals with one specialist area. For example, war correspondent, political correspondent, South-East Asia correspondent).

2 Conduct a brief class discussion on these statements. Encourage a range of views. Prepare by thinking of a couple of recent news stories in advance which support or contradict the statements.

3 Pre-teach these key words and phrases from the interview. You could do this by providing definitions and / or example sentences yourself, or getting students to use dictionaries.

Answers

do somebody justice = represent someone fairly
a pack (of wild animals) = a group
inconspicuous = not attracting attention
off-beat places = unusual and remote places that other people don't go to
a patch (of land) = a small piece
a skirmish = a brief fight between small groups of soldiers
to shrink = to get smaller. Often used to describe clothes that get smaller when washed
subtlety = small distinctions – if something is subtle then it is not immediately clear, it has many layers of meaning or reference
focused = concentrated on one particular thing

Alternatively, you could combine some of this vocabulary in a prediction task. Write the following words and phrases on the board:
inconspicuous   extrovert   focused   adventurous in love with danger   always travelling to off-beat places a loner   motivated by money   biased   objective an observer of life

Ask students in pairs to check the words, then decide which ones best describe the qualities of a foreign correspondent. Listening to see if they predicted correctly could make a straightforward first listening task.

4 **T 6.3** Play the recording. Ask students to answer the questions. Let them check their answers in pairs before checking with the whole class.

Answers
Part one
1 She asks him whether being described as an adventurous foreign correspondent is a fair description of him. He answers by saying it is a flattering description, and that he is adventurous in the sense of doing things alone, inconspicuously, in exotic places, and not travelling with the journalistic pack.
2 He is adventurous, inconspicuous, a listener and observer, who likes to work alone in off-beat places. He isn't a 'pack' journalist who follows the big news stories with all the other journalists.
3 The Watergate affair and Nixon's resignation. (In 1974 President Richard Nixon was forced to resign from office as President of the United States following the Watergate scandal. A break-in at the National headquarters of the opposition Democratic Party, the Watergate building in Washington D.C., resulted in allegations that the President was involved. He denied it and there was a cover-up.)
4 He likes remote places, especially islands.

Part two
5 The public's lack of interest in things foreign.
6 Because of the British Empire, or memories of it, the British had an interest in what was happening abroad.
7 It is the only newspaper that still has a lot of foreign correspondents.
8 He thinks it's unfortunate that it has taken over. It does not take time to look at the background, the whole picture, the subtleties of a story. It makes the story then leaves.
9 News reporting where you look behind the story.
10 It has meant less foreign news coverage, and less money for foreign correspondents to spend.

T 6.3 See SB Tapescripts p138

Language work

5 Ask students in pairs to discuss the meaning of the excerpts. Refer them to the tapescript on SB p138 if they wish to see the phrases in context.

Sample answers
* *I was very much in the thick of things* = I was right in the middle of the action / events
* *a more fulfilling time personally* = a more rewarding time that satisfied my personal ambitions
* *I've never made a virtue out of danger* = getting into dangerous situations isn't something I've held to be good or virtuous in itself

* *the echoes of empire* = the distant memories of the British Empire, which effectively ended after the Second World War
* *the little essay which illuminates brilliantly the inner workings of some distant place* = the short piece of writing that explains exactly why things happen in the way they do in a place that we don't know much about
* *newspapers have become more market-driven, and less of a public service* = newspapers have to react to what 'the market' wants – in other words, they have to sell large numbers and compete with rival newspapers. In the past, many newspapers felt they were there to inform and educate the public about world events – now they just give the public what they want in order to sell more copies.
* *their hands are tied* = they are not free to do as they wish

6 Read the example, then ask students in pairs to find other examples of understatement in the tapescript.

Answers
I really don't like pack journalism (He hates it)
a patch to cover from Tehran to Bangkok (a huge area)
wandering really (not wandering, but travelling with an important purpose)
I've covered a reasonable number of wars and skirmishes and things (for *reasonable*, read *enormous*)
Most readers aren't particularly interested (aren't interested at all)
the little essay (the very important essay)
my friends who remain foreign correspondents now are not the sort of happy bunch that we were (very miserable and angry, in fact)

What do you think?

Sample answers
In some ways TV creates the news simply by deciding to focus on something as a story. If there is some good video footage of an event, for example an accident, it becomes a big news story because the TV channel are keen to show the video clip as often as possible.
Arguably, TV creates the news by invading the privacy of famous people, in which case the presence of the cameras becomes the main story. Some TV news channels also start campaigns against crime, etc.

EXTENSION ACTIVITY

If you have access to a camcorder, you can make your own TV news in class. Otherwise you can prepare a radio broadcast by recording it on audio cassette. Bring in a pile of today's newspapers. If this is a problem, ask each student to bring in a copy of today's newspaper with them for the lesson. Or you could photocopy relevant bits of an English language newspaper for students to refer to, though make sure your school has permission to photocopy newspapers.

Divide students into groups, with four to six people in each group. Write the following 'roles' on the board:

1 International news reporter
2 National news reporter
3 Local news reporter
4 Interviewer
5 Sports reporter
6 Weather forecaster

Ask the students to decide which person in each group will take which role. If you have a small class, and decide on using groups of four, miss out the sports and weather roles.

Ask students to look at the newspapers, decide which story to cover, and rewrite the stories to make a fairly short, spoken news item. Monitor and prompt. Remind students to use language from the *Language Focus* section of this unit. You will need to help the students with role 4 in particular. Tell them that they are going to interview someone in the school about their job, then write up a summary of the interview for the broadcast. Ideally, provide them with a portable cassette recorder so that they can record their interview. If this all seems impractical, they can always interview you.

Ask students to prepare to make the broadcast, and practise reading the items aloud with natural stress and word linking. Make sure the groups decide in what order each person is going to speak. The first speaker will need to introduce the news programme.

Introduce a few key phrases that students may need:
It's 10 o'clock, and here's the news.
This is _____ in London.
And now over to _____ in Moscow.
_____ is our reporter in New York.

When the students are ready, set up the classroom for the news programme. If you are using a camcorder, have a table with a chair behind it for the newsreader. Get the weather person to draw a map of the country you are in on the board. If you are using an audio cassette, make sure all students have easy access to the machine. Otherwise, let students work together to decide how they are going to do this. It is up to them how they want the news programme to look and/or sound.

Play the broadcast to another class.

ADDITIONAL MATERIAL

Workbook Unit 6
Exercise 6 Nouns formed with a verb and preposition
Exercise 8 Phrasal verbs and nouns formed from them

THE LAST WORD (SB p62)

Responding to news

Lead in by writing on the board *I've just won the lottery!* Ask students to respond to your news. See what they come up with.

1 Ask students in pairs to match the statements and responses.

T 6.4 Play the recording so that students can check their answers and identify the additional comments in the recording.

Answers and tapescript
1 A Guess what! I won £5 million on the lottery!
   B You're kidding! Really? That's amazing!
2 A My grandfather died last week.
   B Oh, no! I'm so sorry to hear that. You were very close, weren't you?
3 A One of my students told me I was a lousy teacher.
   B What a cheek! I hope you told him where to get off.
4 A Here we are! Home at last.
   B Thank goodness for that! I thought we'd never make it.
5 A I'm broke since I bought all those designer clothes.
   B Tough. It's your own fault. Serves you right.
6 A Have you heard that Jim's leaving to go to another job?
   B Good riddance. He was always useless.
7 A I missed the last bus and had to walk home. I didn't get home till midnight.
   B What a drag! You must have been really fed up.
8 A When I get a job, I'm going to be a millionaire. I'll have three houses and ten cars.
   B In your dreams. Fat chance you have of being able to afford a caravan and a bike.
9 A I'm going on holiday to Barbados for two weeks with my girlfriend.
   B Nice one! Can I come too?
10 A My six-year-old daughter painted me a picture for Father's Day.
   B Bless her! Isn't that sweet?
11 A I'm fed up with revising. Let's go out for a beer.
   B Now you're talking! A cold beer would go down a treat.
12 A Susan says she never wants to see you again.
   B So what? I don't care. I wouldn't go out with her if she were the last person on earth.
13 A My team lost again last weekend.
   B Where's the surprise? They lose every weekend. They're rubbish.

14 A Dad, I'm going to an all-night party. Is that OK?
   B Over my dead body. You've only just turned twelve! No way!

2 Ask students in pairs to match the responses in B to what they express.

Answers
k surprise at someone's lack of respect
l sympathy
h no sympathy
m pleasure that someone is leaving
f no surprise
a no concern
g relief
d I like what you're saying.
n Isn't she cute?
j How boring!
e I'm impressed!
i I don't believe you.
b What you're saying won't happen.
c I won't allow this to happen.

3 Ask students to cover the responses and try to remember the conversations, then practise them in pairs.

4 **T 6.5** Play the recording. Ask students to listen and reply using responses from exercise 1, and then to continue the conversations. For the first two or three, you may need to elicit responses from individuals in the class. However, once they have got the idea, students should have lots of responses.

Sample answers and tapescript
1 My sister's been married seven times. (*You're kidding!*)
2 My dog died last night. (*Oh no! I'm so sorry to hear that.*)
3 My teenage daughter told me she thought I was boring, stupid, and old-fashioned. (*What a cheek!*)
4 When I told little Katie that her grandma had gone to heaven, she asked when we could visit! (*Bless her!*)
5 One day I'm going to be a famous film star, just you watch. (*In your dreams.*)
6 I can't come out tonight. My dad says I have to do my homework and tidy my room. (*What a drag!*)
7 My girlfriend has dumped me! All because I said girls were stupid. (*Where's the surprise?*)
8 Dad. I know you don't like Malcolm, but I love him and I'm going to marry him. (*Over my dead body.*)
9 I failed the exam because I overslept and missed half of it. (*Tough.*)
10 After last week's argument, my flatmate's decided to leave. (*Good riddance.*)
11 We've been given an extra week to hand in our essays. (*Thank goodness for that!*)
12 My parents bought me a new car for my birthday. (*Nice one!*)

13 How would you feel about going to the cinema this evening, then out for a pizza? (*Now you're talking!*)
14 I'm going to tell the teacher what you said. (*So what? I don't care.*)

5 **T 6.6** Play the recording. Ask students to listen for the second speaker's attitude.

Answers and tapescript
In all responses, **B**'s attitude is one of sarcasm.

T 6.6
1 **A** Pete. I crashed your car. Sorry.
  B Great. That's all I needed. Thank you very much.
2 **A** When you come on Saturday, we're going to have an ice-cream.
  B Ooh! How exciting. I can't wait.
3 **A** You know that guy Parkinson, the millionaire? Apparently he's been sent to prison for tax evasion.
  B Well, ain't that a shame! My heart bleeds for him.
4 **A** I have finally understood how this machine works.
  B You're so clever, you are. I don't know how you kept it secret for so long.

Ask students in pairs to look at the tapescript on SB p138 and practise the conversations, with **B** trying to sound as sarcastic as possible.

6 Ask students in pairs to make conversations from the chart. Get some students to act out their conversations. The rest of the class have to say whether they sound sincere or sarcastic. There is no right or wrong answer here – any of the responses could be used.

Don't forget!

Writing Unit 6 A letter to a newspaper (SB pp124–125)

Workbook Unit 6
Exercise 7 Nouns with a special meaning in the plural
Exercise 9 Pairs of nouns, adverbs, and verbs

Stop and check 2 (TB pp 145–146)
Progress test 1 (TB pp 151–152)

7

Modal auxiliary verbs
Rhyme and reason
Breaking the rules of English

Words of wisdom

Introduction to the unit

The theme of this unit is words of wisdom – the wise advice that people give you to help you through life. The main reading text is an open 'letter' from a well-known BBC correspondent, Fergal Keane, to his newborn son. Originally a scripted radio 'letter', it is a moving message of love and hope from a father to a son. The main listening texts are ten 'vox pop' extracts in which a variety of people recall the best words of wisdom they were ever given.

Language aims

Modal auxiliary verbs This unit looks at modal auxiliary verbs, a rich and subtle area of English. The unit focuses on expressing degrees of probability, and on the complex way that modal past forms are made.

Students will be familiar with many of the concepts that modal verbs express, but not all. The use of *will* and *should(n't)* to express probability may be new, as will some of the less common past structures, *would* for characteristic behaviour, and the past forms of *need*.

Here are some potential confusions between one modal and another.

1   Misusing *can* for possibility
    Students of some nationalities will use *can* where they should use *might* or *could*: *it can rain tomorrow so bring an umbrella*. Take time to check and correct this area. *Can* is used to talk about general possibilities: *It can rain in Spain in the winter.*

2   Confusing *must* and *have to*
    Must is used for personal obligations: *I must go, or I'll be late. Have to* is used for external obligations, rules, regulations, laws: *You have to drive on the left in the UK.* It is, however, a subtle area, and mixing modals here will not result in a major error.

3   Confusing *mustn't* and *don't have to*
    Mustn't expresses a prohibition: *You mustn't smoke in the factory. Don't have to* says that something is not necessary, but optional: *You don't have to bring a bottle of wine to the party, but you can if you want to.* This can be a confusing area for students whose first language uses these structures differently.

The aim here is to build awareness, and get students manipulating the forms. Make sure that students get a feel for using modal verbs more often in their spoken English.

Grammar Reference 7.1–3 on SB p153 looks at the areas of meaning expressed by modal auxiliary verbs. It is a good idea for you to read this carefully before teaching the grammatical section of this unit.

Vocabulary The *Vocabulary* section involves guessing which words can be used to complete a poem. There is also work on guessing the meaning of vocabulary in the *Reading* section.

The last word This section looks at various grammatical rules that many people think should be followed when constructing sentences in English. Students are asked to consider whether or not these rules are valid.

Notes on the unit

STARTER (SB p63)

1 Ask students to look at the pictures and names, and tell the class what they know about the people.

2 Ask students to read the quotations then discuss them in pairs. Conduct a brief whole-class feedback. Do students know any other quotations these people are famous for?

> **Answers**
> 1 Although some tasks in life seem impossibly difficult, it is only necessary to make a start on them in order to make their completion a possibility.
> 2 A reminder that it is non-material gifts that are the most valuable.
> 3 This is a clear indication that the older generation's complaints about the younger generation are nothing new.
> 4 The argument in favour of weapons as a means of deterring war.
> 5 This highlights the gap between cultures, which leaves one society bewildered by the leisure pursuits of another's (e.g. bull-fighting and fox-hunting).
> 6 An ironic way of portraying the enormous development that takes place during adolescence and young adulthood. Young people can be very arrogant, and here the speaker assumes that it is his father who has changed so much during this period.
> 7 Einstein saw that ever more destructive weapons would be developed before the next World War, so destructive that there would be no technology left to fight another war with.
> 8 The more you try to control love, the more you destroy it.
> 9 'An eye for an eye' is an Old Testament idea of punishment, but if it is followed rigorously, we all become literally and metaphorically blind.
> 10 A typical Woody Allen line. He complains about all the suffering in life, and yet still manages to complain that life is too short.

3 Do this as a relaxed open-class discussion.

> **BACKGROUND NOTE**
>
> **Confucius (551–479 BC)**
> Chinese philosopher who founded Confucianism. He appealed to reason, not the supernatural, and taught love, respect, and forgiveness of one's fellow man.
>
> **Buddha (563–483 BC)**
> Buddha, whose family name was Siddhartha Gautama, was born on the border of what is now India and Nepal. He had many disciples in his lifetime, and practised meditation in search of enlightenment. He was the founder of Buddhism.

> **Socrates (469–339 BC)**
> Greek philosopher who lived in Athens, and, having been sentenced to death, drank poison to kill himself.
>
> **George Washington (1732–1799)**
> Washington was commander-in-chief of the American army during the War of Independence against the British government. He became the first President of the United States.
>
> **Jane Austen (1775–1817)**
> Jane Austen was an English novelist who wrote about the personal relationships of the English middle classes. Her novels are witty, satirical, and have great imaginative power. Her best-known novels are *Emma* and *Pride and Prejudice*. She never married.
>
> **Mark Twain (1835–1910)**
> Samuel L. Clemens was a journalist and author. His most famous novels, written under the pseudonym Mark Twain, are *Tom Sawyer* and *Huckleberry Finn*.
>
> **Albert Einstein (1879–1955)**
> A scientific genius whose chief claim to fame rests upon his theory of relativity ($E = mc^2$). He spent most of his life in Switzerland, before moving to the USA in 1933 when the Nazis came to power in Germany.
>
> **Dorothy Parker (1893–1967)**
> An American writer and critic famous for her satirical short stories and sardonic verse.
>
> **Martin Luther King (1929–1968)**
> An Afro-american clergyman who led the non-violent movement for racial equality, which was instrumental in getting the Civil Rights Act of 1964 passed in the United States. Famous for his passionate speeches ('I have a dream …'), he was assassinated in 1968 in Memphis.
>
> **Woody Allen (1935–)**
> An American writer-director-comedian, famous for the shy, inept character he plays in many of his films. His most famous films are *Annie Hall*, *Manhattan*, and *Hannah and Her Sisters*.

READING AND LISTENING (SB p64)

Letter to a newborn son

This is an authentic listening text, originally broadcast on BBC radio in 1996. It is quite long, and has been broken down into three parts. Students listen and read the first and third parts and answer comprehension and interpretation questions. Only the middle section is exploited as a listening, with a true or false exercise. It is scripted, elegiac in tone, yet not particularly high in terms of vocabulary use, so students at this level should not have too many problems with comprehension. The topic is heartbreakingly moving, so it is worth considering how more emotional members of your class might react.

1 Read the introduction as a class. Then ask students in pairs to read the extracts and answer the questions. In the feedback, get students to predict the 'personal story'.

Answers
1 He is *upside down* and *inside out*. In other words, his thoughts and emotions have been totally changed. He is feeling proud (*first baby born ...*), and reflective about his own life, his experiences, and the lives of children he has met in his job.
2 It is the name of a year in the Chinese calendar.
3 He has been to war zones and seen natural disasters, and has seen darkness, danger, and suffering.
4 Students' own ideas. (There is possibly a connection with the relationship he had with his father.)

2 **T 7.1** Give students a moment to read the questions, then play the recording while they read.

Answers
1 It is very time-consuming, having to work while holding the baby (one-handed typing), feeding, winding, and nappy changing.
2 Metaphorically, he is saying that the rules of their daily lives have been transformed by having to look after a baby.
3 Because it is a boy, and the first boy born in the year of the pig, which is good Feng Shui – a positive sign.
4 No. It is better than he expected.

3 **T 7.2** Give students a few moments to read the statements. Play the recording, and ask them to mark each statement true or false. Let students check in pairs, and correct the false answers, before checking with the whole class.

Answers
1 True
2 True
3 True
4 False. Andi Mikail was hurt in war (*wounds ...*); Domingo and Juste suffered from malnutrition; Sharja was a victim of war – she had lost her parents and home; three young children from Rwanda died in an attack during the civil war there.

T 7.2 See SB Tapescripts p139

4 **T 7.3** Give students a few moments to read the questions, then ask them to read and listen for the answers. Ask students to discuss their answers in pairs before checking with the whole class.

Answers
1 A young woman (Fergal's mother): She is walking to the hospital in a snowbound big city to have a baby. She is walking because she has no money, because her husband has spent it on alcohol.
A taxi driver: He sees the young woman in a shop doorway and takes her to the hospital for free.
An alcoholic man (Fergal's father): He lived away from his family in a one-roomed flat, dying of alcoholism.
A baby boy (Daniel): He was born in the Adventist hospital.
2 **Mother**: *... the best thing she has ever seen ...*
Father: *... weeps with joy when he sees his son ... ; ... truly happy ...*
Both: *... young and in love with each other and their son ...*
3 His father was an alcoholic, who lost his family, and died alone in a one-roomed flat. Fergal is understanding and loving towards him. He attaches no blame to him – it just was. He sees his problem being a disease, which eats away at you, which you cannot do anything about.
4 He regrets not being there when his father died, to share final words, and he hopes that his father might somehow know of his grandson's birth.

5 **T 7.1** – **T 7.3** Play the whole recording. Ask students in pairs to summarize each part.

Sample summaries
Part one
Fergal Keane is sitting, holding his baby, and typing this 'letter' in the early morning in Hong Kong. He writes of how happy he and his wife feel, how their lives have changed, and how they had looked forward to the baby's birth.

Part two
Fergal writes about how the birth of Daniel has made him re-evaluate his life and his values. He writes about how it has made think about the terrible plight of less fortunate children who he has seen while doing his job.

Part three
He writes about his own birth, the death of his father through alcoholism, the regret he feels that he was not there when his father died, and the hope that his son's birth has brought.

Vocabulary work

6 Ask students to find the words and phrases in their text, then explain them to their partner. They may need to refer to a dictionary, but make sure students guess from context first. Then ask them to discuss what the pronouns refer to. Monitor this activity carefully, and help any students with difficulties. Check with the whole class.

Answers

1 *He* refers to the baby, Daniel.
  winded = patted on the back to bring up the baby's wind
  cradled = held gently in the arms
2 *He* refers to Fergal.
  gambled = took risks
  veering = moving dangerously and uncontrollably (like a car veering across the motorway towards the other lane)
3 *He / his* refer to Andi Mikail.
  dust = small particles of sand or dirt
  wounds = injuries caused by guns, knives, or bombs
4 *He* refers to Juste.
  malnutrition = lack of food
5 *It* refers to the classroom.
  ransacked = people have run through it, breaking everything and stealing things
6 *They* refers to the mother and her three children in Rwanda.
  huddled = sitting close together, often because they are cold, poor, hungry, or afraid
  clung = held very tight, often in desperation
7 *She* refers to Fergal's mother, *his* refers to Fergal's father.
  pawned = gave to a pawnbroker in return for money, the idea being that she could buy things back later if she had money
8 *He* refers to Fergal's father.
  hungover = suffering from an excess of alcohol drunk the day before
  broke = having no money
9 *their* refers to the man's and his family's (lives).
  cancer of alcoholism = here, alcoholism is described as a disease which slowly eats away at your body until you die

What do you think?

Answers

• *So much that seemed essential to me has, in the past few days, taken on a different colour.*
  He means that the experience of having a son, and the first few days of his son's life, have made him re-evaluate his life and his values.
• Fergal's relationship with his son will probably be much closer than the one he had with his own father.
• He wants to show his son that life is very complicated and that there are many ways in which people can get hurt, both physically and emotionally. He wants him to look sympathetically at the mess that people often make of their lives, saying that it is a result of 'getting lost'. He also wants him to remember that life is very precious, and that his life can be a new beginning which breaks the old patterns.

LANGUAGE FOCUS (SB p66)

Modal auxiliary verbs

Don't forget to look at the *Language Aims* section on TB p64, which looks at problems students may have. You should also read Grammar Reference 7.0 on SB p00.

Modal verbs in the present and future

LANGUAGE INPUT

1 Ask students in pairs to match the sentences with the explanations.

Answers

It will be difficult.	All evidence points to this. I predict this strongly.
It must be difficult.	I have a lot of evidence that it is.
It could be difficult.	I'm not sure but it's possible.
It may be difficult.	I'm not sure but it's possible.
It might be difficult.	I'm not sure but it's possible.
It can be difficult.	There are times when it is difficult.
It can't be difficult.	I have a lot of evidence that it isn't.
It shouldn't be difficult.	If everything goes according to plan.

In the feedback, you could double check by asking check questions: Which modal do we use to say that we expect this not to be difficult? (*shouldn't*) If we are sure, but it is a personal opinion, which do we use – *will* or *must*? (*will*) If we are sure, based on a logical interpretation of events, which do we use – *will* or *must*? (*must*)

2 Read through the examples as a class, then elicit other examples.

Refer students to Grammar Reference 7.1 on SB p153.

1 Ask students in pairs to read the sentences and tick those which express a degree of probability. Do the first two as an example to get students started. Ask students in their pairs to discuss what the other uses are.

Answers

1 ✓ (a logical interpretation of events)
2 ✗ (obligation)
3 ✗ (ability)
4 ✓ (evidence that it isn't going to happen)
5 ✓ (possible)
6 ✓ (possible)
7 ✗ (permission)
8 ✓ (possible)
9 ✗ (refusing permission)
10 ✓ (reasonable expectation)

11 ✗ (mild obligation)
12 ✗ (willingness)
13 ✓ (assumption based on strong evidence)
14 ✗ (refusing – unwillingness)
15 ✗ (ability)
16 ✓ (generally possible)

Modal verbs in the past

LANGUAGE INPUT

1 Ask students in pairs to look at the way modals expressing probability are formed in the past. Ask them to give you more examples.

2–3 Look at the examples as a class, then ask students in pairs to discuss the meanings of the modals.

Answers
She could / was able to … = past ability
He wouldn't … = past unwillingness / refusing in the past
You should have seen … = past mild obligation
He would … = past habit (expresses characteristic behaviour)
I needn't have brought … = an action that was completed but was not necessary

Refer students to Grammar Reference 7.2 on SB p153.

2 Ask students in pairs to complete the sentences, using past forms of modals.

Answers
2 I had to stop smoking …
3 He should have stopped smoking …
4 We were able to go …
5 It'll have been Paul.
6 She needn't have given me a lift …
7 She didn't need to give me a lift …
8 My niece couldn't read …
9 We would have got lost if we hadn't.
10 He would just sit staring into space.

3 Ask students in pairs to discuss the differences in meaning.

Answers
1 *He must be on his way* is a logical interpretation of events – perhaps the speaker has phoned him, and there is no answer, so logically …
I must be on my way expresses a personal obligation. The speaker is saying that they are obliged to leave, perhaps because they are late for something else.
2 *I must stop smoking* is a personal obligation. The speaker is imposing an obligation on him / herself.
I have to stop smoking expresses an obligation imposed from outside, often a rule or regulation.

3 *They must share a flat together* expresses a logical interpretation of events. The speaker has, perhaps, seen the two often coming out of the same building.
We must share a flat together expresses a personal obligation. It is a way of saying that something would be a really good thing to do.
4 *You don't have to buy her chocolates* means that it is not necessary. There is no obligation.
You mustn't buy her chocolates means it is prohibited. Perhaps she will react allergically to them.
5 *The exam will have started* is an assumption that the exam started some time ago.
The exam will be starting is an assumption that the exam is just about to start at this moment.
6 *He can't be married* is saying that there is evidence that this is not true.
We can't be married is saying that there is some problem, e.g. legal, obtaining permission.

4 Ask students in pairs to extend the sentences in exercise 3 to illustrate the meaning.

Sample answers
2 I must stop smoking because I feel unfit and unwell.
   I have to stop smoking because my doctor has told me to.
3 They must share a flat together because they both have the same address on their forms.
   We must share a flat together. We get on so well and it would save us both money.
4 You don't have to buy her chocolates. She will be happy enough if you just say thank you.
   You mustn't buy her chocolates. She's allergic to them.
5 The exam will have started, so there is no point going.
   The exam will be starting, so you'd better hurry up and get there quickly.
6 He can't be married. He's too young and isn't wearing a ring.
   We can't be married because we are too young.

Dilemma!

The aim of this activity is to encourage lots of speaking in a competitive group game. Inherent in this game is the use of the second conditional, which can be revised here in preparation for the contrast of *would* for fact and non-fact in Unit 7. Insist on students using correct conditional forms. There should be lots of result clauses and short answers, for example:

I'd give it back.
I wouldn't. I'd keep it.
I don't think you would. I think you'd try to find out who it belonged to.

There is also an opportunity to use some of the modals practised in this unit, for example:

I think I might …
You couldn't do that, because …

Photocopy and cut up the cards on TB pp136–139. There are sixty in all. Divide the class into groups of four or five then hand each group eight or ten different cards.

1 Give students time to read through the instructions and their cards. Monitor each group and make sure they all know what they are doing.

Before starting the game, model an example by saying: *Imagine I have the card about the taxi driver. I choose Maria. I think Maria would take the money to the police station. So I write,* Maria would take the money to the police station. *When it is my turn to speak, I read the card to Maria and she has to tell me what she would do. If she says what I have written, I score the point. If she says something different, I can challenge her by saying how I think she would react, and giving evidence to prove my point.*

2 Make sure students sit so they can see each other. Ask one student to begin. Decide whether the group has won a point or not, and write it on the board, before moving to a student from the next group. Go from group to group, asking a different student each time to speak.

The majority of the actual speaking will come when the questioner challenges the person who has said what he / she would do.

The winner is the group that scores most points. If there is time, you could hand out more cards to keep the game going.

ADDITIONAL MATERIAL

Workbook Unit 7
Exercise 1–4 Modal auxiliary verbs
Exercise 6 Stress and intonation of modal verbs

Words of wisdom

This is an intensive listening activity in which students must listen to ten short extracts from ten different speakers with a variety of accents, and pick out key information.

1 **T 7.4** Ask students to listen to the speakers and make notes under the different headings. Pause the recording after each speaker to allow students time to write answers.

Answers

Name	Words of wisdom	Given by whom?
1 Elaine	Love, home, and work are important – as long as two out of three are OK, you can deal with the third	father
2 Lizzie	You should allow friends three faults before casting them off	Ex-husband
3 Justin	Always go shopping on a full stomach	himself
4 Claire	Travel is the best education next to books	grandmother
5 Henry	It's better to travel hopefully than to arrive	Gran'pa
6 Simon	Always follow your heart, especially with freedom and love	mother
7 Fiona	This too will pass – it'll be over soon	grandmother
8 Chris	WP – willpower	grandmother
9 Sue	Love many, trust a few, always paddle your own canoe	mum
10 Martyn	Dust it off – just do it	An American actor friend

T 7.4 See SB Tapescripts p139

2 Ask students to discuss their notes with a partner. Which words of wisdom do they like? Conduct a brief whole-class feedback.

3 Ask students to share their personal words of wisdom with the class.

VOCABULARY AND PRONUNCIATION (SB p68)

Rhyme and reason

This is a light-hearted lesson in which students have to guess missing words in a text, based on context, 'feel', pronunciation, and rhythm.

> **BACKGROUND NOTE**
> The poem was written by the famous nineteenth-century writer, Lewis Carroll, author of *Alice in Wonderland*, and several works of 'nonsense' verse. It is a parody of a didactic poem for children: *The Old Man's Comforts And How He Gained Them*, written by the Lakeland poet Robert Southey in 1799. Many contemporary readers would have been familiar with the original, making Carroll's parody even more amusing.

1 Ask students in pairs to read the poem to each other and decide on the missing words.

> **GLOSSARY**
> Note that some of the vocabulary in the poem is a little archaic and mock-formal:
> *incessantly* = without stopping
> *uncommonly* = unusually
> *Pray* = please tell me
> *sage* = wise man
> *locks* = hair
> *a shilling* = old British currency
> *suet* = hard fat used to make soft puddings
> *give yourself airs* = pretend to be more important than you are
> *stuff* = here, nonsense
> *Be off* = go away

2 **T 7.5** Discuss as a class what the answers might be. Then play the recording. Which pair was closest?

> **Answers and tapescript**
> 'You are old, Father William,' the young man said,
> 'And your hair has become very white;
> And yet you incessantly stand on your **head**
> Do you think, at your age, it is **right**?'
>
> 'In my youth,' Father William replied to his son,
> 'I feared it might **injure** the brain;
> But, now that I'm perfectly sure I have **none**,
> Why, I do it again and again.'
>
> 'You are old', said the youth, 'as I **mentioned** before,
> And have grown most **uncommonly** fat
> Yet you turned a back somersault in at the door –
> Pray what is the reason of that?'
>
> 'In my youth,' said the sage, as he shook his grey **locks**,
> 'I kept all my limbs very **supple**
> By the use of this ointment – one shilling the box –
> Allow me to sell you a couple?'

> 'You are old,' said the youth, 'and your jaws are too weak
> For anything tougher than **suet**;
> Yet you finished the goose, with the **bones** and the beak –
> Pray, how did you manage to do it?'
>
> 'In my youth,' said his father, 'I took to the law,
> And argued each **case** with my wife;
> And the muscular strength which it gave to my **jaw**,
> Has lasted the rest of my life.'
>
> 'You are old,' said the youth, 'one would hardly suppose
> That your eye was as **steady** as ever;
> Yet you balanced an eel on the end of your nose –
> What made you so **awfully** clever?'
>
> 'I have answered three questions, and that is enough,'
> Said his father. 'Don't give yourself **airs**!
> Do you think I can listen all day to such **stuff**?
> Be off, or I'll kick you downstairs!'

3 Play the recording of the first two verses again and ask students to mark the stresses.

> **Answers**
> 'You are <u>old</u>, Father <u>William</u>,' the <u>young</u> man <u>said</u>,
> 'And your <u>hair</u> has be<u>come</u> very <u>white</u>;
> And <u>yet</u> you incessantly <u>stand</u> on your <u>head</u>
> Do you <u>think</u>, at your <u>age</u>, it is <u>right</u>?'
>
> 'In my <u>youth</u>,' Father <u>William</u> re<u>plied</u> to his <u>son</u>,
> 'I <u>feared</u> it might <u>injure</u> the <u>brain</u>;
> But, <u>now</u> that I'm <u>perfectly</u> <u>sure</u> I have <u>none</u>,
> Why, I <u>do</u> it a<u>gain</u> and a<u>gain</u>.'

Ask students in pairs to practise reading the two verses aloud, copying the rhythm and stress of the poem on the recording. You could get students to mark where they think strong stresses and pauses might go in the other verses before reading them out, too.

In this poem, the words at the end of each line are always strongly stressed.

4 **T 7.6** Read and listen to the children's poem as a class.

5 Ask students in pairs to write their own poems, then read them out. You could put some poems on the classroom walls, or even make a class anthology of nonsense poems.

ADDITIONAL MATERIAL

Workbook Unit 7
Exercise 7 Revision: word puzzle

Breaking the rules of English

1 Read the quotations as a class and answer the question.

Answers
The point is that applying prescriptive rules is pedantic and often results in unnatural-sounding English.

2 Ask students in pairs to read the 'rules' and correct them.

Answers
1 A preposition is a terrible word with which to end a sentence. (*with* is a preposition)
2 Remember never to split an infinitive. (not *to never split*)
3 Don't use any double negatives. (*Don't* and *no* are both negatives)
4 Do not ever use contractions. (*Don't* is a contraction)
5 Never start a sentence with a conjunction. (*And* is a conjunction)
6 The words *anciently* and *weird* break the rule.
7 Foreign words and phrases are not fashionable / trendy. (*chic* is a French word)
8 Avoid the passive voice wherever possible. (*to be avoided* is a passive construction)
9 A rhetorical question, as here, is one which doesn't require an answer.
10 Reserve the apostrophe for its proper use and omit it when it's not necessary. (not *it's proper use. it's* = it is)
11 ... Fewer and fewer people do. (not *less people*, as *people* is countable)
12 ... to see if you miss any words out. (the word *miss* was missed out)
13 John and I are careful to use subject pronouns correctly. (*Me* is an object pronoun)
14 Verbs have to agree with their subjects. (not *has to*)
15 You've done well to use adverbs correctly. (*good* is an adjective)
16 If *any* word is incorrect at the end of a sentence, it is an auxiliary verb. (not *is* at the end of the sentence)
17 Steer clear of incorrect verb forms that have sneaked into the language. (*snuck* is an irregular past participle of *sneak* in American English)
18 Take the bull by the horns and avoid mixing your idioms (this idiom is mixed with *A bird in the hand* ...).
19 Tell the rule about *whom* to whom you like. (*whom* is used as an object pronoun)
20 Ultimately, avoid clichés completely. (*At the end of the day* and *like the plague* are clichés.)

3 Ask students in pairs to discuss which rules they think are valid.

Answers
Sentences 3, 10, 12, 14, 15, and 18 are clearly wrong, and so the rules that forbid them can be considered 'good' rules.
Most native speakers would agree that 13 is strictly speaking incorrect, although it is very often heard.
The other rules are more dubious:
1, 2 Ending a sentence with a preposition (e.g. *What are you listening to?*) and splitting infinitives (e.g. *He wanted to quickly go though everything.*) are common in English. Splitting infinitives often avoids ambiguity.
4 Contractions are preferred in informal English, although they should not be used in formal written English.
5 *And*, *But*, and *So* are commonly used to begin sentences in English.
6 A useful rule, but with many exceptions.
7, 20 Using foreign words and clichés is perfectly acceptable, though of course excessive use would amount to poor style.
8 The passive voice is the norm in many contexts, especially in more formal and scientific English.
9 Rhetorical questions are often used to create an effect.
11 It has only recently become common, even in educated circles, to use *less* with countable nouns. To many it is still considered incorrect, and language learners should learn to differentiate between *less* and *fewer*.
16 As shown in Unit 1, English sentences often end with an auxiliary in order to avoid repetition.
19 Most people consider *who* to be an acceptable alternative to *whom* in spoken English, and in fact the use of *whom* will sound ridiculously formal in an informal context. In formal written English, *whom* should be used as the object pronoun.

4 Discuss this as a class.

Don't forget!

Writing Unit 7 Describing a personal experience (SB p126)

Workbook Unit 7
Exercise 5 Listening – A father's advice on marriage
Exercise 8 Compound adjectives
Exercise 9 Prepositions in questions
Endquotes

Song
Father and son (TB p140)

8

Metaphors and idioms
Real and unreal tense usage
Softening the message

Altered images

Introduction to the unit

The theme of this unit is art and artists, the images artists create, and what influenced them. The main reading text is about Walt Disney, and how his difficult childhood influenced his creation of the world of Disney that we see today. The listening text is an interview with American painter and sculptor, Joe Dudley Downing. He describes how his life and experiences have been central to the development of his work.

Language aims

***would* and real and unreal tense usage** This unit looks at the various uses and meanings of the modal auxiliary verb, *would*. Referring to facts in real time, it can be used to express past habits, typical behaviour, future in the past, and refusal on a past occasion. With reference to non-fact, it is used to help form second and third conditionals.

The *Language Focus* section aims to make sure students can recognize the different uses by getting them to analyse different sentences, then checks their ability to use them in sentence completion and gap-fill exercises. The emphasis within the unit is on recognizing and using forms involving *would*. In Grammar Reference 8 on SB p154, however, all aspects of the three main conditional forms are analysed.

> **WATCH OUT FOR ...**
> **Use and contractions**
> *   *would* expresses past habits, but not past states
> *   *would* can express irritating or characteristic behaviour
> *   *would* expresses future in the past
> *   *would* expresses a refusal
> *   *would* helps form second and third conditionals
> *   *would* is often contracted to *'d*, and the pronunciation of *I'd* or *we'd* can be problematic.

Using *would* to express past habits Many students will have studied *would* for past habits in contrast with *used to*, which can be used to express past habits and past states. *Would* cannot be used with a state verb, so **When I was young I would live in the country* is incorrect.

Students may over-stress *would*. Remind them that *would* is often contracted in this use, and that when stressed it implies that the behaviour described is irritating: *He would sit around doing nothing all day*.

Using *would* to express future in the past Often this use is quite formal, and very much a written use. This is typical of the example from the text: *Later, Walt would paint a nostalgic picture of life in Missouri*.

In spoken English, *would* is very common to report words and thoughts: *He told me he'd be there. I hoped you'd phone. I knew you wouldn't like it*.

In the part of the *Language Focus* section that looks at real and unreal tense usage, the emphasis is on testing students' ability to recognize when past forms are referring to real time, and when they aren't. It also gets students to recognize when *'d* means *would* and when it means *had*. Two of the most common recurring form problems here are the wrong use of *would* in the *if* ... clause, and mistaking *had* for *would*.

Pronunciation of the contracted *would* form may be tricky for some students. You may wish to drill the pronunciation of *I'd* /aɪd/, *we'd* /wiːd/, and/or *they'd* /ðeɪd/ before students practise using the forms in speaking exercises.

Grammar Reference 8 on SB p154 looks at all the uses of *would* and at conditional forms. It is a good idea for you to read this carefully before teaching the grammatical section of this unit.

Vocabulary The *Vocabulary* section looks at metaphors and idioms. There is also a lot of work on guessing the meaning of vocabulary in the *Reading* section.

The last word In this unit, this section looks at ways of softening the message – expressing ourselves in polite, tactful ways. This involves using *would*, past tense, and continuous forms.

Notes on the unit

STARTER (SB p71)

1 Discuss the questions briefly as a class Clearly, the answers will be students' own opinions. The purpose of art might be to reflect the artist's thoughts and feelings; to mirror or reflect reality in a thought-provoking way; to highlight the beauty of life; to shock.

2 Ask students in pairs or threes to discuss the pictures. Some students may be very opinionated about this subject, and others may have little to say. Conduct a brief whole-class discussion, and find out what students think.

3 **T 8.1** Ask students to listen to the descriptions, and decide which picture the speakers are describing. Ask students to remember phrases used by the speakers. You could let them look at the tapescript on SB p139.

Answers
1 A photograph of an Afghan girl by Steve McCurry
2 *Mother and child* by Henry Moore
3 The TGV station at Avignon
4 Tracy Emin's bedroom (this art installation of the artist's unmade bed was a contender for the prestigious Turner Prize)
5 *La Grande Jatte* by Georges Seurat

The film still from *Casablanca*, starring Humphrey Bogart and Ingrid Bergman, is not described.

T 8.1 See SB Tapescripts p139

4 Ask students to compare their own reactions to the pictures with those of the people on the recording. Discuss as a class.

LISTENING AND SPEAKING (SB p72)

At home with an artist

This is a long, intensive listening, an interview with the American artist, Joe Dudley Downing. The listening is broken into three sections, exploited by a variety of comprehension and interpretation tasks.

1 Ask students in pairs to look at the pictures and discuss Joe's style, then discuss briefly with the whole class.

2 Read the biodata as a class, then ask students in pairs to prepare questions to ask Joe. Suggest one or two to get them started, for example *Have you always wanted to be a painter? What inspires you to paint?*

3 Ask students to read through the statements. Check that they understand all the vocabulary before they listen.

> **GLOSSARY**
> *quilts* = thick, hand-made bed covers
> *country bumpkin* = a naïve and unsophisticated person from the countryside
> *optometry* = the profession of looking at people's eyes and prescribing glasses for them. *Optometrist* is an American word – in British English, the word *optician* is used.

T 8.2 Play part one of the interview. Ask students to listen and correct the statements. Let them check their answers in pairs before checking with the whole class.

Answers
1 He had no knowledge of art until he was twenty-two.
2 There were no paintings of any kind.
3 His mother made the quilts and showed him the beans she was shelling.
4 She loved the colours in the beans.
5 He had to go to war when he was 18.
6 He had his nineteenth birthday in France.
7 He had no real desire to be anything, but he had to do something.
8 He loved big city life and it was like a second birth.
9 He says he would have eventually gone to some museum and seen some paintings.

T 8.2 See SB Tapescripts p140

4 Ask students to read through the questions.

> **GLOSSARY**
> *abstract painter* = a painter who doesn't paint recognizable figures and scenes
> *follow his bent* = follow what he was naturally good at
> *keep the pot boiling* = here, make enough money to live

T 8.3 Play part two of the interview. Ask students to listen and answer the questions. Let students check their answers in pairs before checking with the whole class.

Answers

1 No. He did landscapes, still life (which he still loves) and portraits in the beginning – they were part of his development. He did collages in his free time when he lived in Paris – they were his first abstract work and the foundation of his whole painter's life. He didn't aim to be an abstract painter, but what he did naturally took him in that direction – in that way, he followed his bent.
2 He worked as a secretary for an American law firm.
3 Though his style is developing, all his work has something in common which you can see in everything he does.
4 The desire to create.
5 They look similar – green, velvety, and beautiful. Joe painted little landscapes on pieces of green lasagne at a dinner party, and gave them to the guests. The next day his hostess was upset because the lasagne had dried and cracked, so he promised to make another painting on something that looks like green lasagne. He eventually found some pale green leather that is used for making gardener's gloves.

T 8.3 See SB Tapescripts p140

GLOSSARY

landscape = picture of, for example, a country scene
still life = painting of, for example, a vase of fruit
portrait = painting of a person
collage = a picture made by, for example, sticking lots of pieces of material together

---

5 **T 8.4** Play part three of the interview. Ask students to listen and answer the questions. Let them check their answers in pairs before checking with the whole class.

Answers

1 It changes for the worse – in other words, it becomes developed for tourism.
2 It's a long way south of Paris. It's an agricultural village that produces wonderful fruit and vegetables.
3 Because he wants the place to himself – he doesn't want to share it with tourists.
4 A friend, because Joe can't drive, and therefore she had to do all the driving. *Lugging* means carrying something heavy, like a suitcase.
5 He went for a walk in the village and followed a dog. It led him to the house.
6 Because it was in ruins; 'RUINS FOR SALE'
7 He is back in a rural setting. Ménerbes has the same number of people as Horse Cave, Kentucky, and the people even look the same.
8 No. Except for having to fight in the war.

T 8.4 See SB Tapescripts p140

What do you think?

Sample answer
Fate has played a large part in Joe's life. He was taken to see *La Grande Jatte* by Seurat in a museum, and that made him want to paint. A friend insisted on stopping in a small French village because she was tired of driving. Next morning he saw 'ruins for sale', and this became the house where he has spent much of his life.

Talking about a work of art

This is best done in the form of a presentation. Ask students to think of a favourite work of art, and give them a few minutes to make notes in response to the questions and prompts. Then, ask students to stand up and tell the class about their work of art. In a large class, ask students to make presentations in groups. Listen carefully and note any key errors, which you can discuss at the end of each presentation. Encourage students to ask the speaker questions at the end of each presentation.

Alternatively, you could set this as a homework task. Ask students to bring in a picture of the work of art they like the most, and to prepare a short presentation, which they can make to the rest of the class.

VOCABULARY (SB p74)

Metaphors and idioms

1 Ask students to read conversation **A**. Ask *What's the situation?* (two old friends meeting up and catching up on news).

   T 8.5 Play the recording. Ask students to listen to conversation **B** and notice in what way it is different from **A**.

Answer
In conversation **B**, more idiomatic and metaphorical language is used.

2 Ask students to look at the tapescript on SB p140. Ask them in pairs to find and underline the metaphors, explain their literal meaning, and then find the paraphrases of the metaphorical meanings in conversation **A**.

Answers and tapescript

Metaphor	Literal meaning	Paraphrase of literal meaning
Time flies	it goes through the air	time goes so fast
slaving away	working like a slave for his / her owner	working extremely hard

snowed under	unable to get out because of heavy snow	have an awful lot of work to do
keeping our heads above water	managing to avoid drowning in deep water	just about coping
tighten our belts	fastening your belt tighter	make a lot of economies
picked up	retrieved from the floor	improved
sleepy	having difficulty staying awake	where not much happens
tied up	unable to move because you've been tied with rope	very busy
bitten off more than we can chew	taken such a big mouthful of food that you can't chew it	given ourselves more work than we can manage
must dash	have to run fast	must go

T 8.5 **Conversation B**

A Hi, Annie! I haven't seen you for ages.

B I know. **Time flies**, doesn't it?

A It's true. Work as busy as ever, is it?

B Yes, I'm **slaving away** as usual, but we're a bit **snowed under** at the moment. We're just about **keeping our heads above water**, but it isn't easy. How about you?

A OK. Business was bad this time last year, and we really had to **tighten our belts**, but things have **picked up** since then. You've moved, haven't you? Where are you living now?

B We've bought an old house in a **sleepy** little village. You must come and visit us.

A I'd love to, but we're a bit **tied up** at the moment. Does it need much doing to it?

B Everything. I hope we haven't **bitten off more than we can chew**.

A You'll be fine. Anyway, I **must dash**. Lovely to see you again.

B And you. Bye.

3 Ask students in pairs to find and underline the metaphors in each sentence, and to work out the metaphorical meaning from context. Go round monitoring and helping as necessary.
You may wish to let students do the first ten, then feedback on the answers, before doing the second ten.

A NOTE ON DICTIONARY USE
You may wish to use this exercise (and the next one) as a way of developing students' ability to use monolingual language learner's dictionaries. Bring in a class set, or make sure all students have the same or a similar dictionary. Ask students to decide which key word in each idiom would be best to look up. For

example, you are more likely to find the meaning of the first metaphor by looking up *point* rather than *finger*. (Indeed, if you look up *finger* in the *Oxford Advanced Learner's Dictionary*, it refers you to *point* in order to find this expression). Make sure students guess from context, then use dictionaries to check their ideas.

Answers

	Metaphor	Literal meaning	Metaphorical meaning
1	*to point the finger at*	to indicate with your finger	to put the blame on
2	*had a few hiccups*	a hiccup is a sudden, involuntary gulp-like sound in your throat	had a few small problems
3	*broke his heart*	stopped his heart functioning	hurt him very deeply
4	*takes your breath away*	gives you difficulty breathing	to leave you stunned and unable to speak
5	*scarred her for life*	a scar is the physical mark left by a cut or burn	caused her permanent psychological damage
6	*came to me in a flash*	a flash of light	it suddenly occurred to me
7	*glowing with pride*	to glow like a fire or light	visibly very, very proud
8	*sparked my interest*	a spark is a tiny flame that can start a fire	awakened my interest
9	*being overshadowed*	blocked from the light by something bigger than you	appearing inferior in comparison to
10	*it dawned on me*	dawn is when the sun rises	I realized
11	*stormy relationship*	with frequent rain, thunder, and lightning	a relationship in which people row a lot
	blazing rows	a blazing fire burns strongly	very angry rows with lots of shouting
12	*blossomed*	flowers blossom when they begin to open up	developed successfully

13	*in floods of tears*	there are floods when it rains so much that the rivers burst their banks	crying a lot, uncontrollably
14	*the root of*	the underground base of a plant or tree	the fundamental cause of
15	*haven't the foggiest idea*	on a foggy day you can't see anything clearly	really don't know or understand
16	*reach a crossroads*	come to a junction of four roads	reach a point in life when an important choice has to be made
17	*followed in his father's footsteps*	walked behind his father	did what his father did (professionally)
18	*rambling speech*	you ramble when you walk with no planned direction	long-winded and poorly-planned speech
19	*going round in circles*	following the same circular path	making no progress at all
20	*great strides*	very big steps forward	very significant and rapid progress

4 **T 8.6** Play the recording. Ask students to listen and answer the questions. Conduct a brief whole-class feedback. Find out how many idioms students can remember, but don't teach them at this point.

Answers and tapescript
Two friends are talking about Pete – his inheritance, his girlfriends, his life.

T 8.6
A I hear Pete's aunt left him everything.
B Absolutely right, he inherited a fortune **out of the blue**.
A He knew nothing about it then. How exciting!
B You bet! When he heard about it, he was **over the moon**.
A So what's his problem now?
B Well, he's **in deep water** because he spent the whole lot in a month and then his girlfriend walked out on him .
A You're kidding. I thought he'd asked her to marry him?
B He was going to ask her, and then he **got cold feet**.
A So what next?
B Looks like he'll have to **pull his socks up** and get a job.

A And a new girlfriend. What about that girl he used to work with? Mm... Miranda, Marilyn – no, that's not it, erm, her name's **on the tip of my tongue**.
B You mean Melissa. Whatever you do, *don't* mention Melissa! She told him he was **a waste of space**, money or no money.
A Oh dear, I'm glad you told me, otherwise I might have **put my foot in it**.

5 Ask students to replace the words in italics with idioms from the recording. Let them check their answers in pairs.

T 8.6 Play the recording again. You may need to play and pause if students have problems catching the idioms.

Answers
1 It came out of the blue
2 over the moon
3 in deep water
4 got cold feet
5 pull his socks up
6 Her name is on the tip of my tongue
7 a waste of space
8 put my foot in it

6 Ask students in pairs to use phrases from exercises 3, 4, and 5 to replace the words.

Answers
1 followed in my mother's footsteps
2 hiccups
3 have a stormy relationship
4 over the moon
5 'd reached a crossroads in life
6 going round in circles
7 took his breath away
8 blossomed
9 got cold feet
10 the foggiest idea
11 glowing review
12 in deep water

READING (SB p75)

The man behind the mouse

The reading is a biographical article about the maker of animated films, Walt Disney. The tasks involve prediction and reading for specific information. There is also a lot of work on developing passive vocabulary, and a pre-view of the use of *would* in structures expressing hypothesis.

1 Lead in by asking students about Disney films and Disneyland®. You could put students in groups and see which group can name the most Disney films.

Sample answers

Some classic famous Disney films are: *Fantasia, Snow White and the Seven Dwarfs, Bambi, Dumbo, The Jungle Book, The Lady and the Tramp, The Aristocats, 101 Dalmations, The Little Mermaid*. More recent films include *Beauty and the Beast, The Lion King*, and *Aladdin*.

2 Ask students in pairs to decide which words and expressions describe Disney's world. All ideas and opinions are relevant here, of course; and, as the aim is to create a prediction task for the first reading, you need to elicit students' opinions without expressing your own too strongly.

Sample answers

Disney films are often described as **magical**, **idealized**, and **romanticized**, and they are certainly **imaginative**. The world of Disney, as seen in Disneyland®, is a **fantasy land**, and any element of the real world is an **airbrushed reality**. (If a photo is *airbrushed* it means that people or images that you don't want are improved, or removed altogether, so *airbrushed reality* is a negative phrase meaning that reality has been distorted so that it only shows what you want.) The Disney film studios could be described as a **dream factory**, producing stories with **harmonious** outcomes and **happy endings**. While the films may contain characters who are **cruel** and **violent**, the overall tone is not **harsh**. They do not leave the audience feeling troubled, and do not have any association with a **tormented childhood**.

3 Ask students to read the opening lines of the article and say what their first impression is of Walt Disney's childhood.

Answer

It was an unusually hard life for an 8-year-old.

4 Ask students to read the rest of the article and decide which of the words in exercise 2 relate to Walt Disney himself.

Answers

The life of Walt Disney had a **troubled** beginning, as he suffered a **harsh** and **tormented childhood** at the hands of his **cruel** and **violent** father. Walt later **romanticized** this childhood, presenting it as an **airbrushed reality**.

5 Ask students in pairs to rephrase the sentences to express the truth. Encourage them to rephrase, according to what they remember from the first reading, then look back at the text, find the relevant section, and check and correct what they have written.

Answers

1 He had a dirt-poor upbringing, and, although, there were small pleasures, it wasn't idyllic – he had to work hard, and his father beat him. He had no real childhood in fact.
2 He was close to his brother Roy, but his father was violent, and he doesn't mention his mother at all.
3 He was very close to Roy, who comforted him as a child, and worked with him as an adult.
4 He invented his lost childhood in his work. He didn't put any of his hard childhood experiences into his work.
5 He worked very hard for his success, suffering a nervous breakdown due to overwork.
6 He was helped by Ub Iwerks, another artist who first drew Mickey Mouse, a distributor who financially supported his first project, and his brother Roy, who handled the business end of the Disney empire.
7 Walt was married to his work and slept in the studio when his second daughter took to crying all night. He died of lung cancer when he was 65.
8 Mickey Mouse was first drawn by Ub Iwerks. Walt did the voice. His wife didn't like the first name of the mouse, Mortimer, so that is why it was changed to Mickey.
9 Success followed success, but there were personal hiccups: overwork, nervous breakdown, disappointments in his family life.
10 He oversaw every nut and bolt, and would not be dissuaded when people told him it was too costly.

Language work

6 Ask students in pairs to discuss who might have said what about what. Again, students should look back at the text to check their answers. Note that this exercise anticipates the *Language Focus* work on *would* and unreal tense usage.

Answers

1 Walt or Roy Disney about his father.
2 Roy Disney about his father and the way he beat his children.
3 Walt Disney about his poor family, and the fact that they didn't have enough money for pencil and paper.
4 Walt's parents about him working for the Red Cross in France during World War I.
5 Lillian or Walt Disney about changing Mortimer to Mickey Mouse.
6 Lillian Disney on the birth of their second daughter.
7 Walt Disney about his second daughter, Sharon, who cried all night.
8 A doctor / Roy / Walt's family after Walt was diagnosed with lung cancer.

Ask students to say whether the contractions are *would* or *had*.

Answers

1	would	5	had
2	had	6	would, had
3	would, had	7	would, had
4	had, would	8	had

7 Ask students in pairs to discuss the meaning of the highlighted words in the text.

Answers

traipse = walk slowly and unwillingly when you are tired
sneak = to go into secretly, without being seen
catnap = short sleep during the day
brunt = the main part of something unpleasant
nostalgic = viewing the past in a sentimental way
sketching = drawing quickly
rocking = moving gently from side to side
forged = made an imitation in order to deceive people
sissy = weak, effeminate
premiered = showed at a cinema for the first time
overnight sensation = became successful immediately
fits of rage = episodes of violent anger
prolifically = producing many works
oversaw every nut and bolt = supervised every detail of the project
irrepressible drive = a determination that could not be stopped

What do you think?

Sample answers
- He did three part-time jobs to pay for his studies; he pushed himself ever harder; he suffered a nervous breakdown; he oversaw the building of Disneyland®. What drove him was his desire to recreate the 'idyllic' childhood that he never had.
- Perhaps an unhappy childhood is a stimulus to work hard and be creative: such people are driven to create the life they never had, to prove something, to be successful in order to forget about or make up for the unhappiness of their childhoods.
- Apart from imagination and drive, creative geniuses often have a clear vision of what they want, and refuse to compromise their vision.
- Unlike Walt Disney, Joe Downing doesn't seem to be a workaholic or driven. He thinks you should follow your natural 'bent' and not try to control everything. Joe's childhood was poor, but beautiful and loving.

LANGUAGE FOCUS (SB p78)

Real and unreal tense usage

Don't forget to look at the *Language Aims* section on TB p71, which looks at problems students may have. You should also read Grammar Reference 8 on SB p154.

would

LANGUAGE INPUT

1–2 Ask students in pairs to look at the examples and match *would* to its uses.

Answers
past habits b
refusal on a past occasion c
the future in the past a

Refer students to Grammar Reference 8.1 on SB p154.

1 Ask students in pairs to discuss which use of *would* is being expressed in each sentence.

Answers

1	refusal on a past occasion	5	past habit
2	past habit	6	future in the past
3	future in the past	7	refusal on a past occasion
4	past habit	8	future in the past

In the feedback, check the form: *would / wouldn't* + infinitive without *to*. Point out that we tend to contract *would* to *'d*. If we stress *would* for past habit, it suggests criticism and irritation. Sometimes, we use *would*, not *'d*, simply because it is difficult to say *'d* after some nouns, for example *Disney would* ... , not *Disney'd* ... . To express refusal on a past occasion, *wouldn't* can be used not only to express the idea of a person refusing to do something, but also a machine 'refusing' to work.

2 Ask students to use their own ideas to complete the sentences. Do the first as an example. You could set this for homework.

Sample answers
1 stop crashing.
2 often take me out, even when he was tired.
3 change my ways.
4 listen to my phone conversations.
5 win easily.
6 do it when I got home.

Past tenses to express unreality

1 Ask students in pairs to look at the examples and discuss the questions.

> **Answers**
> The first sentence is a second or unreal conditional. The second sentence is a third or past conditional.
> **Rule of form**
> Second conditional: *If* + past (*if* or condition clause), *would* + infinitive (result clause)
> Third conditional: *If* + Past Perfect (*if* or condition clause), *would* + *have* + past participle (result clause)
> **Rule of use**
> The second conditional expresses a hypothetical condition and its probable result.
> The third conditional expresses a situation which is contrary to reality in the past.

2 Ask students in pairs to decide the 'reality' of each example of tense usage for non-fact, and complete the sentences.

> **Sample answers**
> Past Simple for hypothesis about a present state. (= But I smoke more than twenty cigarettes a day, and I can't give up.)
> Past perfect for a past hypothesis. (= But she did. And she said something tactless or embarrassing.)
> *would* for hypothesis about a present action. (= But you never do. And you say really stupid things that often hurt other people.)
> *could* for hypothesis about a present state. (= But I can't. I've never had a lesson.)
> Past Perfect for past hypothesis. (= But we didn't. And now we're going to be really late.)

Refer students to Grammar Reference 8.2–7 on SB pp154–156.

3 Ask students in pairs to decide which sentences refer to real past time.

> **Answers**
> 2, 3, and 6

4 Ask students in pairs to decide which sentences refer to real past in the past.

> **Answers**
> 2, 4, and 6

5 Ask students in pairs to complete the conversation. Do the first one as an example.

T 8.7 Play the recording so that students can check their answers. Ask students in pairs to practise the conversation, making sure they pay attention to the pronunciation of short forms and contractions.

Answers and tapescript

1	hadn't come	17	'll … have
2	've … seen	18	'd have liked
3	wouldn't be	19	to spend
4	was / were	20	had
5	's	21	hadn't
6	wouldn't … wash	22	'd be staying
7	was getting	23	'd love
8	'd been driving	24	to have seen
9	wanted	25	thought / were thinking
10	hadn't	26	wasn't / weren't
11	'd … be driving	27	'd suggest
12	would have been	28	did
13	'd set off	29	wouldn't moan
14	could have arrived	30	wouldn't mind
15	would have had	31	was / were left
16	won't get	32	'd … do

T 8.7

Amy Ugh! This hotel is horrible. I wish we hadn't come here. I've never seen such a dirty hotel in my life! It wouldn't be so bad if the bathroom was clean, but it's filthy. I wouldn't even wash my socks in it.

Seth I know, but it was getting late, and we'd been driving all day, and I wanted to stop. If we hadn't, we might not have found a hotel and we'd still be driving. That would have been awful. At least this is better than nothing.

Amy Well, I wish we'd set off earlier. Then we could have arrived in London today, and we'd have had a whole day to go round the galleries and museums. As it is, we won't get there 'til tomorrow lunchtime, and we'll only have a few hours.

Seth I'd have liked to spend more time in London, too, but I had to go to work this morning. If I hadn't, we'd be staying in a top London hotel now instead of this dump.

Amy I'd love to have seen a show, but we can't, so that's all there is to it. Anyway, it's time we thought about getting something to eat. If it weren't so late, I'd suggest going into town, but if we did, we might not find anywhere. It's quite late already.

Seth I wish you wouldn't moan about everything. I wouldn't mind, but you're so indecisive. If it were left up to you, we'd never do anything or go anywhere.

Amy OK, OK. I'm sorry. Let's go.

ADDITIONAL MATERIAL

Workbook Unit 8
Exercises 1–4 Tense usage for fact and non-fact
Exercise 6 Pronunciation – Conditional sentences
Exercise 7 Revision: metaphors and idioms
Exercise 8 Metaphors and idioms to do with the body

Softening the message

Lead in by writing on the board *Lend me some money*. Then ask students to think of ways of asking you for money in a very polite and tactful way. See which student can come with the politest (accurate) way of asking for money.

1 Read through the introduction as a class, then ask students in pairs to number the lines in order of directness, with 1 as the most direct, and to decide what makes a message more or less direct.

T 8.8 Play the recording to check the correct order. Ask students to repeat the lines and copy the intonation.

Answers

a
- 3 I wonder if you could help me?
- 2 Could you help me?
- 1 Can you help me?
- 4 I was wondering if you could possibly help me? I'd be very grateful.

b
- 1 Do you mind if I open the window?
- 2 Would you mind if I opened the window? It's so stuffy in here.

c
- 1 I want to speak to you.
- 2 I wanted to have a word with you, if that's all right.

d
- 3 If I were you, I'd dye it black.
- 4 I'd have thought the best idea would have been to dye it black, but it's up to you.
- 2 You could dye it black.
- 1 Dye it black.

What makes a message softer and less direct?

- Using hypothesis: *would, could,* and conditional forms. This distances the speaker – they are only speaking hypothetically – and so makes the message less direct.
- Using past tenses: *I wanted to* ... Again, this creates a sense of distance.
- Using the continuous: *I was wondering* ... This suggests the potentially temporary nature of the suggestion.
- Using indirect phrases: *I wonder if* ...
- Using apologetic phrases: *I'd be very grateful*; *It's up to you*; *if it's not too much trouble*

In the feedback, it may be worth discussing with students whether their own language softens the message in this way. Many students find these expressions uncomfortable to use because in their language they would sound ridiculously subservient. Point out that, unlike most languages, English does not have a polite *you* form. Consequently, *Dye it black*, an imperative which some languages can express with a polite form or an informal form, just sounds bossy or rude in English.

Refer students to Grammar Reference 8.8 on SB p156.

2 **T 8.9** Ask students to listen and discuss in pairs what softens the message in each conversation.

Ask students to look at the tapescript on SB p141 and practise reading the conversations aloud. You could play the recording again so that they can copy the intonation and sentence stress.

Answers and tapescript

1 Using *I'd like*, not *I want*.
2 *I would think* distances the speaker by saying they are not certain. *I'd say* uses the conditional *would*, which makes it even less direct. *I'd have thought* is a hypothetical past form, and thus softens the message considerably.
3 Using past tenses and the continuous form.
4 Using continuous forms. Notice the use of the continuous to express the future as a matter of course (irrespective of personal volition). Using *should* and *would*. Using *Don't you think*, which politely says that you want another person's opinion – but the decision is theirs.

T 8.9

1 A I'd like to book a table, please.
  B Certainly. What name was it?
2 A How old's Peter?
  B I would think he's about 60.
  C I'd say he's about 65.
  D I'd have thought he was nearer 70.
3 A I was wondering if you'd like to go out tonight?
  B Mmm! What were you thinking of?
  A I thought we could try that new pasta place.
4 A What time will we be setting off on Monday?
  B I was thinking of leaving about 8.30.
  A Don't you think we should leave a bit earlier to avoid the rush hour?
  B That'd be fine.

3 **T 8.10** Ask students in pairs to rephrase the sentences. Then play the recording so that they can check their answers.

In the feedback, get students to practise saying the sentences to their partner. Or you could get them to listen and repeat some of the phrases from the recording.

Answers and tapescript

1 Would you mind if I used your phone?
2 If I were you, I wouldn't paint the wall red.
3 Wouldn't it be better if we went in my car?
4 Would it be possible for you to ring back later? / Could you possibly ring back later?
5 Don't you think we should phone to say we'll be late?
6 I was hoping you might give me a lift to the station.
7 I would think she's French. / I'd have thought she was French.
8 I was wondering if you'd like to come to the cinema with me?
9 Would you mind filling in this form?
10 I wouldn't be surprised if it rained this afternoon.
11 I was thinking of going for a walk. Anyone interested?

12 I just thought I'd pop in to see if you needed anything.

13 I'd say it's a bad idea. / I'd have said it was a bad idea.

14 I'd have said that apologizing to her would be the best idea.

15 I gave her a present. You'd have thought she could have said thank you.

4 Ask students in pairs to write some conversations. Depending on how much time you have, you could ask them to choose one situation to write about, or get them to write a conversation for each situation. Go round monitoring and helping as students prepare. When they have finished writing, give students a few minutes rehearsal time to practise rhythm and intonation, then ask some pairs to come to the front and act out their situation. If your students enjoy this kind of thing, you could ask them to memorize the conversations they have prepared, which usually gives the acting out of conversations more edge. Don't forget to listen and note errors, and feedback at the end.

T 8.11 Play the recording so that students can compare their conversations.

Sample answers and tapescript
T 8.11

1 **A** Hi, Jenny. You all right?

   J Uh huh. You?

   A Er ... yeah. OK. Listen, Jenny. Are you doing anything tonight?

   J Gosh! Er ... I don't know. Why?

   A Well, I was wondering if you'd maybe ... you know ... if we could go out somewhere ... if you ... if you'd like to.

   J Well, er ... What did you have in mind?

   A Oh, I don't know. We could have a bite to eat, or we could take in a film. What do you fancy?

   J Well, that would be really nice. We could meet at the new bar on the High Street and take it from there. What do you think?

   A OK. Nice idea. What time ...?

2 **A** Hello. The Bedford Hotel. Karen speaking. How can I help you?

   B I'd like to book a room, please.

   A Certainly, sir. I'll just put you through to reservations. It's ringing for you.

   B Thank you.

   R Reservations. Robert speaking. I understand you'd like to book a room.

   B That's right. For three nights starting Wednesday the fifteenth of this month.

   R For how many people?

   B Just me. I wonder if it would be possible to have a room at the back of the hotel. I'm afraid I can never get to sleep if I hear the traffic.

   R I'll just see what I can do, sir. Yes ... that's certainly possible. Your name was?

   B Brown. Jonathan.

   R Thank you sir. Would you mind giving me a credit card number ... ?

3 **A** So what do you think of it?

   B It's fantastic!

   A It needs a lot doing to it, though. What do you think of the colour scheme?

   B It's too dark. Browns and blues and reds. You could do with something brighter. If I were you, I'd go for cream or white. You can't beat cream, it goes with everything.

   A Mm ... maybe. What about the kitchen?

   B Well, this is a bit of a disaster area, isn't it? I'd have thought the best idea would be to rip it all out and start again. I know it would be expensive, but at least you'd end up with a kitchen that suited you. No?

   A Don't you think I should wait a bit before I do that?

   B Well, you could, but I wouldn't. I was thinking you could go to Ikea and get a whole new kitchen.

   A Wow! Would you come with me?

4 **A** Hello.

   B Hi. Can I speak to Amanda, please?

   A She's out at the moment. Sorry.

   B Ah, OK. Would you have any idea when she might be back?

   A I'd have thought she'd be back by 8.00. She usually is on a Tuesday.

   B Would you mind giving her a message? Could you say that Andy phoned, and I'll try her again after 8.00?

   A Fine.

   B Would that be OK?

   A Sure.

   B Thanks a lot. Bye.

   A Bye.

Don't forget!

Writing Unit 8 Reviewing a film or book (SB p127)

Workbook Unit 8
Exercise 5 Listening – the pictures in my house
Exercise 9 Synonyms – break
Exercise 10 Phrasal verbs and their Latin-based synonyms

9

Verb patterns
Homonyms, homophones, and homographs
Telling jokes

History lessons

Introduction to the unit

The theme of this unit is history. The main reading texts are eye witness accounts of major historical events. The main listening text is an interview with two survivors of the First World War, who describe the Christmas Truce of 1914, when German and British troops briefly stopped fighting and crossed no-man's-land to meet each other. There is also a listening text in which an eye witness describes the terrorist attack on the World Trade Center in New York on September 11th 2001. There are opportunities for students to describe their own personal histories, and tell jokes.

Language aims

Verb patterns This unit looks at verb patterns. The problem, of course, is in getting the form right. There are few rules. Students must simply learn, practise, and remember the various patterns.

The unit looks at the following areas:

1 Verb patterns with the gerund
   The gerund, or -*ing* form, is used after prepositions, phrasal verbs, and certain other verbs. A key problem is recognizing when *to* is a preposition (*look forward to* + -*ing*).

2 Verb patterns with the infinitive
   The infinitive is used after certain verbs, and after certain verbs + object. A key problem is to remember that *to* must be omitted after some verbs (*make, let, help, dare*).

3 Verb + *that* + clause
   These structures are quite complex. Students have problems remembering that, as with reported speech, the verb in the clause goes one tense back when the main verb is in the past. *Suggest* has alternative forms, which need to be learnt separately. And, since not all verbs can be used in this pattern, students are likely to make errors such as **I want that I go* due to L1 interference.

4 Verb + -*ing* or verb + infinitive?
   Some verbs can take both forms (*like, love, start*) with minimal change of meaning. Other verbs can also take both forms, but with a significant change of meaning (*remember, regret, see*).

Grammar Reference 9.1–6 on SB pp156–157 looks at verb patterns. It is a good idea for you to read this carefully before teaching the grammatical section of this unit.

Vocabulary The *Vocabulary* section looks at homophones, homonyms, and homographs There is also work on categorizing vocabulary in the *Reading* section.

The last word This section generally looks at main stress when telling jokes, and responding in conversations.

Notes on the unit

STARTER (SB p81)

1–2 Ask students in small groups to look at the pictures, and decide which events are being illustrated.

Ask students in their groups to put the events in chronological order, and have a guess at exactly when they happened.

Answers

First Olympic games held in Greece (8)	776 BC
Great Wall of China (1)	built 221 BC, but some of it was begun even earlier. Most of what we see today was built between 14th–16th centuries AD
Leonardo da Vinci paints the *Mona Lisa* (2)	1519
American War of Independence begins (5)	1775 (Declaration of American independence made on 4 July 1776)
Storming of the Bastille – start of the French Revolution	14 July 1789
Charles Darwin publishes *On the Origin of Species* (6)	1859
Gottlieb Daimler and Karl Benz produce the first automobiles	1885
The First World War begins	July–August 1914
US drops first atomic bombs on Hiroshima and Nagasaki (3)	5 and 9 August 1945
AIDS becomes major health threat throughout world	first appeared in 1979
Berlin Wall demolished (7)	November 1989
Terrorist attack demolishes World Trade Center in New York (4)	11 September 2001

3 Ask students to decide individually which three events are most important. Then ask them to compare and justify their ideas in their groups. You could do this as a pyramid discussion. Ask each group to agree on a list of three. Then ask one person from each group to present their list to the class, and justify why. Then agree on a class list of three.

4 Have a brief open-class discussion. You could do this by eliciting from students or writing on the board some recent events, then asking students to say which they think will go down in history and why.

I was there

1 Ask students to say where the events fit chronologically.

Answers

The destruction of Pompeii: 24 August 79 AD (after the Great Wall of China was built)
The first transatlantic radio message: 12 December 1901 (after Gottlieb Daimler and Karl Benz produced the first automobiles)
The sinking of the *Titanic*: 14–15 April 1912 (after Gottlieb Daimler and Karl Benz produced the first automobiles)
The first aeroplane flight across *the Channel: 25 July 1909 (after Gottlieb Daimler and Karl Benz produced the first automobiles)
The first men on the moon: 20–21 July 1969 (after the bombing of Hiroshima and Nagasaki)

the Channel refers to the English Channel, the stretch of water between England and France.

2 Ask students in pairs to match the extracts to the events. Then ask students to quickly scan the texts to check their answers. Give them a time limit of three minutes, about 30 or 40 seconds a text, to make sure they just scan.

Answers
1 The sinking of the *Titanic*
2 The first aeroplane flight across the Channel
3 The first men on the moon
4 The destruction of Pompeii by Mount Vesuvius
5 The first transatlantic radio message

3 Divide students into groups of four or five. Ask each student to choose two or three texts, read them, and answer the questions. Make sure that each text is read by at least one person in the group. When students have finished reading, ask them to share their information with other members of the class. Conduct a brief whole-class discussion. Rather than going through all the answers, check understanding by asking check questions about each text, for example *When was Pompeii destroyed? Was Neil Armstrong a protagonist or an observer?*

Answers
The eruption of Vesuvius
1 24 August 79 AD
2 Pliny the Younger. He is an observer – he saw the eruption from a distance, and left Pompeii before it struck the town.
3 Natural – an earthquake. Bad. A great cloud like an umbrella pine tree rose to a great height. There were fire and flames, ashes, and the sea was sucked away from the shore. The black cloud covered the sea. The buildings shook with violent shocks.

4 The citizens of Pompeii. They panicked, screamed, and cried out to the gods.

5 The importance of Pompeii is not in the event itself, but in the fact that it was recorded, and that excavations have uncovered the well-preserved city, and the bodies of the people who died in the earthquake.

The first radio signal across the Atlantic

1 12th December 1901

2 Guglielmo Marconi. He is a protagonist – he has devised and is doing the experiment.

3 Man-made – the first radio signal across the Atlantic. Good. He is on a cliff in Newfoundland, surrounded by crude instruments, listening through an earpiece to the letter 'S' being sent in Morse code.

4 Marconi, his assistant Kemp, and somebody sending the message from Cornwall.

5 It was an 'epoch in history' – after that, mankind would be able to send messages without wires all over the world.

The first flight across the Channel

1 25th July 1909

2 Louis Blériot. He is a protagonist – the man flying the plane.

3 Man-made – the first flight across the Channel. Good. After examining his plane, at first light, Blériot takes off and flies steadily towards England at 40 mph. He is followed by a support ship, goes slightly off course, then sees the white cliffs of Dover. He lands and is greeted by soldiers, a policeman, and two Frenchmen.

4 Blériot, the crew of the *Escopette*, and, on his arrival in England, soldiers, a policeman, and two Frenchmen.

5 It was one of a number of heroic early flights, each of which improved the technology and showed the potential of aeroplanes. Today, flying is an everyday occurrence.

The *Titanic*

1 15th April 1912

2 A survivor, Mrs Bishop – an observer in the sense that she had escaped in a lifeboat, and was watching the *Titanic* go down from afar.

3 Natural and man-made – the man-made ship is sinking because it hit an iceberg. Bad. The ship is gradually moving downwards at a greater and greater angle until eventually it is standing upright in the water, then it suddenly sinks. The people on board are panicking and screaming, rushing to and fro.

4 A great mass of passengers, panicking and screaming. Mrs Bishop and her fellow passengers – they just watched and didn't go to the rescue.

5 It was important because it was such a shocking disaster at the time. The *Titanic* had been proudly declared to be 'unsinkable', and its loss shattered the myth that technology was enabling humans to become masters of nature. It is the most famous of all 'ship sinkings', and many novels and films have been written or made about it.

The first men on the moon

1 21st July 1969

2 Neil Armstrong and Buzz Aldrin – protagonists – they were astronauts on Apollo 11, and the first men on the moon.

3 Man-made. Good. The astronauts describe the beauty of the moon – its shape, colours, odours.

4 Armstrong and Aldrin. They reacted with wonder and awe, describing the beauty of the moon.

5 It was one of the most significant technological achievements in history. Although the exploration of space has continued, it has done so at a slower pace than anticipated in 1969. However, many products and inventions we are familiar with today were a direct result of technological achievements made during the space race.

Vocabulary work

4–6 Ask students in their groups to categorize the nouns, verbs, and adjectives. Encourage them to find the words in the texts they have read, and guess or check the meanings from the context. Some words, such as *bow* and *cart*, have many meanings, so it is important that students concentrate on the meanings of the words as they appear in the texts. Let them use dictionaries, and explain words to each other. In the feedback, concentrate on explaining words students are not sure about.

Answers

Nouns	Verbs	Adjectives
'amplifiers	blaze	crude
'ashes	blot out	lunar
bow (/baʊ/ here, *front of a boat*)	cart (here, *carry*)	over'whelmed
	de'ploy	'panic-stricken
coils	'jettison	'pungent
con'densers	shriek	'stranded
mob	slant	unim'peded
'snowdrift	slide	'violent
stern (*back of a boat*)	swarm	'wailing
	sway	
trunk (*body of a tree*)	toss	
valves	whirl	

Technical words

First radio signal: amplifiers, coils, condensers, valves
the Titanic: bow, stern

Listening

7 Read the introduction and set the scene. You could get students to guess what recent major historical event the speaker may have witnessed, just to create interest.

T 9.1 Play the recording and set the gist questions: *Which major historical event was it? Where was he at the beginning of his story? From where did he watch events unfold?*

Ask students in groups to describe to each other what Justin saw, and to describe their own experiences of the day.

Discuss the repercussions of this event as a class. The students may have their own angle on this, but their answers are likely to include: stock market uncertainty, travel and security procedures, changed mood of America, tension with and within Muslim communities, the war on terrorism, the invasion of Afghanistan, the war on Iraq, and whatever consequences there have been since the time of writing.

Answers
The terrorist attack on the World Trade Center, 11 September 2001.
At the beginning of his story, Justin was on the New York subway. He watched events unfold from his office block, which was near the Twin Towers.

T 9.1 See SB Tapescripts p141

Personal history

Give students a few minutes to select and prepare to talk about an important event in their life. Then put them in goups to ask and answer questions about it. Go round monitoring and helping as necessary. At the end, ask one or two students who heard particularly interesting stories from other group members, to summarize them for the class.

VOCABULARY AND PRONUNCIATION (SB p86)

Homonyms, homophones, and homographs

The aim here is to introduce students to a common feature of English: the way the same word can have a variety of meanings, or a variety of pronunciations. It gets students to think about the non-phonemic spelling of words, and includes dictionary work.

- *homonym*: same pronunciation, same spelling, different meaning
- *homophone*: same pronunciation, different spelling, different meaning
- *homograph*: different pronunciation, same spelling, different meaning

LANGUAGE INPUT

1 Model the pronunciation of *bow* /baʊ/ and *bow* /bəʊ/. Ask students to listen and repeat.
   Then ask students in pairs to look at the examples, read the sentences aloud to each other, answer the question, and think of their own examples.

Answers
2 The cast took their **bows** ... (n) / the Japanese **bow** ... (v)
3 The ribbon made a beautiful **bow** in her hair.
   Robin Hood used a **bow** and arrow to fight.
4 The front of a ship is called the **bow**.
   You play the violin with a **bow**.

2 Read as a class, and point out the pronunciation of *bow* /baʊ/ and *bough* /baʊ/. Ask if anyone knows what *bough* means.

Answer
Bough means the bottom part of the branch of a tree.

Homonyms

1 Ask students in pairs to find and check homonyms. Encourage them to guess meaning from context before checking in their dictionaries.

Answers
1 *branches*: here, local offices belonging to a large company. In the 'Vesuvius' text, the 'arms' of trees.
2 *trunk*: here, a big, heavy box used to carry clothes on long journeys – rarely used nowadays. In the 'Vesuvius' text, the cloud of dust from Vesuvius is metaphorically described as rising like the *trunk* (the main body) of a tree.
3 *pine*: here, a verb meaning to miss someone and feel very unhappy as a result. In the 'Vesuvius' text, a *pine* is a type of tree.
4 *stern*: here, very strict and serious. In the 'Titanic' text, the back of the ship.
5 *deck*: here, it has the same meaning as pack of cards. In the 'Titanic' text, it means the floor of a ship, where people walk.

2 Ask students in pairs to identify the homonyms, and write their own sentences.

Sample answers
1 A *swallow* is a type of bird / It's difficult to *swallow* food with a sore throat.
2 *To spot* is to catch sight of something / I love dalmatians – such beautiful *spotted* dogs.
3 A *rash* promise is made without thinking / I've got a terrible *rash* on my neck. I must be allergic to something. It's red and itchy.
4 A fire *drill* is a fire practice / Could you *drill* a hole in the wall, please, dad? I want to hang a picture there.

5 *To scrap* is to throw away / Do you have a *scrap* of paper I could use to write down this phone number before I forget it? (Also: a *scrap book* full of newspaper and magazine cuttings, and *he got into a scrap* (a physical fight)

6 *To ramble* is to speak in a confused way / My father loves *rambling*. Every weekend, he goes walking in the hills with his friends.

Homophones

3 Ask students in pairs to say the words, and think of homophones.

Answers

whale /weɪl/	sight /saɪt/
world /wɜːld/	higher /ˈhaɪə/
fought /fɔːt/	court /kɔːt/
air /eə/	saw /sɔː/

4 Ask students in pairs to complete the sentences.

Answers

1a 2a 3b 4b 5b 6b 7b 8a

Homographs

5 **T 9.2** Play the recording. Ask students to listen and write the homograph they hear and note the different pronunciations.

Answers and tapescript

1 We're sitting at the back, in **row** 102. (/rəʊ/)
 We've had another **row** about our finances. (/raʊ/)

2 That was never him singing **live**. He was miming. (/laɪv/)
 Live and let **live** is my philosophy. (/lɪv/)

3 **Close** that window! There's one helluva draught. (/kləʊz/)
 (*helluva* is a common way of writing *hell of a* in this informal expression.)
 You're not **close** to getting the answer. (/kləʊs/)

4 I soon got **used** to working the late night shift. (/juːst/)
 I don't trust **used** car-dealers. I'd never buy a car from one. (/juːzd/)

5 It's impossible to **tear** open this packet. Give me a knife. (/teə/)
 A single **tear** ran silently down her cheek as she waved goodbye. (/tɪə/)

6 He always looks so **content** with his lot. (/kənˈtent/)
 The **content** of your essay was excellent but there were rather a lot of spelling mistakes. (/ˈkɒntent/)

7 The head teacher complained to the parents about their son's **conduct** in class. (/ˈkɒndʌkt/)
 General Macyntire has been appointed to **conduct** the next stage of the war. (/kənˈdʌkt/)

8 Could you **record** the next episode for me? I'm out that night. (/rɪˈkɔːd/)
 He's broken the Olympic world **record** for the 100 metres. (/ˈrekɔːd/)

6 Divide the class into Groups **A** and Groups **B**. There should be no more than four or five students in a group.

Ask each group to look up their words in their dictionaries, find the two different pronunciations, and write sentences. This means they need to look at the phonemic script representation of each word, not just the meaning. Go round monitoring and helping as necessary.

When students are ready, mix them up so there are some Group **A** students and Group **B** students together, then ask them to read out their sentences, and teach each other the homographs.

In the feedback, point out that the change in pronunciation is often due to shifting word stress, from nouns, which tend to stress the first syllable /ˈrefjuːz/, to verbs, which tend to stress the second syllable /rɪˈfjuːz/.

Sample answers
Group A

wind /wɪnd/: The cold *wind* blew in from the north.
wind /waɪnd/: It's time to finish. Can we *wind* the discussion up?
refuse /rɪˈfjuːz/: I *refuse* to help you any more. You are lazy and need to take responsibility for yourself.
refuse /ˈrefjuːz/: *Refuse collector* is the official term for a dustman.
defect /ˈdiːfekt/: I took the machine back to the shop because it had a *defect*.
defect /dɪˈfekt/: During the cold war, spies used to *defect* from the Soviet Union to the USA, and vice versa.

Group B

wound /wuːnd/: After the fight, one man had a terrible *wound* in his side.
wound /waʊnd/: She *wound* some tape around the handle to make it stronger. (past of *wind* /waɪnd/)
minute /ˈmɪnɪt/: Wait a *minute*! I'm coming.
minute /maɪˈnjuːt/: Some living creatures are *minute* – you need a microscope to see them.
object /ˈɒbdʒekt/: What's that strange *object* you're holding?
object /əbˈdʒekt/: I'm sorry, but I *object* in the strongest terms to what you are saying.

LISTENING AND SPEAKING (SB p87)

Peace and goodwill

This listening is in two parts. The first is a short extract from the film *Oh, what a lovely war!* The accents, jargon, and grammatical inaccuracy are typical of the speech of working class soldiers at the time. The students don't need to understand every word, they just need to get an idea of what it is about. The second extract is long, and again, the accents of the old men being interviewed are strong, and they use jargon of the time. However, the intensive gap completion task which students are asked to complete should guide them to a close understanding of the recording.

1   Lead in by asking students what recent major wars or conflicts they can name. Then focus on the First World War or Great War. *When was it? What were the reasons for it? What do you know about it? What do the following words refer to: trench* (long, deep hole dug in the ground), *truce* (agreement to stop fighting), *rifle* (gun with a long barrel), *sentry duty* (period of time when a soldier is on guard), *the Western Front* (area of Belgium and France where the trench battles were fought)?

BACKGROUND NOTE

Oh, what a lovely war!

Based on a theatrical production, the film *Oh, what a lovely war!* was directed by Richard Attenborough in 1969. It is a harsh attack on war, contrasting the patriotism of those at home in Britain with the realities of trench warfare at the front. The film is in the style of a musical, with black comedy.

The First World War or Great War

It started in 1914, following the assassination of Archduke Franz Ferdinand of Austria in Sarajevo. Germany, Austria-Hungary, and Turkey fought against Britain, France, Russia, and their allies. The war soon became a stalemate of attritional trench warfare. Casualties were enormous. Russia withdrew from the war following the revolution of 1917, the same year that the Americans joined the war on the side of the British and French. Germany and Austria surrendered, and an armistice was signed on November 11th 1918.

---

2   **T 9.3** Play the recording. Then ask students to discuss the questions in pairs.

GLOSSARY

… they're coppin' it = they're under heavy attack
Nah = No
innit = isn't it
Let's 'ear yer! = Let's hear you – sing louder
'E 'eard us! = He heard us!
Fröhliche Weihnacht = Happy Christmas

Answers
1   The First World War or Great War. The British are fighting the Germans.
2   Jerry (for the Germans), and Tommy (for the British).
3   In a trench.
4   It's warm and friendly – they wish each other Happy Christmas.
5   Students' own ideas. (You could teach the expression *to fraternize with the enemy*.)

T 9.3   See SB Tapescripts p142

---

3   **T 9.4** Read the introduction, and ask students to look at the sentence extracts, and think what the missing words might be. Play the recording. You may need to play it a second time, pausing where there are missing words. Let students check their answers in pairs before checking with the whole class.

Answers
1   German trenches
2   carol
3   no-man's land
4   cigars
5   grudge (bad feeling), grudge
6   pals (friends)
7   bury, buried
8   strengthen

T 9.4   See SB Tapescripts p142

---

4   Ask students to discuss the questions in pairs before discussing briefly with the whole class.

Answers
1   They heard Germans singing a carol, then one of the Germans called out to them.
2   They sang carols to each other.
3   The open space between the British trench and German trench, which both sides were fighting over.
4   They were cordial (friendly), shared goodies (nice things) such as cigars and tobacco, helped each other bury their dead, and the British borrowed German tools to strengthen their defences.
5   Six weeks.
6   A soldier from Stuttgart who Harold Startin befriended.

What do you think?

Sample answers
• Reasons for enemies becoming friends in war: mutual respect, shared experience, an awareness that the conflict is between governments rather than ordinary soldiers, a desire to make amends for all the killing.
• Students own answers. It may be more difficult for officers to become friends as they are less likely to come into contact with each other. However, if they do, they are very likely to have mutual respect for each others' position and rank.

LANGUAGE FOCUS (SB p88)

Verb patterns

Don't forget to look at the *Language Aims* section on TB p81, which looks at problems students may have. You should also read Grammar Reference 9.1–6 on SB pp156–157.

1   Ask students in pairs to complete the sentences, following the verb pattern rules. If they can't remember which verb is missing, ask them to guess.

Answers

Verb + infinitive

The buildings seemed to be swaying to and fro.

We finally decided to leave the town.

The lights continued to burn until it sank.

I attempted to land my plane.

I placed the earphone to my ear and started to listen.

Verb + object + infinitive

They had trained us to hate the Germans.

I had ordered the destroyer to go to sea.

They helped us bury our dead. (*they helped us to bury* ... is also correct here)

It made the moon appear blue-grey. (*make* is always followed by the infinitive without *to*)

Verb + preposition + -*ing*

The Germans joined in singing with the British.

Not speaking German didn't stop him from making friends.

Verb + adjective + infinitive

We were terrified to see everything changed.

Refer students to Grammar Reference 9.1–6 on SB pp156–157.

2 Ask students to read the dictionary entry.

Note that this extract comes from the *Oxford Advanced Learner's Dictionary*. If your students have different dictionaries, or you use a different class set, you may wish to research *agree* in those dictionaries.

GLOSSARY

[V] = verb used alone

[V **speech**] = verb + noun phrase + direct speech

[V to inf] = verb + *to* infinitive

[V that] = verb + *that* clause

[VN] = verb + noun phrase

[VN **that**] = verb + noun phrase + *that* clause

Ask students in pairs to correct the incorrect sentences.

Answers

1 ... I *agree*.

2 ✓

3 They agreed *that* fighting ...

4 ✓

5 They always agree *with* each other on ...

6 ✓

7 Is this plan agreed *by* everyone?

8 They agreed *with* me about the time ...

3 Ask students to read the dictionary entry.

Ask students in pairs to correct the incorrect sentences.

Answers

1 He persuaded his mother *to* lend ...

2 ✓

3 ✓

4 You'll never persuade me *to take up* ...

5 ... I was persuaded *by* all their arguments.

4 Ask students in pairs to decide which verb is correct, then ask them to change the other forms to make correct sentences. Do the first as an example.

Answers

1 He used to be a soldier; He enjoys being a soldier; He is used to being a soldier; He would rather be a soldier.

2 We are thinking of selling our flat; We are trying to sell our flat; We have decided to sell our flat; We had better sell our flat.

3 They wanted us to go; They stopped us going; They hoped (that) we would go; They let us go.

4 I suggested that he meet her. (*I suggested that he should meet her* is also correct); I am looking forward to meeting her; I happened to meet her; I avoided meeting her.

5 Did you see him do it? Did you mind doing it? Did you remind him to do it? Did you manage to do it?

6 She promised not to laugh; She didn't feel like laughing; She made me laugh; She couldn't help laughing.

7 Why were you forced into resigning? Why didn't you dare (to) resign? Why were you made to resign? Why are you threatening to resign?

8 He helped me learn English; He is keen to learn English; He encouraged me to learn English; He can't stand learning English.

You can give students a photocopy of the Verb patterns tables on TB p142.

Point out exceptions: *hoped* is followed by a clause with *would* + infinitive, which expresses a hypothetical idea. *Suggest* has alternative forms, and *make* in the passive takes *to*.

5 **T 9.5** Play the recording. Pause after each conversation, and ask students to complete the phrases using different verb patterns. Let students check their answers in pairs before checking with the whole class.

Answers and tapescript

1 She was delighted to get the job.
   He congratulated her on getting the job.

2 She was concerned about her car / about the strange sound her car was making.
   He urged her to get her car serviced.

3 She was annoyed about missing the last bus. / that she had missed the last bus.
   They offered her a lift.

4 She complained that they were making too much noise.
   They denied (that) they were making a lot of noise.

5 She promised to be home by midnight. / (her father) (that) she would be home by midnight.
   He threatened not to let her out for a month if she wasn't (home).
6 She accused him of making all the mess.
   He apologized for making the mess.
7 He's really scared of having to speak in public.
   She advised him to take deep breaths before he starts. / before starting.
8 He boasted of climbing right to the top / that they had climbed right to the top in record time.
   He challenged him to show him the proof / to prove it.

T 9.5
1 'Oh great! I got the job!'
   'Well done! I knew you would.'
2 'My car's making this strange rattling sound.'
   'It sounds bad. You should really get it serviced.'
3 'Oh no! I've missed the last bus!'
   'Don't worry. We'll give you a lift.'
4 'Will you lot stop making so much noise!
   'We're not. We're just talking quietly'
5 'Don't worry, dad. I'll be home by midnight.'
   You'd better be, because if you're not, you're grounded for a week!'
6 'Did you make all this mess?'
   'I'm sorry, really I am.'
7 'I get so nervous when I have to speak in public.'
   'Take deep breaths before you start.'
8 'We climbed right to the top in record time.'
   'Where's the proof ?'

6 Ask students to complete the sentences. Let students compare their answers in pairs before checking with the whole class.

Sample answers
1 I remember being frightened of the dark when I was young.
2 I'll never forget seeing the Grand Canyon for the first time.
3 I like staying in and reading when it's raining.
4 I'm thinking of going skiing next year.
5 I find it difficult to remember verb patterns.
6 I mustn't forget to feed the cat.
7 I've always tried to be a patient person.
8 I'm looking forward to seeing my best friend on Saturday.
9 I try to avoid having arguments.
10 Our teacher always makes us speak English in class.

EXTENSION IDEA
A nice variation on this type of personalisation exercise is to ask students to complete it with information about themselves, but make half of the sentences true, and half of them false (but believable). After you have checked that their sentences are grammatically correct,

put students into pairs or groups and ask them to read their sentences to each other. The other student(s) have to decide which sentences are true and which are false.

ADDITIONAL MATERIAL

Workbook Unit 9
Exercises 1–4 Verb patterns
Exercise 6 Jokes based on homophones and homonyms

THE LAST WORD (SB p90)

Telling jokes

1 Ask students in pairs to match the questions with the answers.

Answers

1 h	6 d
2 c	7 f
3 a	8 g
4 j	9 e
5 i	10 b

2 **T 9.6** Play the recording and ask students in pairs to explain the jokes to each other.

Answers
1 *Sir Cumference* sounds like *circumference*.
2 *Knights* is a homophone of *nights*.
3 *Held up* has two meanings: literally to hold up something heavy, metaphorically, to hold up (i.e. to rob at gun point) a bank or shop.
4 *Arkitect* sounds like *architect*. Noah built an ark.
5 *An arrow* sounds like *a narrow*. A narrow escape means a lucky escape.
6 *Kahn't* sounds like *can't*. This Genghis can't conquer anything.
7 *Blown apart* (by a mine) sounds similar to the English pronunciation of *Buonapart* /ˈbəʊnəpɑːt/
8 *Sioux* is a homophone of *sue*, which means to take someone to a civil court.
9 *The Cs are* sounds like *the Caesar*.
10 The idiomatic expression *lies in ruins* means failed completely. Literally, buildings lie in ruins when they have fallen down.

3 **T 9.7** Play the recording. Ask students to notice which words are stressed. The key stress here is on the emphatic auxiliary verb, *did*.

Ask students in pairs to practise telling the jokes to each other. Make sure that the person responding uses the auxiliary verb emphatically and correctly, and encourage students to groan at the jokes.

4 **T 9.8** Ask students to look at the conversations and mark the main stresses. Play the recording. Ask students to compare their ideas, then to practise the conversations in pairs.

Answers and tapescript

1 **A** Have you heard the one about the old man and his dog?

   B I told you it!

2 **A** I invited Anna but she isn't coming.

   B I told you she wouldn't.

3 **A** Peter hasn't told anybody.

   B He told me.

4 **A** I hope you didn't tell Clara.

   B I didn't tell anyone.

5 **A** Who told Clara?

   B I didn't tell her.

6 **A** John won't like it when you tell him.

   B If I tell him.

7 **A** It's the worst film I've ever seen.

   B Tell me about it!

8 **A** He dumped me.

   B I don't want to say 'I told you so'!

5 Ask students to tell the class any jokes in English they know.

Don't forget!

Writing Unit 9 Personal profile (SB p128)

Workbook Unit 5
Exercise 5 Listening – Henry VIII
Exercises 7–8 Vocabulary
Exercise 9 Prepositions in passive sentences
Exercises 10–11 Comparisons with *as … as* and *like*

Stop and check 3 (TB pp 147–148)

Verb patterns tables (TB p142)

10

Sports vocabulary
Intensifying adverbs
The body • Clichés

The body beautiful

Introduction to the unit

The theme of this unit is sport and the body. The main reading text is an article about how sport has become a world-wide obsession. The main listening texts are conversations about ballerina Darcey Bussell, and Olympic rower Steve Redgrave, detailing their careers, their training programmes, and their diets.

Language aims

Intensifying adverbs This unit looks at intensifying adverbs and the verbs and adjectives they collocate with. While some adverbs collocate with some verbs or adjectives because of a link in meaning (see Unit 3), with many others there are no rules that dictate why certain combinations are possible or not. Here are a few possibilities.

extremely	angry, difficult, important, sorry
awfully	nice, cold
terribly	sorry, ill, worried
pretty	big, hard, good
rather	stupid, tired, expensive
fairly	useful, large, good
totally	ridiculous, different, unexpected
completely	relaxed, different, unrecognizable
entirely	mistaken, obvious
simply	ridiculous, awful, wonderful
utterly	exhausted, unbearable, terrified
pretty	impossible, fantastic, amazing

These collocations can only be learnt through memorizing and practising. Consequently, the *Language Focus* section in this unit provides plenty of practice.

> **WATCH OUT FOR ...**
> **'Gradability' and collocation**
> Students need to think about:
> • which adjectives are gradable, and which extreme
> • which adverbs collocate with gradable and extreme adjectives

There are three key areas students need to understand.

1   The difference between gradable and extreme adjectives.
    A **gradable** adjective expresses a quality that can exist in different intensities, for example *clever* – you can be *quite* or *very* clever.

    An **extreme** adjective expresses a quality whose intensity is already, and is only, extreme, for example *brilliant* – you can be *absolutely* brilliant, but not *very* or *fairly* brilliant.

    Errors can occur when students come across a gradable adjective which they think expresses a strong emotion or intensity, and therefore treat as if it were extreme, for example, *~~absolutely upset~~* or *~~absolutely ugly~~*.

2 *Very* collocates with gradable adjectives, *absolutely* collocates with extreme adjectives, and *really* collocates with most adjectives.

3 The uses of *quite*, and the importance of stress and intonation to carry its meaning.

It's quite good. = It's better than expected. (up a bit)

It's quite interesting. = But not as interesting as expected. (down a bit)

It's quite ridiculous. = It's completely ridiculous. (up to the top)

Grammar Reference 10.1–3 on SB p157 looks at intensifying adverbs. It is a good idea for you to read this carefully before teaching the grammatical section of this unit.

Vocabulary The *Vocabulary* section looks at words to do with the body, both in terms of their literal meaning, and how they are used as verbs. It also looks at verbs to describe actions involving parts of the body. There is also work on guessing the meaning of vocabulary in the *Reading* section.

The last word In this unit, this section looks at the meaning of some common clichés in English.

Notes on the unit

STARTER (SB p91)

1 Make this a competition. Divide students into groups of three or four, and ask them to complete the two lists. Which group can think of ten sports for each list the quickest?

> **Sample answers**
> **Competitive**
>
> | | | |
> |---|---|---|
> | squash | wrestling | netball |
> | boxing | judo | karate |
> | tennis | table tennis | badminton |
> | golf | football | volleyball |
> | basketball | rugby | cricket |
> | baseball | hockey | ice hockey |
> | lacrosse | athletics | horse racing |
> | motor racing | polo | showjumping |
>
> **Individual**
>
> | | | |
> |---|---|---|
> | yoga | aerobics | *skateboarding |
> | *swimming | *surfing | *diving |
> | *skiing | *snow boarding | *waterskiing |
> | *windsurfing | *sailing | *canoeing |
> | *rowing | jogging | *gymnastics |
> | *ice skating | *roller skating | *weightlifting |
> | *shooting | *archery | *cycling |

> | | | |
> |---|---|---|
> | *rock climbing | *mountaineering | rambling |
> | *orienteering | skydiving | |
>
> *Of course, these sports can also be played competitively.

2 **T 10.1** Play the recording. Ask students to identify the sports described.

> **Answers and tapescript**
> **1** Horse racing. Clues: names of horses; *straight; winning post; photo finish; third place*
> **2** Football. Clues: *ball; half; passes; dribbles; shoots; goalkeeper; corner kick; striker; heads; net; goal; two – nil*
> **3** Tennis. Clues: *deuce; serves; returns; net; volleys; cross-court; down the line; advantage; match point; opponent; backhand; Game, set, and match; 6–4, 6–2*
> **4** Boxing. Clues: *bell; round six; ring; punch; canvas; count; knockout; World Heavyweight title*
> **5** Baseball. Clues: *Giants; runs; inning; base; home run; pitches; 3-run homer*
> **6** Golf. Clues: *eighteenth hole; three par; shot; green; putts; tournament*
>
> **T 10.1** See SB tapescripts p143

3 Ask students to discuss the questions in their groups before discussing briefly with the whole class.

READING AND SPEAKING (SB p92)

The age of sport

1 Ask students in groups of three or four to discuss the sports the different nationalities are renowned for.

> **Sample answers**
> **Australians**: swimming, tennis, surfing, and the team sports, cricket, rugby league, rugby union.
> Reasons could be the general love of sport, the warm climate, the competitive nature of the people, and the excellent facilities and sports training in Australia.
> **Brazilians**: football, volleyball. Brazil were Football World Cup winners in 1994, finalists in 1998, and winners again in 2002.
> Reasons could be that football is almost a religion, everybody plays, and the population is large. The warm climate and outdoor culture mean that young Brazilians spend a lot of time practising on the beach, where volleyball is also a popular sport.
> **African-Americans**: boxing, basketball, athletics, particularly sprinting.
> Reasons could be natural build and athleticism, role models in the sport, the attraction of sports which don't cost a lot to practise, and excellent facilities and training in the USA.

The Chinese: gymnastics, table tennis.

Reasons could be that size and physical stature are not so important in these sports, which suits the smaller physical stature of the Chinese.

Kenyans: middle-distance running.

Reasons: natural build, living at altitude, role models who offer an escape from poverty, and the fact that it is a national sport, with large training camps provided.

Russians: gymnastics.

Reasons: the old USSR provided a huge state-sponsored programme to train youngsters rigorously in this field.

2–3 Ask students about sport in their country. *Who is the most highly-paid sportsperson? What are the biggest sporting events? Which sports are important in their country? Which sports do people do, and which do they watch? Is there a sport unique to their country?*

At the time of writing, Michael Schumacher is reputed to be the most highly-paid sportsman in the world. The Formula One driver is estimated to earn $80m a year.

4 Ask students to read the paragraph headings, and write down what they think the text might be about. Discuss students' ideas as a class.

5 Ask students to read the text and in pairs to discuss and answer the questions. Encourage them to try to remember the answer, then look back at the relevant section of the text to read closely and check.

Answers
1 Like strawberries, sport used to be seasonal. Now, you can get both all year round.
2 Sport was fun and amateur. It had a specific audience. You did not see sport on TV all the time, or have so much in newspapers, and it had nothing to do with fashion, showbiz and business.
3 It had its own limited and specific place in life. Now it invades all areas of life: fashion, showbiz, business.
4 It has increased access for TV audiences, and made sports richer via advertising, sponsorship, and fees. It has not been beneficial.
5 It is an example of how many people can participate in sport.
6 They come from an ordinary background and are self-made people.
7 Like gladiators, they display their supreme skill in an arena.
8 Spontaneous uncertainty – we don't know who is going to win.
9 They are the only truly global occasions.
10 Most people are becoming satiated and disillusioned with sport.

Vocabulary work

6 Ask students to find the words and phrases in the text, and work out their meaning. Ask students to discuss their answers with a partner. Rather than going through all the words in the feedback, ask students if there any words that they were not sure about and would like to have explained in more detail.

Answers
Paragraph 1
ubiquitous = appearing everywhere
proliferation = rapid increase
cultural icons = people in the world of sport or arts that people look up to as role models

Paragraph 2
self-made people = people who have worked to become very rich – they haven't inherited money
seek fame and fortune = try to be rich and famous
spontaneous uncertainty = here, it means that at any moment (in a sporting match) we don't know what will happen next
gut-wrenching experience = emotionally very stressful
thronging mass = a huge number of moving people

Paragraph 3
untold riches = extreme wealth
saturated = completely filled, so that there is no room for any more

Paragraph 4
package = sell themselves as a 'package' of many different products
mirrored = reflected

Paragraph 6
sheer volume = incredibly large amount (*sheer* is used to emphasize a noun)
greed and over-exposure = wanting too much money and being on TV too often
satiated = having had so much of something that we don't want any more
disillusioned = disappointed because something isn't what you expected

What do you think?

Sample answers
• Arguably, the wealth of individuals in some sports can make the sport poorer. It's more difficult to relate to top sports stars as heroes, when we know they are super-rich and probably doing it for the money; performance-enhancing drugs are prevalent because of the amount of money in sport; amateur notions of fair play, being a good loser, etc. are lost in professional sport, which is all about money; cheating and match-fixing are part of professional sport.

- Arguably, men are more interested in sport. Perhaps it's because sport plays to aggressive, competitive instincts in men (instincts which were developed by men when they were hunters and warriors). It may also be that in many cultures team sports are the only way for men to meet each other, bond, and share an emotional experience.

LANGUAGE FOCUS (SB p94)

Intensifying adverbs

Don't forget to look at the *Language Aims* section on TB p90, which looks at problems students may have. You should also read Grammar Reference 10.1–3 on SB p157.

> **LANGUAGE INPUT**
>
> Read through the examples as a class. Ask students if they can think of any intensifying adverb and verb / adjective collocations that they know and regularly use. Ask students to read Grammar Reference 10.1–3 on SB p157.

1 Ask students in pairs to choose the two correct adverbs.

> **Answers**
> 1 totally / quite
> 2 totally / strongly
> 3 sincerely / seriously
> 4 perfectly / completely
> 5 really / quite

2 Ask students in pairs to choose the one correct adverb.

> **Answers**
> 1 absolutely   4 really
> 2 totally   5 thoroughly
> 3 entirely

3 Ask students to match gradable adjectives with extreme adjectives.

> **Answers**
>
> | Gradable | Extreme |
> | --- | --- |
> | stupid | ridiculous |
> | expensive | exorbitant |
> | pleasant | delightful |
> | unusual | extraordinary |
> | upset | devastated |
> | clever | brilliant |

Ask students which group of adjectives can be used with which intensifying adverbs.

> **Answers**
> *Very* can be used with gradable adjectives.
> *Absolutely* can be used with extreme adjectives.
> *Really* can be used with both.
> *Quite* can be used with both, but with different meanings (see below).

T 10.2 Play the recording. Ask students in pairs to practise the sentences. You could do this as a prompt drill. Write on the board: *Annabel / Sonia, book / film, meal / company, mother / father, house / garden, shoes / dress*. Nominate individuals, and ask them to produce the sentences from the recording from the prompts. You may need to model sentences once or twice until students can remember them. Make sure the students emphasize stress and intonation.

T 10.2
1 Annabel is very clever, but Sonia is absolutely brilliant.
2 I thought the book was really stupid, but the film was quite ridiculous.
3 The meal was very pleasant, and the company absolutely delightful.
4 My mother was quite upset, but my father was really devastated.
5 Their house was really unusual, but the garden was quite extraordinary.
6 Her shoes were quite expensive, but the dress was really exorbitant.

4 **T 10.3** Play the recording. What does *quite* mean in each sentence?

In the feedback, point out the stress and intonation on *quite* in each sentence. In the first, the stress is on *quite*, and the intonation goes down. In the second, the stress is on the adjective, *clever*, and the intonation on *quite* goes up. In the third, there is stress on *quite* as well as the adjective, and the rising intonation is exaggerated.

Ask students in pairs to practise saying the sentences to each other.

> **Answers and tapescript**
>
> 1 The holiday was quite good, but I wouldn't go back. (*down a bit*)
>
> 2 James is quite clever. Cleverer than me, anyway. (*up a bit*)
>
> 3 The answer is quite obvious. I'm surprised you can't see it. (*up to the top*)

5 Ask students in pairs to choose the two correct adverbs.

T 10.4 Play the recording. Ask students to listen and check their answers, then practise the sentences in pairs.

Answers and tapescript
1 Kate thinks maths is hard, and she's *absolutely* right / *quite* right.
2 Personally I find maths *totally* impossible / *quite* impossible.
3 She's *absolutely* terrified / *completely* terrified of dogs.
4 I was *very* pleased / *terribly* pleased to hear you're getting married.
5 I'm sure you'll be *extremely* happy / *really* happy together.

6 Ask students in pairs to choose the adverb that goes with the adjective.

T 10.5 Play the recording. Ask students to listen and check their answers, then practise the sentences in pairs.

Answers and tapescript
1 This wine is *rather* pleasant. You must try it.
2 I'm *absolutely* determined to lose weight.
3 The film was *quite* interesting. You should see it.
4 The restaurant was *quite* nice, but I wouldn't recommend it.
5 If you ask her, I'm *pretty* sure she'll say yes.

7 Ask students in pairs to write some questions and replies following the examples in the Student's Book. Ask a few pairs to act out their conversations for the class.

ADDITIONAL MATERIAL

Workbook Unit 10
Exercises 1–2 Intensifying adverbs
Exercise 7 Extreme adjectives
Exercise 8 Pronunciation – Making the most of extreme adjectives

VOCABULARY AND SPEAKING (SB p95)

Words to do with the body

1 Ask students in pairs to label the picture. Encourage them to use a dictionary.

Answers

1	forehead	14	chest	27	wrist
2	brain	15	rib	28	groin
3	eyebrow	16	armpit	29	knuckle
4	temple	17	heart	30	thigh
5	cheek	18	kidney	31	thumb
6	lip	19	stomach	32	bone
7	earlobe	20	liver	33	knee
8	jaw	21	vein	34	calf
9	chin	22	muscle	35	shin
10	neck	23	intestines	36	ankle
11	throat	24	spine	37	heel
12	shoulder	25	waist	38	toe
13	lung	26	hip		

2 Ask students to complete the sentences. Do the first as an example. Let students check their answers in pairs before checking with the whole class.

Answers

1	headed	6	elbow
2	shoulder	7	thumb
3	foot(s)	8	handing
4	eyeing	9	nosing
5	face	10	kneed

3 Ask students in pairs to match the action to the part of body. If students are unsure about any words, use mime to show the meaning.

Ask students to say why we do these things.

Answers

tickle: fingers	to make someone laugh
stroke: hand; fingers	to calm someone down when they are upset; to show affection to animals
nudge: elbow	to get someone's attention
thump: fist	to hit someone in a fight
sniff: nose	to stop your nose running when you have no handkerchief
slap: palm of hand	to hit someone in the face, often when they have said something rude to you
munch: mouth; teeth	to chew food
smack: palm of hand	to hit someone, usually on the bottom or legs, because they are rude or naughty – usually by a parent to a child
pinch: finger and thumb	to annoy someone
squeeze: fingers; hands	to show someone you are happy to see them; to get something out of a plastic container (e.g. toothpaste)
grin: mouth; lips	to show you are pleased with yourself
rub: hands; fingers	to warm your hands; to make something feel better or warmer; to show your delight at some good news
clap: hands	to show your appreciation of a performance
pat: hand	to comfort, support, or congratulate someone
hug: arms	to hold someone very close, with affection
frisk: hands	to search someone to see if they are carrying a weapon
shove: hands and arms	to push someone out of the way angrily
spit: mouth; lips; throat	to clear your mouth of a bad taste

wink: eye; eyelid	to catch someone's attention; to show you like them; to share a secret joke with someone
scratch: fingers; nails	to get rid of an itch; to hurt someone when you are angry

4 Ask students in pairs to take it in turns to test each other on the vocabulary by miming actions for the other student to identify.

LISTENING AND SPEAKING (SB p96)

The rower and the ballet dancer

This is a jigsaw listening activity, and requires careful preparation before the lesson (see 4 below). It involves two conversations between friends, one about famous British ballerina, Darcy Bussell, and one about British Olympic rower, Steve Redgrave. The task is to take notes while listening to one of the conversations, then compare information with someone who listened to the other one.

1 Ask students in pairs or small groups to discuss the questions, then have a brief open class feedback.

2 Ask students to discuss the questions briefly in pairs. In the feedback, elicit ideas.

Sample answers
Highs: winning, fame, sense of achievement, pushing themselves to the limit.
Lows: they train hard, they have to watch their diet, they have to push themselves to the limit, they have to sacrifice a social life.

3 Ask students to look at the photographs and read about the two people. Ask them to read the quotations. Who says what?

Answers
Steve Redgrave: 'When you get tired ...'
Darcey Bussell: 'Of course the worst thing ...'

4 **T 10.6** and **T 10.7** This is a jigsaw listening, so this will take careful preparation before the lesson. You will need two CD or cassette players, and two recordings of the conversations. Divide students into two groups, Group A and Group B, and ask one group to go to another room to listen to their recording. Nominate one person in each group to be in charge of playing and pausing the recording while students make notes to answer the questions. This frees you up to go back and forth between rooms, making sure everything is going smoothly.

5 When students have finished, bring them back together in the classroom, and rearrange them in AB pairs. Ask students to compare answers about their person.

Answers
Steve Redgrave
1 Steve is one of Jez's all-time sporting heroes.
2 Winning a fifth medal gold at the Sydney Olympics, and winning a knighthood.
3 Diabetes.
4 Trained eight hours a day, seven days a week, for 25 years.
5 Porridge, pasta, potatoes, red meat, eggs, and chocolate.
6 His body goes numb and his mind goes blank – he doesn't even hear the crowds cheering him on.
7 His dedication to rowing nearly cost him his marriage.
8 His wife Ann and children Natalie, Sophie, and Zak.
9 He plans to make use of his fame by raising money for children's charities, running the London Marathon to raise £5 million.
10 They are flatmates. Jez once tried rowing at university, and is thinking of doing the London Marathon.

Darcey Bussell
1 They are interested in Darcey because they are ballet students.
2 Having whole ballets created especially for her.
3 Pain in the back, calves and bottom. Tendonitis in the ankles. Feet suffer terribly.
4 She rehearses nearly ten hours a day. When not rehearsing, she exercises for hours and has physio to keep her limbs supple.
5 Carbohydrates like pasta, cereals, and baked potatoes.
6 She has an adrenaline rush when she's on stage.
7 She's had to give over her whole life to it.
8 Her daughter Phoebe and husband Angus.
9 To have more children.
10 They are friends who've been going to ballet classes since they were three.

T 10.6 See SB Tapescripts p143

T 10.7 See SB Tapescripts p143

What do you think?

Sample answers
- Students' own opinions
- To succeed in sport you have to be: single-minded, driven, hard-working, focused, ambitious, competitive, a little aggressive. There are many reasons why people do it, ranging from a love of the game, a desire to win, to a desire to be rich, famous, and successful.
- Famous examples of sports people burning out include young female tennis players like Tracy Austin, Andrea Jaeger, and Jennifer Capriati. Capriati was a top player at 15, then got in trouble with the law because of drugs, only to return to become a Grand Slam-winning player.

How healthy and fit are you?

The aim here is to get students talking about health and fitness.

1 Read out the statement and the questions, then discuss them as a class. Most students will probably disagree with the statement.

> **Sample answers**
> You can pull muscles, have a heart attack from over-exercising, put too much stress on bones and joints.

2 Ask students to read through the quiz, and check any unknown words. Ask students to think how to turn the statements into questions, so that they can interview their partner. Put students into pairs to ask and answer the questions.

> **GLOSSARY**
> *calorific intake* = number of calories you eat
> *food supplements* = usually pills containing vitamins, iron, etc. to supplement (add to) your diet
> *sugar consumption* = the amount of sugar you eat
> *exercise aerobically* = any exercise which increases your heart rate significantly and strengthens your heart and lungs
> *actively cultivate* = develop in a positive, deliberate way
> *meditate* = to empty or concentrate your mind in order to relax or as part of a religious exercise

When they have finished, ask students to work out and compare their scores, and decide on priorities for action. Conduct a brief whole-class feedback.

What do you think?

Discuss the questions as a class or in small groups.

> **Sample answers**
> Naturally, the answer here is a personal opinion. Arguably, although the results are not very scientific, they do give you a rough idea of how healthy you are, and can prompt people to change their lifestyle and eating habits for the better. On the other hand, they may worry people unnecessarily, make people feel they are fine when they should change their diet or lifestyle, and they encourage our twenty-first century preoccupation with our lifestyles.

ADDITIONAL MATERIAL

Workbook Unit 10
Exercise 4 Listening: Sports – love them or loathe them?
Exercise 5 Revision: words to do with the body

Clichés

1 Read the introduction as a class. Ask students if they can think of any English clichés.

> **T 10.8** Play the recording. Ask students to read and listen, and identify the clichés.

> **Answers**
> 1 Easier said than done.
> 2 At the end of the day …
> 3 Don't do anything I wouldn't do.

2 Ask students in pairs to match a line in **A** with a line in **B**. Ask them to identify the clichés and discuss what they mean.

> **T 10.9** Play the recording so that students can check their answers. Ask students if they can provide any clichés from their own language and translate them.

> **Answers and tapescript**
> 1 b *Accidents will happen.* (These things happen – no point worrying about it.)
> 2 d *Better safe than sorry.* (It's better to take precautions, even if they seem unnecessary, rather than risk something bad happening.)
> 3 f *You can say that again.* (I agree completely.)
> 4 a *A change is as good as a rest.* (Doing something different, like changing your job, is as relaxing or invigorating as going on holiday.)
> 5 i *Better late than never.* (Although, he / she did it late, this is better than not doing it at all.)
> 6 j *… just what the doctor ordered.* (This is exactly what is needed in this situation.)
> 7 c *No pain, no gain.* (If you don't work hard and suffer, you won't be successful.)
> 8 e *… these things come in threes.* (Bad events tend to come in a succession of three.)
> 9 h *The mind boggles. It doesn't bear thinking about.* (I can't believe it. / It's too difficult to really consider it.)
> 10 g *It takes all sorts.* (The world is full of different people, and we should let them get on with what they want to do.)

> **T 10.9**
> 1 Mum! Tommy's broken the vase!
> Never mind. Accidents will happen.
> 2 I just need to go back in the house and make sure I've turned off the iron.
> Good idea. Better safe than sorry.
> 3 It's been raining non-stop for weeks! Do we need some sunshine!
> You can say that again.

4 Work's awful at the moment, and I have to go away on business this weekend!
Oh, well. A change is as good as a rest.

5 I got a card from Jerry a week after my birthday.
Oh, well. Better late than never.

6 We're having a complete break for a fortnight.
Sounds like just what the doctor ordered.

7 Took me ten years to build up my business. Nearly killed me.
Well, you know what they say. No pain, no gain.

8 Larry's failed his exams, Amy's got chicken pox. Whatever next?
Oh dear! They say these things come in threes, you know.

9 They've got ten kids. Goodness knows what their house is like.
The mind boggles. It doesn't bear thinking about.

10 Bob's a weird bloke. Have you heard he's going to walk across Europe?
It takes all sorts.

8 I've spilt red wine on your carpet. I'm really sorry.

9 I've lost the car keys, I've burnt the meal, and the washing machine has packed up. How bad is that?

10 My daughter is on a cabbage soup diet. She eats nothing else.

Don't forget!

Writing Unit 10 Entering a competition (SB p129)

Workbook Unit 10
Exercise 3 The position of adverbs
Exercise 6 Verbs of movement
Exercise 9 Phrasal verbs – Particles and meanings

3 **T 10.10** Play the recording and ask students in pairs to choose a suitable cliché to respond with. Discuss the answers in class.

Answers and tapescript
1 Well, it takes all sorts.
2 No pain, no gain.
3 You can say that again.
4 Oh, well. Better late than never.
5 Oh well. A change is as good as a rest.
6 Better safe than sorry.
7 Sounds like just what the doctor ordered.
8 Never mind. Accidents will happen.
9 They say these things come in threes, you know.
10 It doesn't bear thinking about.

T 10.10
1 My uncle has never married. He lives in a caravan. He eats only cheese, and he has twenty-five cats.
2 James Herriot had three jobs and wrote non-stop for five years before his book became a best-seller.
3 Isn't it lovely when the kids are in bed, the house is quiet, and we can relax!
4 I finally got a date for my knee replacement operation. I've had to wait eighteen months.
5 I really wanted to stay at home for New Year, but my in-laws are insisting that we go to stay with them.
6 When I go abroad, I make sure I have life insurance, medical insurance, and personal possessions insurance.
7 We had a fabulous holiday. Two weeks sitting round a swimming pool, reading and relaxing.

11

Relatives and participles
Compound nouns and adjectives
Idiomatic expressions

The ends of the earth

Introduction to the unit

The theme of this unit is remote places. The main reading texts are about three islands, Greenland, Tristan da Cunha in the South Atlantic, and Zanzibar. The main listening text is a story, told by a journalist, about a chance meeting on a train journey through a remote corner of China.

Language aims

Relatives and participles This unit looks at using relative clauses and participles, two grammatical ways of forming complex sentences.

Relative clauses

> **WATCH OUT FOR …**
> **Form and use**
> In terms of form and use, there is a lot for students to grasp:
> * A defining relative clause is essential to the meaning of the sentence.
> * A non-defining relative clause adds extra information.
> * We use *who* for people, and *which* for objects.
> * The pronoun we use depends on whether it is replacing subject or object, person or thing.
> * *What* means 'the thing that'.
> * Relative clauses are often very complex sentences.

Watch out for the following problems:

1   Students need to be able to distinguish between defining and non-defining relative clauses.

A defining relative clause is essential to the meaning of the sentence: *The neighbour who lives opposite is rich.* (it tells us *which* neighbour). A non-defining relative clause adds extra, non-essential, information. It is mainly found in written English. The clause comes after a comma, and can be omitted without affecting the meaning of the main clause: *My next-door neighbour, who has six children, is rich.* (my neighbour is rich – and incidentally has six children).

A common error which students make when manipulating these forms is to define a noun which is already completely identified, for example **My best friend who lives in London is coming at the weekend*. Students think the clause here is defining the friend, but it isn't (the word *best* has already told us which friend it is), it's just adding extra information, and should be *My best friend, who … .* Compare *the man who …* (needs defining), with *my brother, who …* (we already know who you're talking about).

2   Students may have problems manipulating relative pronouns.

In English, we use *who* for people and *which* for objects, but other languages use the same pronoun for both, changing the form depending on the gender of the noun. Watch out for errors such as *the people which … .*

Which pronoun to use and when, depending on whether it is replacing subject or object, person or thing, makes this area of language tricky. Students often avoid omitting the pronoun when it defines the object of the clause, and say, for example, *the place which I went to … ,* which is correct, but not the most natural spoken use.

Many languages avoid putting a preposition at the end of the sentence. As a result, students often say, *the school at which I studied* rather than *the school I studied at*, which feels wrong to them, but is actually much more natural spoken English.

Students get confused by the complexity of the sentence, inserting subject pronouns when the relative pronoun is already expressing the subject: *~~The doctor who he helped me~~* …

3 *What* can cause problems. It means 'the thing that' and is not synonymous with *that*, which merely repeats the meaning of the noun that comes before it. However, in some languages, the word for *that* and *what* is the same. Watch out for errors such as *~~Everything what you need is~~* …

Participles Present participles describe actions still happening. Past participles describe actions that have happened. They are used as reduced relative clauses: *I saw a man (who was) sitting by the side of the road*; in adverb clauses: *He woke up feeling ill* (*feeling ill* is adverbial, describing how he woke up); and after certain verbs: *go swimming*. Participle clauses can also express the ideas of *because*, *as a result*, *if*, and *after*, areas which are dealt with in detail in Grammar Reference 11.4–7 on SB p159.

Using these structures correctly is complex and demanding, and requires lots of practice from students. Perhaps the key problem area to watch out for is making sure that the subject of the participle clause and the main verb are the same, as here:
Bill Bryson was born in the US. He has written books about his travels in many different countries. ⇨
Born in the US, Bill Bryson has written books about his travels in many different countries.

This, however, is not possible:
Bill Bryson was born in the US. His books are about his travels in many different countries. ⇨
~~Born in the US, Bill Bryson's books are about his travels in many different countries.~~

Because these sentences have two different subjects, they cannot be joined with a participle. It would suggest that Bill Bryson's *books* were born in the US!

Grammar Reference 11.2–7 on SB pp158–159 looks at participles and relatives. It is a good idea for you to read this carefully before teaching the grammatical section of this unit.

Vocabulary The *Vocabulary* section looks at compound nouns and adjectives formed from weather words. It also looks at adjective word order. There is work on prepositions in geographical expressions in the *Reading* section.

The last word This section looks at expressions and idioms using the nouns, *earth*, *ground*, *floor*, *land*, *soil*, and *world*.

Notes on the unit

STARTER (SB p99)

1–2 Ask students to work in small groups of three or four to do the quiz.

T 11.1 Play the recording so that students can check their answers. Find out which group got most correct, and what extra information students learned about each question.

Answers and tapescript

1 **How old is the earth?**
The current scientific estimate for the age of the earth is 4.6 billion years. There are numerous indicators that the earth was in existence billions of years ago but it is still impossible to prove exactly how many.

2 **The earth is considered to have a maximum of seven continents. What are they?**
A continent is one of several major land masses on the earth. These are Africa, Antarctica, Asia, Australia, Europe, North America, and South America. Many geographers and scientists now refer to just six continents, where Europe and Asia are combined (since they're one solid land mass).

3 **How many countries are there in the world?**
There are 193 countries in the world. East Timor is the most recent country, having gained independence from Indonesia in 2002.

4 **Which continent has the most countries?**
Africa is home to 53 independent countries, representing more than 25% of the countries of the world. The largest African country is Sudan.

5 **What is the population of the world?**
The population of the world is 6.1 billion people and it is growing all the time. Current research indicates that about five people are born every second, while two people die, leaving us with a population increase of three new human beings per second.

6 **Which country has the largest population?**
China. It is home to more than 1.2 billion people. India is currently the world's second most populous country with 1 billion people, but by 2040, India is expected to have the largest population.

7 **What proportion of the earth is covered by water?**
71% of the Earth's surface is covered in water, which maintains the temperature of the planet. Of the 71% , 97% is salt water, 3% is fresh water, of which 1% is drinking water.

8 **How many oceans are there? What are they?**
Most often the world is divided into four major oceans – the Pacific Ocean, Atlantic Ocean, Arctic Ocean, and the Indian Ocean. Some consider there to be five oceans – the fifth being the Antarctic Ocean.

9 **How much of the earth's land surface is used to grow food?**
Only 11% of the land surface is used to grow food. 31% is forest, 27% is desert and wilderness, 26% is pasture land. 5% is urban.

10 **Where is the world's largest desert? What is it called?**
The Sahara Desert in Northern Africa is the world's largest desert. At more than 9 million square kilometres, it is slightly smaller than the size of the United States.

11 **What's the difference between a political and a physical map?**
A political map shows human-created features such as boundaries, cities, roads, and railroads. Physical maps display the natural features of the earth – the location and names of mountains, rivers, valleys, ocean currents, and deserts.

12 **Which is the world's largest island?**
At 2,175,600 square kilometres, Greenland is the world's largest island. Australia also meets the definition of an island but it is large enough to be considered a continent.

3 Ask students in their groups to read the 'howlers' and explain the mistakes.

Answers
1 A *boomerang* is a type of Australian aboriginal weapon.
2 A big *dame* is a large woman. The student meant *dam*.
3 *Mosquitoes* are malaria-carrying insects. The student meant *Muscovites*.
4 *Sewage* means untreated waste. The student meant *Suez*.
5 The *Pyramids* are monumental tombs in Egypt. The student meant *Pyrenees*.
6 *Irritating* means annoying. The student meant *irrigating*.

READING AND SPEAKING (SB p100)

Three island stories

This is a jigsaw reading in which students read a text for specific information, then share their information in an interactive speaking stage.

1 Ask students in groups of three to discuss the questions. In the feedback, ask individuals who have been to interesting or exotic islands to describe them.

2 Ask students to match the pictures to the islands, and share any information they know about the places. The aim here is to set the scene for the reading by finding out how much students know about these islands, so, in the feedback, encourage students to share any interesting information they may have.

Answers
First picture: Greenland
Second picture: Zanzibar
Third picture: Tristan da Cunha

3 Ask the groups of three to decide who is going to read each text. Ask them to read quickly, and to underline three interesting or surprising things. Give students a time limit of, say, four minutes, to make sure they read quickly. Ask students to briefly tell each other what they underlined in their text.

4 Ask students to answer the questions as a group. A good way to do this is to get one student to lead the discussion, and ask the questions, while the others contribute by looking back at their texts to provide the answers.

Answers
1 *Greenland*: named by Eric the Red to encourage settlers, even though the island is not green.
Tristan da Cunha: named after explorer, Tristao da Cunha.
Zanzibar: forms half the name of the country of which it is a part, Tanzania.
2 *Tristan da Cunha*
3 *Tristan da Cunha*
4 Arguably, *Tristan da Cunha*: self supporting, thriving economy, low income tax, no unemployment.
5 *Zanzibar*: colonized by Egyptians, Arabs, Portuguese, Chinese, Dutch, British.
6 No. *Greenland*: Inuit and Danish; *Tristan da Cunha*: English; *Zanzibar*: Swahili
7 *Greenland*
8 *Tristan da Cunha*
9 Most colourful: *Zanzibar* – spices, golden beaches, coral reefs, fertile soil
Least colourful: *Greenland* – ice, grey granite, tiny pockets of greenery in winter
Reasons: climate in Zanzibar means abundant vegetation, ethnic mix means different styles of often colourful dress.
10 Probably, *Zanzibar*.
11 *Greenland*: tombs are shallow and dead people have to be stored because you can't dig the soil in winter; seasonal depression results in alcoholism and suicide.
Tristan da Cunha: the surrounding seas are rich in fish, enabling a strong fishing industry; opportunity to be self-supporting is reflected in the islanders' character.
Zanzibar: desirability as a strategic location has led to incredible ethnic mix; temperate climate has enabled production of spices, also potential for tourism.
12 *Greenland*: heavy Danish influence remains in terms of language and consumer goods.
Tristan da Cunha: the capital is called Edinburgh because of the visit of the Duke of Edinburgh in 1867; the people speak English and have English names because it was once a British colony.
Zanzibar: mixture of ethnic backgrounds because it has been ruled by so many different nations; maintains the language and the tradition of a thriving export trade.

Check answers briefly with the whole class.

Language work

5 Ask students in pairs to complete the sentences, and decide which island is being described. When they have finished, let them check their answers by looking back at the texts.

Answers
1 in, from, of (Tristan da Cunha)	8 out of, to (Zanzibar)
2 from, to (Greenland)	9 into (Greenland)
3 up of (Greenland)	10 with, to (Zanzibar)
4 off (Zanzibar)	11 under (Tristan da Cunha)
5 in, to (Greenland)	12 at about (Zanzibar)
6 by, to (Greenland)	13 of, on (Zanzibar)
7 on, after (Tristan da Cunha)	

What do you think?

Answers
Students' own answers.

VOCABULARY AND LISTENING (SB p104)

Compound nouns and adjectives: Weather words

1 Ask students in pairs to make compound nouns and adjectives using the weather words. Ask them to check their ideas in their dictionaries.

Answers
Nouns
sun roof, sunstroke
raindrop, rainfall, rainstorm
windfall
snow cap, snowdrift, snowdrop, snowfall, snowflake, snow plough, snowstorm
iceberg, ice cap

Adjectives
sunburnt, sun-drenched, suntanned
rain-soaked, rainswept
wind-blown, windswept
snow-capped
ice-capped

2 Ask students in pairs to complete the sentences.

Answers
1 rainfall
2 sunstroke
3 snowstorm, snowdrifts, snowploughs
4 sun roof
5 iceberg
6 snow-capped
7 sunburnt / suntanned, windswept

---

8 snowflake
9 raindrops
10 sun-drenched, rainswept / windswept

Adjective order

3 Ask students in pairs to look at the examples and answer the questions. Do the first as an example. Check answers and rules with the whole class.

Answers
1 Factual: *old, thatched*; opinion: *beautiful*.
2 Factual: *golden, Mediterranean*; opinion: *glorious*.
3 Factual: *huge, grey, granite*; opinion: *amazing*.
4 Factual: *old-fashioned, English*; opinion: *strange*.
5 Factual: *storm-tossed, Atlantic*; opinion: *wild*.
6 Factual: *man-eating, polar*; opinion: *dangerous*.

Rules
Value adjectives (which indicate personal opinion) come first, followed by size, age, shape, colour, origin and material.

Refer students to Grammar Reference 11.1 on SB p157 and ask them to check their ideas.

4 Ask students to put the adjectives in order, then check with a partner before checking with the whole class.

Answers
1 He gave us some delicious, home-made, wholemeal bread.
2 A funny, little, old, Irish lady arrived.
3 I bought a gorgeous, red and white, striped silk shirt.
4 She's just had a lovely, fat, bouncing baby boy.
5 He showed me into a delightful, light, airy, high-ceilinged living room.
6 I met a trendy, young Venezuelan art student. (*or* young, trendy)
7 She's wearing shiny, tight-fitting, black, leather trousers. (*or* tight-fitting, shiny, black)
8 It's an exquisite, sweet-smelling, apricot-coloured rose.

5 Ask students in pairs to add extra information to the sentences in exercise 4. Point out that we do this by using clauses beginning with *with*, a relative pronoun (*who* or *which*), or a past or present participle.

T 11.2 Play the recording. Ask students to listen and compare their answers.

Answers and tapescript
1 He gave us some delicious, home-made, wholemeal bread, which was still warm from the oven.
2 A funny, little, old Irish lady arrived, wearing a big feathered hat.
3 I bought a gorgeous red and white striped silk shirt with gold buttons.
4 She's just had a lovely fat bouncing baby boy with lots of brown tufty hair.

5 He showed me into a delightful, light, airy, high-ceilinged living room with all-white furniture and carpets.
6 I met a trendy, young Venezuelan art student who's living in London at the moment.
7 She's wearing shiny, tight-fitting, black, leather trousers with back pockets.
8 It's an exquisite, sweet-smelling apricot-coloured rose covering the whole wall.

Farflung spots

6 These are short, authentic 'vox pops' in which six people, with a variety of accents, briefly describe farflung places they have visited. Lead in by explaining that a farflung spot is a distant and remote place.

T 11.3 Play the recording. Ask students to listen, and try to write down where the people went, and any adjectives they hear as they listen.

Ask students in pairs to discuss the answers to the questions, using the adjectives they have noted down.

Answers
1 **Sean**
  1 Salar de Uyuni in the south of Bolivia
  2 Drove for two days across an enormous salt plain.
  3 It was completely white, with incredible, strangely-coloured lakes and chocolate caramel-covered mountains.
2 **Lucy**
  1 Nundle – a little place, out in the sticks (very remote) in Australia, with a sheep station
  2 She danced in a disco.
  3 She remembers how absolutely gorgeous it was dancing under the stars as she brushed her teeth in the outside toilet.
3 **Jerry**
  1 Iceland
  2 Went on a bicycling trip, saw really strange landscapes with glaciers and volcanoes.
  3 Felt like the end of the world: incredibly empty, strange volcanic smells, constant very high winds.
4 **Claire**
  1 Moose Factory in Canada
  2 Visited the tiny island community.
  3 In the winter you can drive across the ice to the island, but in summer you travel by boat.
5 **James**
  1 Lost City in Colombia
  2 A three-day hike into the jungle, in the tropical rainforest. Visited a village buried in the jungle.
  3 Beautiful rock terraces. It was an amazing trip, like an Indiana Jones adventure.

6 **Belinda**
  1 Underwater in Sardinia
  2 Snorkelled.
  3 She felt really small, out of her depth and shocked and terrified by what she saw.

T 11.3 See SB Tapescripts p144

7 Ask students to discuss the questions in small groups of four or five. Go round monitoring and helping as necessary.

8 Ask students to write about a place they have visited. A good way of doing this is to ask students to prepare brief notes under the headings, *Where did you go? What did you do and see?* and *Why was it unusual and memorable?* Encourage them to use factual and opinion adjectives. The actual writing of the description could then be set as a homework task.

LISTENING AND SPEAKING (SB p105)

A meeting in the desert

This is an intensive listening activity – an anecdote about an unusual meeting on a train journey in a desert in the far west of China. The tasks involve true and false, prediction and comprehension questions, and break down the listening into three bite-sized sections. Students have already heard Simon Winchester in Unit 6, talking about journalism.

1 Read the introduction as a class, then put students in pairs to predict the story from the illustrations. Ask three or four pairs to share their predictions with the class in feedback. Take the opportunity to pre-teach key words: *watering tower, sand dunes, business card.* And check that students know who Anthony Trollope was (a nineteenth century British author who wrote novels about provincial life in England).

2 **T 11.4** Play part one of the story. Ask students to listen and correct the false statements. Let them check their answers in pairs before checking with the whole class.

Answers
1 False. He went with a friend called George Robertson.
2 True
3 False. They stopped in a desert town 150 miles west of Urunchi.
4 False. The Chinese woman spoke impeccable English.
5 True

T 11.4 See SB Tapescripts p145

Ask students to predict what happens next. Try to encourage a number of different suggestions from the class.

3 **T 11.5** Play part two of the story. Ask students to listen to see if their predictions were correct, then work in pairs to answer the questions.

Answers
1 To find out how long she has to practise her English with the stranger.
2 The Chinese woman asks the narrator, Simon Winchester, if he would care to discuss the novel with her.
3 Simon Winchester struggles to converse about Trollope's novel, which he read many years ago, and scribbles his name on the back of his friend's business card to give to the woman as the train leaves. (*scribble* means to write quickly and untidily)
4 The Chinese lady scrabbles on her hands and knees to find and pick up the business card in the sand. (*scrabble* means to move your hands around quickly, without much control)
5 Because he tells her he loves her and wants to stay with her.
6 a *odds and ends*
　 b *hands and knees*

T 11.5 See SB Tapescripts p145

Ask students to predict the end of the story. Again, try to encourage a number of different suggestions from the class.

4 **T 11.6** Play part three of the story. Ask students to listen to see if their predictions were correct, then work in pairs to correct the false statements.

Answers
1 False. She is writing to thank him for the meeting.
2 True
3 False. She calls it a ghastly (horrible) little town.
4 False. She cycles thirty miles.
5 True
6 False. She occasionally speaks to a migrant worker, but it seems unlikely that she would speak to him about Trollope.
7 False. She talked to him about her passion – Trollope.
8 False. They are the best of friends and have been for years.

T 11.6 See SB Tapescripts p145

5 Ask students in pairs to retell the story, using the pictures. Go round monitoring and helping as necessary.

LANGUAGE FOCUS (SB p106)

Relatives and participles

Don't forget to look at the *Language Aims* section on TB p98, which looks at problems students may have. You should also read Grammar Reference 11.2–7 on SB ppp158–159.

Defining and non-defining relative clauses

LANGUAGE INPUT

Ask students in pairs to underline the relative clauses in the sentences, and answer the questions.

Answers
a Here's somebody who speaks English.
b The Chinese lady, who speaks impeccable English, lives in the desert.
c She works for a company which organizes adventure holidays.
d They made a railway journey across the desert to Kazakhstan, which sounded fascinating.
e The friend who he travelled with is a doctor.
f The islanders were taken to what was referred to as 'civilization'.

1 b and d make sense without the relative clause.
　 a, c, e, and f are defining relative clauses (f is a defining relative clause, because here *what* means 'the thing that ...').
　 b and d are non-defining.
2 a, c, and e – because they are defining relative clauses.
3 e – because it is the object pronoun of a defining relative clause.
4 e – *The friend with whom he travelled is a doctor*. It makes the sentence sound very formal.
5 The commas make the speaker pause.

Refer students to Grammar Reference 11.2–3 on SB p158.

1 Ask students in pairs to discuss the differences between the sentences.

Answers
1 S1: The sailors below deck drowned. The others didn't.
　 S2: The non-defining clause is inside commas. All the sailors drowned. Their cabins happened to be below deck.
2 S1: The non-defining clause is inside commas. I only have one sister. She is a travel agent and afraid of flying.
　 S2: I have more than one sister. It is the one who works as a travel agent who hates flying.
3 S1: The non-defining clause is expressed formally by having the preposition *after* before the object relative pronoun, *whom*.
　 S2: The non-defining clause is expressed informally by using the object relative pronoun, *who*, with the preposition at the end of the clause.
　 Both sentences mean the same, although the first sentence is more formal, written English. The second is much more common in spoken English.

4 **S1:** *that* is used as the subject after *everything* – many things happened.

 S2: *what* is used as a relative pronoun in place of 'the thing that' – only one thing happened.

5 **S1:** *which* replaces the object of the preceding clause, 'the place'.

 S2: *where* is used instead of the whole phrase, *the place in which*.

 Both sentences mean the same, although the first sentence is more formal, written English. The second is much more common in spoken English.

6 The idea of the defining relative clause in S1 *who seeks adventure*, is expressed by a present participle in S2, *seeking*.

 Both sentences mean the same.

7 In S1, *fringed* is a reduced past participle, expressing the idea of *which are fringed* in S2.

 Both sentences mean the same.

2 Ask students in pairs to look at the sentences, and decide how they should be completed. Conduct a brief whole-class discussion, then ask students to write possible sentence completions.

T 11.7 Play the recording. Ask students to listen and compare their ideas.

> **Answers and tapescript**
>
> 1 D I don't like children who always have to be the centre of attention.
> 2 ND The journey from work to home, which usually takes half an hour, took over two hours yesterday.
> 3 B Politicians who make extravagant promises aren't worth listening to.
>   Politicians, who make extravagant promises, aren't worth listening to.
> 4 ND The Taj Mahal, which took twenty-two years to complete, is built from exquisitely carved white marble.
> 5 D These are the photographs I was telling you about.
> 6 D We docked at the small port on the coast of East Africa where my parents lived twenty years ago.
> 7 B My cousin, who's a real thrill-seeker, went hang-gliding at the weekend.
>   My cousin who's a real thrill-seeker went hang-gliding at the weekend.
> 8 D We went on a cycling holiday in Wales, where there are some really steep hills.

3 Ask students to complete the text. Let them check their answers in pairs before checking with the whole class.

> **Answers**
>
> 1 The part of Britain I most like to visit is **where** (the place in which) I was born in the north-east of England.
> 2 I was born in Sunderland, **which** is on the coast and **where** there used to be a large ship-building industry.
> 3 My sister, **whose** husband is an artist, still lives in the town, **which** is the reason **why** I often return there.
> 4 My grandfather, **who** worked in the shipyards, went to London only once in his life and that was **when** the Sunderland football team won the FA Cup in 1973.
> 5 The Wear Bridge, **whose** outline you can see from miles around, spans the estuary of the River Wear, and, **where** once dockyards and warehouses stood, there are now trendy restaurants and yacht clubs.
> 6 My brother-in-law, **who** has travelled widely and **whose** paintings depict many exotic places, still prefers to paint **what** is most familiar to him – the grey, stormy North Sea.
> 7 **What** I like most **when** I visit my home town are all the memories **that** / **which** come flooding back.

4 Give students three or four minutes to write notes about their home town. Ask them to give their notes to their partner, then take it in turns to ask and answer questions about each other's town, using the notes as prompts. Go round monitoring and helping as necessary.

Participles

Go through the Language Input box. Refer students to Grammar Reference 11.4–7 on SB p159.

5 Ask students in pairs to match the ideas in the Language Input box to the participles in the sentences.

> **Answers**
>
> 1 because   5 if
> 2 at the same time   6 because
> 3 after   7 because / so that / with the
> 4 because   result that
>   8 at the same time

6 Ask students in pairs to complete the sentences.

> **Answers**
>
> 2 saving; saved   6 Breaking; Broken
> 3 Taking; Taken   7 Giving; given
> 4 booked; Booking   8 worn; wearing
> 5 hurting / injuring; hurt / injured

ADDITIONAL MATERIAL

Workbook Unit 11
Exercises 1–3 Relative clauses
Exercises 4–6 Participles
Exercise 7 Listening – Simon Winchester: how I became a journalist

THE LAST WORD (SB p108)

What on earth!

1 Ask students in pairs to complete the sentences.

Answers

1	land	4	floor	7	earth
2	earth	5	world	8	world
3	soil	6	floor	9	earth

2–3 Ask students in pairs to match the lines in **A** and **B**. Let them use a dictionary if necessary.

T 11.8 Play the recording so that students can check their answers. Ask students to practise the conversations in pairs.

Answers and tapescript
1c 2d 3h 4b 5a 6i 7e 8f 9g

T 11.8

1 **A** I'm cleaned out! This new jacket cost the earth.
  B Come on! It's good to spoil yourself every now and then.
2 **A** Believe me, that guy's really going places.
  B Don't I know it! He landed that consultancy job that we all applied for.
3 **A** The holiday's over. It's back to the real world.
  B You can say that again. Back to earth with a bump!
4 **A** What? You're not coming out on Saturday night!
  B I can't. My dad caught me smoking and I've been grounded for two weeks.
5 **A** Hey! Great to see you! I thought you weren't going to be able to make it.
  B I nearly wasn't. I had to move heaven and earth to get here.
6 **A** We're throwing caution to the wind and emigrating to Oz.
  B Don't your folks already live down under?
7 **A** Come on, you know you want to go out with me really.
  B In your dreams. Not if you were the last man on earth!
8 **A** Can you follow these instructions? Where on earth do all these screws go?
  B Don't ask me. I was totally floored by the last lot I read.
9 **A** I don't want to drink, so I'll do the driving tonight.
  B Great! That suits me down to the ground.

GLOSSARY

cost the earth = very expensive
going places = heading for success
back to earth with a bump = suddenly back to ordinary reality after an exciting time
grounded = not allowed out
move heaven and earth = work extremely hard to remove obstacles
down under = Australia (from the geographical point of view of Britain)
Not if you were the last man on earth = under no circumstances
totally floored = unable to understand it at all
That suits me down to the ground = That's perfectly convenient for me

4 Ask students in pairs to write similar conversations using the expressions from exercise 2. Put pairs of students together to read their conversations to each other.

Don't forget!

Writing Unit 11 Describing a journey (SB p130)

Workbook Unit 11
Exercise 8 Pronunciation – word stress
Exercise 9 Adjective order
Exercise 10 Geographical features
Exercise 11 Synonyms – *shine* and words with a similar meaning
Exercise 12 Prepositions in set phrases

12

Linking devices
Synonyms and antonyms 2
Euphemisms

Life goes on

Introduction to the unit

The theme of this unit is how we see the passage of life. The main reading text is about how we allow our lives to be ruled by man-made time, rather than following our natural clocks. The main listening text is a radio programme about the pilgrimage site, Lourdes, in which a doctor questions how we seek answers to problems in life through miracles.

Language aims

Linking This unit revises a wide variety of different linkers, which are looked at in the Grammar Reference under the headings, result, reason, purpose, contrast, time and condition. Students see examples in context, then restructure sentences to show they know how to manipulate them. A lot of your teaching will be in feedback to the tasks, referring to the Grammar Reference.

This is such a large area of language that it is impossible to focus here on all the possible problems or confusions students might have. They also depend on how linkers in English differ from those in the students' first language.

WATCH OUT FOR …

so and *such*
so + adjective; *such* + noun
Watch out for errors such as, **She is so likeable person that …*

Infinitive of purpose
This is not a natural form in many other languages. Watch out for errors such as **She is here for studying English.*

although, despite, however
The form of these contrast linkers can confuse students. Compare:
Although I was tired, I went to the party. (*although* + clause, clause)
Despite being tired, I went to the party. (*despite* + *-ing*, clause)
I was tired. However, I went to the party. (sentence. *However*, + clause)

Note that we use these contrast linkers to express a surprising contrast. We use *while* or *whereas* when the contrast is not surprising because it is between two different subjects, for example, *I like chips whereas Tom doesn't.* **I like chips, although Tom doesn't* is not correct because the contrast is not surprising. There is no reason why my opinion of chips should have any influence on Tom's.

Grammar Reference 12.1–6 on SB pp159–160 looks at linkers. It is a good idea for you to read this carefully before teaching the grammatical section of this unit.

Vocabulary The *Vocabulary* section looks at synonyms and antonyms. There is also work on guessing the meaning of vocabulary in the *Reading* section, and on euphemisms in *The last word* section.

The last word This section looks at euphemisms commonly in use in English.

Notes on the unit

STARTER (SB p109)

1 Ask students in pairs to look at the picture of Bruegel's *Landscape with the fall of Icarus*, and describe it in detail to each other. Discuss briefly with the whole class. Make sure you pre-teach *ploughman*, *shepherd*, *fisherman*.

2 Ask students to ask you the questions in the Student's Book, and any other questions they would like answered about the picture. The answers you will need are below and in the tapescript.

> **BACKGROUND NOTE**
> *Landscape with the Fall of Icarus* was painted in oil on canvas in about 1558 by Pieter Bruegel the Elder, (1525–1569). It is now in the *Musées Royaux de Beaux-Arts de Belgique* in Brussels.
>
> In the Greek myth, Daedalus and his son Icarus were imprisoned in Minos' labyrinth on Crete. Daedalus fashioned wings fixed to the shoulders with wax, so that he and his son might escape. But Icarus flew too close to the sun, the wax melted, and he fell to his death in the Aegean Sea. Icarus is the character in the bottom right of the picture, only his legs showing as he falls into the sea.

3 **T 12.1** Play the recording. Ask students to listen to the art historian and answer the questions.

> **Answers**
> • The three men: the common men, the ploughman, the shepherd, and the fisherman, are carrying out their everyday pursuits with apparent pleasure, oblivious to Icarus' fall.
> • The central event: it is away from the main event, the ploughing, and you don't see it at once. Icarus' legs are caught at the precise moment that this symbol of human pride is about to disappear for ever.
> • Direction and movement: all of the movement in the picture is away from the main event. The ploughman and shepherd, oblivious, go about their business, as does the fully-rigged boat, also sailing away from the fallen figure.
> • An interpretation of the picture: a warning against pride and ambition. The common man should not search for personal gain, nor have ambitions above his station in life. In the painting we also see life as a process of continuation. No matter what momentous events are happening in the world, near to you or far away, despite wars, death, natural disasters, famine, plagues or earthquakes, life goes on.
>
> **T 12.1** See SB Tapescripts p145

4 Ask students to discuss the questions in small groups before checking briefly with the whole class.

A sideways look at time

1 Ask students to discuss the questions in pairs before discussing briefly with the whole class. Who is the least punctual person in class?

2 Discuss these questions briefly with the whole class.

> **Sample answer**
> To a child of five, one year represents one fifth of his / her whole life. To a person who is 60, one year represents a mere sixtieth of their life, and so can seem to pass relatively quickly. Time seems to fly by when you're enjoying yourself; it drags when you're bored.

3 Ask students in pairs to explain the words to each other by miming them. In the feedback, mime the words yourself to check the meaning.

> **Answers**
> *look sideways* = look to one side
> *winkle sth out* = to force sth out
> *sigh* = let out a long deep breath to show that you're disappointed, sad, or tired
> *blink* = close both eyes very briefly
> *spin* = go round
> *slip* = to lose your footing, e.g. on ice

4 Ask students to guess the meaning of the phrases, and then read the article to check their ideas. Ask them what they think the title of the article means.

> **Answers**
> *clock-time* = time dictated by clocks which has an even, perfectly regular, mechanical beat
> *chronological time* = linear, quantifiable, 'by the clock' time – named after the Greek god, Chronos
> *universal time* = time as defined by the atomic second
> *kairological time* = nature-based time in which your heart tells you when to do something

5 Ask students in pairs to discuss and answer the questions. Encourage them to try to remember the answers from their first reading, then look back at the relevant section to research their answer.

> **Answers**
> 1 Clocks on buildings are everywhere. Receipts have the time you purchased something on them. From the moment the alarm clock wakes us up, we are governed by clocks which count the seconds digitally.
> 2 Hamburgers, fried chicken.
>   Fast knowledge is being able to find things out quickly through, for example, computers and the Internet.
> 3 Co-ordinated Universal Time – time defined by the atomic second, and set by international agreement.

4 Its spin changes by up to a thousandth of a second in some years.

5 The Karen use the forest as a clock, by noticing how the air in the forest changes throughout the day.

6 The Karen know that sunset will come in the time that it would take to walk three kilometres.

7 The time of year is described by the smells of flowers and trees which are present during that period.

8 Adults have learned clock-time. Children live in the present and have no concept of punctuality. Time lasts longer for children.

9 Chronos gave his name to absolute time, linear and quantifiable. Kairos gave his name to timing, opportunity and chance – qualitative time.

10 In the town, time is man-made and linear, defined by the working day. In the country, time is nature-given, defined by sun, stars, or storms.

What do you think?

Sample answers
1 Time-saving devices: computers, phones, washing machine, dishwasher, microwave, car, remote control.
2 Nature's clocks: sunset, seasons, night, day, dawn, dusk, tides, age.

4 **T 12.2** Ask students to read and listen to the poem and answer the question.

Answer
The poem says that time goes quickly if you fear or rejoice, but too slowly if you wait or grieve. For lovers, time is eternal.

LANGUAGE FOCUS (SB p112)

Linking devices

Don't forget to look at the *Language Aims* section on TB p106, which looks at problems students may have. You should also read Grammar Reference 12.1–6 on SB pp159–160.

LANGUAGE INPUT

Read through the examples as a class. Then ask students in pairs to find other examples in the text on SB p111. There are many examples, so ask them to find one example of each way of making links.

Sample answers
1 ... it is added to 'accommodate' the earth's unreliable time. **For** the earch, you see, is too inaccurate ... (paragraph 2)

2 **While** old people sigh over how fast it goes ... , children are incapable of patience ... . (paragraph 6) If you eat biscuits when you're hungry, that is kairological; **whereas** if you eat by the clock, that is chronological time. (paragraph 7)

3 Roughly every year an extra second is needed **to realign** *the* time with that of the earth ... (paragraph 2)

4 Roughly every year an extra second is needed to realign *the* time with **that** of the earth ... (paragraph 2)

5 So the timekeepers of today must tell *the* time from outside the earth itself, **insisting** that there is one time, abstract and universal: ... (paragraph 3)

Refer students to Grammar Reference 12.1–6 on SB pp159–160.

1 Ask students to read the passage and choose the correct linker. Do the first as an example. Let students check answers in pairs before checking with the whole class.

Answers

1 wherever / no matter where	11 whenever
2 so / therefore	12 If
3 As soon as / After	13 When
4 then	14 in case
5 Since / As	15 to avoid / so as to avoid
6 unless	16 even so / all the same
7 in order not to / so as not to	17 Immediately / As soon as
8 Once	18 Working / As I work
9 afterwards / after that	19 As long as / Provided
10 Even though / Although	20 so that

2 Ask students to write a paragraph about a typical day, using linkers. A good way to do this is to get them to write notes first – seven or eight short sentences which say what they typically do. Then ask them to think of ways of ordering and linking the information before writing it up. Alternatively, an interactive way of doing this is to get students to write notes about their typical day, then exchange them with a partner. Students must write up their partner's typical day, using linkers.

3 Ask students to rewrite the sentences. Let them check their answers in pairs before checking with the whole class.

Answers
2 Having seen the film, I read the book.
   After seeing the film, I read the book.
3 As long as you look after this carefully, it will last a lifetime.
   Provided (that) you look after this carefully, it will last a lifetime.
4 The curry was hot, so we couldn't eat it. / The curry was so hot we couldn't eat it.

It was such a hot curry that we couldn't eat it.
The curry was too hot to eat.

5 No matter what you do, don't touch this switch.
Whatever you do, don't touch this switch.

6 I'm not sure whether I like her or not.

7 Even though I'm on a strict diet, I still haven't lost any weight.
I'm on a strict diet. However, I still haven't lost any weight.
I'm on a strict diet. Even so, I still haven't lost any weight.

8 I took an umbrella in case it rained.
I took an umbrella, as I thought it might rain.

9 He was penniless and starving. Nevertheless, he still shouldn't have stolen the food.
Although he was penniless and starving, he still shouldn't have stolen the food.
Despite being penniless and starving, he still shouldn't have stolen the food.

10 Supposing I hadn't gone to the party. I wouldn't have met Jenny. We wouldn't have got married and had three children.

4 Ask students in pairs to combine the sentences. Do the first as an example. Go round monitoring and helping students as they work to put the sentences together.

T 12.3 Play the recording. Ask students to listen and compare their answers.

Sample answers and tapescript
- Salvador Dalí was born in 1904 in a small town, Figueres, in Catalunya, north-east Spain, where his father was a prestigious notary.
- Wanting to study art, Dalí went to the Royal Academy of Art in Madrid, but he was expelled from the Academy twice, as a result of which he never took his final examinations.
- In 1928 he went to Paris, where he met the Spanish painters Pablo Picasso and Joan Miró, and established himself as the principal figure of a group of surrealist artists, whose leader was André Breton.
- By 1929 Dali found the style, consisting of the world of the unconscious recalled during our dreams, that would make him famous.
- In 1927 he met Gala, a Russian immigrant ten years older than Dalí.
- Although she was married to a French poet at the time, she decided to leave her husband as she wanted to stay with Dalí.
- In 1940 Dalí went to the United States, where he stayed for eight years until 1948, when he and Gala returned to Europe, spending most of their time in Spain or Paris.
- When Gala died in 1982, Dalí became deeply depressed, and moved to Púbol, a castle he had bought for Gala.
- He lived in his castle for the rest of his life, dying there in 1989 of heart failure.

ADDITIONAL MATERIAL

Workbook Unit 12
Exercises 1–2 Linking devices
Exercise 7 Revision: word puzzle

LISTENING AND SPEAKING (SB p114)

Do you believe in miracles?

This is a quite a long, intensive listening activity broken down into four bite-sized sections. The first listening task is prediction. The second involves answering comprehension and interpretation questions. The listening is an extract from a radio programme, with sound effects and three different voices.

1 Discuss the questions as a class. Find out if anybody has been on a pilgrimage of some sort.

2 Ask students in pairs to look at the pictures and answer the questions.

Answers
The pilgrims are at Lourdes. They are Christians (Roman Catholics).

3 Ask students to read through the questions in pairs, and discuss the answers, including what they think the answer to last question might be.

Answers
- Lourdes is in France, in the south-west near the Pyrénées.
- It is a place of pilgrimage – the place where the Blessed Virgin Mary appeared to Bernadette Soubirous in 1858.
- About six million Catholic pilgrims a year go there to pray, but mostly to seek a miracle cure because the spring Bernadette discovered in 1858 is said to have healing properties.
- To find out if Lourdes really has healing properties.

4 Ask students in pairs or threes to discuss what they think the words refer to. Encourage them to use dictionaries to check the words. Go round monitoring and helping with defining meaning.

T 12.4 Play the recording. Ask students to listen and check their predictions.

Answers
reverential = showing deep respect. The pilgrims are silent and bow their heads.
introspective atmosphere = an atmosphere where people are silent, lost in their own thoughts, as at Lourdes

in wheelchairs or borne on stretchers = refers to people seeking cures

sanctuary = the sacred place at the heart of a church. Traditionally, a place where people could hide from anyone chasing them.

1858 = the year Bernadette saw her vision

six million people every year = the number of pilgrims who visit Lourdes

paralysed = unable to walk. Here, it describes Jean-Pierre Bély.

multiple sclerosis = multiple sclerosis (MS) is a disease of the central nervous system that causes gradual paralysis. This is what Jean-Pierre Bély was suffering from when he visited Lourdes.

T 12.4 See SB Tapescripts p145

5 **T 12.4** Ask students to read the questions to part one, then play that part of the recording again. Ask students to discuss their answers in pairs before checking with the whole class.

Answers
1 The reverential quiet. It is surprising because there are so many people.
2 100,000 seriously ill people visit Lourdes every year; 30,000 hotel beds; 15,000 permanent residents; 6 million people visit Lourdes every year.
3 Three churches and the famous grotto.
4 Visions of the Virgin Mary.

T 12.4 Ask students to read the questions to part two, then play that part of the recording again. Ask students to discuss their answers in pairs before checking with the whole class.

Answers
5 It is said to have healing properties.
6 Because more and more people come in the twenty-first century, despite having gone through a more intellectual, rational age.
7 They are divided about whether miracles still occur at Lourdes, or only did so in the past.
8 God raising Jesus from the dead.

T 12.4 Ask students to read the questions to part three. Ask students to discuss their answers in pairs before checking with the whole class.

Answers
9 Fatigue, a lack of suppleness and mobility in the hands, pins and needles in the fingertips.
10 In 1984, he had a violent attack that left him partly paralysed. He went into hospital, and the doctors carried out a thorough examination. He was diagnosed as having multiple sclerosis. When he got to Lourdes, everything was turned upside down, and he was sucked into a whirlwind of emotion, of joy, of peace, and an

extraordinary feeling of serenity. The second part of the cure took place back in the sick room. Lying on the bed, he felt terribly cold, like an intense chill in his bones. But slowly it got warmer and warmer, until it felt like a fire burning through the whole of his body. He heard a voice, like an order, 'Get up and walk!' He then found himself sitting up on the bed, and he started to touch the back of his hands. He'd regained mobility and sensitivity in his spine and shoulders, which had been blocked for years.

T 12.4 Ask students to read the questions to part four, then play that part of the recording again. Ask students to discuss their answers in pairs before checking with the whole class.

Answers
11 When it runs out of technological answers, it offers nothing else.
12 It is a concrete place you can visit, which renews belief that something good can come from catastrophe.

What do you think?

Sample answers
• Answers here are very personal, of course, and depend on students' beliefs.
• Different theories of the creation of the inverse: scientific – the Big Bang theory which says that the universe began with a huge explosion; religious – the Judaeo-Christian belief that God created the world in six days. There are also countless creation myths in other cultures.

VOCABULARY AND SPEAKING (SB p115)

Synonyms and antonyms 2

1 Read the example as a class. Then ask students in pairs to complete the exercise.

Answers
1 enormity	6 relieved
2 gradually	7 crafty / clever
3 unreliable	8 phenomenal / extraordinary
4 rough	9 raid
5 mention	10 diseases

2 Ask students in pairs to divide the words into groups. Go round monitoring and helping as necessary.

Answers

	Synonyms	Antonyms
old:	ancient	novel
	antiquated	current
	antique	up-to-date
fair:	impartial	biased
	liberal	prejudiced
	open-minded	bigoted
perfect:	immaculate	faulty
	impeccable	flawed
	faultless	second-rate
unimportant:	trivial	urgent
	petty	vital
	irrelevant	essential

3 Ask students in pairs to match the adjectives from exercise 2 with the nouns that they collocate with.

Answers

faulty machinery	petty crime
vital organs	ancient Greece
novel idea	liberal / biased Press
antique vase	impeccable manners
bigoted racist	flawless / second-rate performance
urgent mail	current affairs

EXTENSION ACTIVITY

Ask students in pairs to choose eight words – one synonym and one antonym from each group – and write sentences which clearly illustrate their meanings, leaving a blank for the word. Monitor to check that the sentences they are writing are do-able. Get pairs of students to swap their sentences and try and complete them. Then ask them to swap back and mark the sentences.

ADDITIONAL MATERIAL

Workbook Unit 12
Exercise 6 Pairs of synonyms

Euphemisms

1 Read the introduction as a class. Ask students if they can think of any other euphemisms.

2 Ask students in pairs to read the newspaper article and complete it with euphemisms from the list.

Answers

1 disadvantaged senior citizen
2 disabled
3 retirement pension
4 leisure garden
5 pass away
6 taking industrial action
7 working to rule (*actually means refusing to work beyond normal working hours)
8 lower income bracket
9 under the weather
10 low IQ
11 jobseeker's allowance
12 Ministry of Defence
13 have a dialogue
14 companion animal

3 Ask students in pairs to discuss the euphemisms.

Answers

1 killed
2 wrong
3 put some money in it because it is overdrawn
4 an argument
5 It's dangerous
6 It's making a loss / bankrupt

4 Ask students in small groups to think of and translate euphemisms from their own language.

Don't forget!

Writing Unit 12 Bringing a biography to life (SB p131)

Workbook Unit 12
Exercise 3 General revision – correcting mistakes
Exercise 4 Listening – Estate agents' euphemisms
Exercise 5 Pronunciation – Sentence stress
Exercise 8 Phrasal verbs – Connections between literal and metaphorical meanings
Exercise 9 Idioms with the word *time*

Stop and check 4 (TB pp149–150)

Progress test 2 (TB pp153–154)

Writing

UNITS 1–12

UNIT 1 Formal and informal letters (SB p117)

1 Read through the 'checklist' as a class.

2 Ask students to read the task. Ask them to look back at the 'checklist' in 1, and plan their letter carefully. They could work in pairs. You may wish to support their preparation by writing some useful phrases on the board, (see below). Students could write their letter for homework.

> **USEFUL PHRASES**
> *Thanks for your letter.*
> *It was great to hear from you.*
> *I'm thinking of …*
> *I wonder whether you could …*
> *Looking forward to hearing from you.*

3 Same procedure as **2**.

> **USEFUL PHRASES**
> *I am writing in response to your advertisement in …*
> *Please find enclosed my curriculum vitae.*
> *I look forward to hearing from you.*

UNIT 2 Story telling (SB p118)

1 Ask students to read the opening paragraphs and answer the questions. Let them discuss their answers in pairs before discussing as a class.

> **Answers**
> 1 The opening lines of each story are fairly short. They engage the reader's attention because they immediately take us to the critical point in each story. The events leading up to this point are described later in the paragraph. In story A the opening creates an atmosphere of monotony, depression and loneliness through the weather, the empty garden and the two birds. In stories B and C the openings create tension and a certain amount of fear / anxiety through the adjectives and adverbs used, through the actions of the main characters, and the deserted locations.
>
> 2 Narrative tenses are used in the stories. Direct speech is used in story C for dramatic effect. It varies the pace of the narrative.
>
> 3 Story A: Joyce and her (possibly dead) husband; story B: Hannah and her (possible) boyfriend Peter; story C: Jes and his schoolfriend Luis.
>
> 4 Joyce is old, probably in her 70s, 80s. We know this because she has 'a wisp of white hair', pictures as companions and very few Christmas cards. Hannah and Pete are probably students in their 20s. They're backpacking around India probably because they don't have much money. Luis and Jes are probably teenagers, as they mention finishing school, and the raid sounds like a dare.

2 Ask students to discuss what happens next in groups or as a class.

> **Answers**
> Students' own answers.

3-4 Ask students to read the rest of the first story and add the adverbs. Then discuss the endings as a class.

> **Answers**
> 2 softly, gently, encouragingly
> 3 instinctively
> 4 gently, slowly
> 5 strangely
> 6 slowly
> 7 encouragingly, softly, gently

5 Ask students to plan their own story in pairs. Read through the advice, then ask pairs to choose which story to finish. They could work in pairs to plan the story in class, then write it up for homework.

UNIT 3 Writing a business report (SB p120)

1-2 Ask students in pairs to discuss which features are typical of report writing. Then ask them to read the report and check their answers.

Answers
1. a state your aims in the introduction
2. a use headings for each section
3. b give mostly facts rather than opinions
4. b use mostly passive tenses
5. b give recommendations based on the facts

3 Ask students to re-read the report and underline words or expressions to introduce recommendations.

Answers
should introduce
should also be considered
would strongly recommend
needs to be
could be consolidated

4 Ask students to read the report and circle ways of reporting opinions.

Answers
1. commented that ...
2. was said to be
3. were generally thought to be
4. was considered to be
5. was felt to be
6. there were some complaints

5 Ask students to use the prompts to report opinions. Let students check in pairs before discussing as a class.

Answers
1. People commented that a colour display screen made no difference.
2. The voice recorder was generally said to be too complicated to use.
3. The text messages were generally thought to be better value for money than making a phone call.
4. Some special features were felt to be unimportant.
5. There were some complaints that the battery life was too short and that recharging it was very inconvenient.
6. Customers commented that the WAP service had limited value.

6 Ask students to rewrite the report using language practised in the lesson.

Sample answer
The aim of this report is to evaluate a new range of Trident mobile phones. Recently there has been a decrease in the number of phone sales, despite improvements to the basic model. Consequently I have been asked to analyse the results of a customer survey in order to explain this trend, and to make recommendations for future improvements.

7 Read through the table as a class, then ask students to prepare and write a report following the paragraph plan.

EXTENSION ACTIVITY
You could generate data for the report by doing your own class survey. Ask students to design a table similar to the one in 7. They can think of their own headings, and they could choose to evaluate PCs, personal CD players or cameras, as well as mobile phones. Ask them to interview three or four classmates, and note their answers in the table, before writing a report based on the data.

UNIT 4 Expressing a personal opinion (SB p122)

Lead-in

Set the scene, and create interest, by asking students a few lead-in questions, e.g. *Do you watch reality TV shows? Which shows are popular in your country at the moment? What do you think of them?*

1 Ask students to read the essay, and tick the ideas (a–g) which appear in it. Ask them to decide which ideas are not relevant to the question.

Answers
ideas which appear in essay:	a, b, d, e
irrelevant ideas:	f, g

2 Ask students to read the essay again and choose the most appropriate adverb or expression of opinion. Let them check in pairs before discussing as a class.

Answers
1	In fact,	6	Presumably,
2	Surely	7	Naturally
3	exactly	8	probably
4	Generally speaking	9	basically
5	Clearly	10	ultimately

3 Ask students to match the sentences, using an adverb or phrase from the box.

Suggested answers
1. f Some people say that the price of fame is too high. *Admittedly* life is difficult if your private life is public.
2. a Famous people complain if there is a sensational story in the newspapers. *Frankly* they shouldn't because they exploit newspapers to get famous.
3. c Celebrities claim it's difficult to make new friends. *Obviously / Naturally* it must be difficult to know what motivates new 'friends'.
4. b People think celebrities have an easy life. *As a matter of fact* most celebrities have to work very hard.

5 e Stalkers pose a real threat to many celebrities. *Naturally / Obviously* they have to spend a lot of money on security.

6 d Why are we obsessed with fame? *Presumably / Naturally / Obviously* it's because it's 'the new religion'.

4 Ask students to prepare carefully by following the paragraph plan and taking notes. Ask them to write the essay for homework.

EXTENSION ACTIVITY

A good way of correcting written work like this is to do it as a class activity. Sit the students in a circle, or in circles, if you have a large class. Then ask them to pass their written work to the person on their right. That person must read, correct (or query with a question mark) any errors, and write a short comment on the bottom, (e.g., *very interesting*). They then pass the work to the next person on their right, and so on until the piece of work is returned to the person who wrote it. As a teacher, you can monitor the activity, answering queries about whether something is correct or not. A variation on this activity is to assign roles to each student in the circle: one student must read for grammatical errors, one must suggest vocabulary changes, another must comment on style and appropriacy, etc.

UNIT 5 Discussing pros and cons (SB p123)

Lead-in

Set the scene, and create interest, by asking students a few lead-in questions, e.g., *Are you married? Do you intend to be? Is it important or necessary to get married these days?*

1 Ask students to read the essay and put the paragraphs in order.

Answers
A 3   B 2   C 4   D 5   E 1

2 Ask students to look at the highlighted words and answer the questions. Ask them which arguments they agree with.

Answers
arguments he agrees with: *It's obvious that … , it's clear that …*
arguments he disagrees with: *it could be argued that … , this is partly true … , it has been suggested that … , some people claim that …*
To illustrate arguments he agrees with: *a stable single-parent environment is healthier than an unhappy marriage; marriage is no longer necessary to a successful relationship*
To illustrate arguments he disagrees with: *marriage brings emotional and financial stability; marriage provides stability for children; marriage is more flexible*

3 Ask students to find linking words and phrases in the text.

Answers
A contrasting point of view: *But in spite of this; On the other hand; Nevertheless*
A reason: *as; precisely because*
A result: *As a result*

4 Ask students to rewrite the sentences, using the words in brackets. Do the first as an example.

Answers
1 It's common for young adults to live at home in some countries, *whereas* in others it's not. / *Whereas* it's common for young adults to live at home in some countries, in others it's not.
2 *On account of* the money they save, many young adults live at home. / Many young adults live at home *on account of* the money they save.
3 *Despite* not having much money, some people prefer to leave home. / Some people prefer to leave home, *despite* not having much money.
4 *Due to* economic circumstances, some people stay at home. / Some people stay at home *due to* economic circumstances.
5 Many young adults live at home *so that* they can save money for their own flat.
6 Some people move out as soon as they can *in order to* have more independence. / *In order to* have more independence, some people move out as soon as they can.
7 *Owing to* their selfish behaviour, one mother evicted her sons. / One mother evicted her sons *owing to* their selfish behaviour.

5 Ask students in pairs to choose one of the essays. Then ask them to work together, making notes, following the advice.

Ask students to write the essay for homework.

EXTENSION ACTIVITY

Ask the class to choose one of the essays. Then divide the class into small groups of three or four. Half the groups must brainstorm arguments *for*. Half the groups must brainstorm arguments *against*. Pair students from different groups so that they can share their *for* and *against* arguments before writing the essay.

UNIT 6 A letter to a newspaper (SB p124)

Lead-in

Set the scene, and create interest, by asking students a few lead-in questions, e.g., *Is using cannabis legal in your country? Do you think that cannabis should be legalized? Why? Why not?*

1 Read the extract as a class. Then ask students to read the letter. Set a gist question: *Is the writer in favour of legalization or against it?*

2 Ask students to match the paragraphs to the descriptions. Then have a brief class discussion – which arguments do the students agree with?

Answers
- B summarizes arguments in the article that the writer disagrees with
- D concludes and restates the writer's point of view
- C puts forward arguments the writer agrees with
- A introduces the reason for writing and states the writer's point of view

The letter puts forward eight arguments altogether.

3 Ask students to complete the letter with the best alternative in each pair. Let students check in pairs before discussing as a class.

Answers

Paragraph A	2	Paragraph C	1
Paragraph B	1	Paragraph D	2

4 Ask students to rewrite the sentences. Let students check in pairs before discussing as a class.

Sample answers
2 It would appear that / It is assumed that young people are encouraged to smoke by their friends.
3 It has been proved that / It would seem that most ill health is caused by lack of exercise and an unhealthy diet.
4 It has been proved that / It is believed that people have been killed by passive smoking.
5 It would seem that the risks of smoking are known.
6 It would appear that the nicotine content in cigarettes has been increased.
7 It could be argued that / It would appear that people can't be frightened into giving up smoking.

5 Read through the task as a class, and elicit a variety of students' views to put on the board. Ask students to prepare their letter, following the paragraph plan. Ask students to write the essay for homework.

UNIT 7 Describing a personal experience (SB p126)

Lead-in

Set the scene, and create interest, by asking students a few lead-in questions, e.g. *Have you ever been helped by a stranger? Has anybody ever gone out of their way to help you?*

1 Ask students to read the two paragraphs and discuss the questions with a partner.

Answers
B describes emotions, the surroundings and the weather
A gives mostly factual narrative
B uses a variety of vocabulary
A uses similar sentence structures throughout
B has more impact on the reader

2 Ask students to choose the most suitable title, and say why.

Answer
b The kindness of strangers

3 Ask students to read the rest of the article and answer the questions. Let them discuss their answer in pairs before discussing as a class.

Answers
1 He felt suspicious because he'd been attacked and robbed when he was travelling in London.
2 Because he genuinely wanted to help someone in distress.
3 Because he'd had a bad experience in London with a stranger.
4 He found out that Robert had lived in Wick all his life, and that most of his family had moved away. He felt Robert was quite lonely.
5 Because his act of kindness, although simple, was extraordinary in today's world.

4 Ask students to rewrite the sentences in a more emphatic way.

Answers
1 Rarely do people help a stranger in trouble.
2 It's mistrust that's the problem.
3 What people worry about is being robbed.
4 The thing that we should do is try to help in some way.
5 Never will I forget the first time a stranger helped me.

5 Ask students to think of an example of kindness. You could elicit some ideas and write them on the board, or get one or two students to tell stories, to get the others started. Then ask the students to follow the paragraph plan, and make notes.

Ask students to write the story for homework.

EXTENSION ACTIVITY
Once the students have written their stories, use them as a springboard for an interview. Put students in pairs to interview each other about their stories, using the questions suggested in the paragraph plan:

Where were you?	*What were you doing?*
Why did you need help?	*Who did you meet?*
How did they help you?	*What happened in the end?*

When they have completed the interview, ask students to exchange and read the stories they have written.

1   Ask students if anybody has seen *Road to Perdition*. What can they tell you about it?

Ask students to read the review and answer the questions.

Answers
The purpose of the review is to inform, evaluate and recommend. The reader will be a magazine or newspaper reader. The language is mostly formal.

2   Ask students to divide the review into paragraphs. Do one as an example. Then ask students to match the paragraphs to the headings.

Answers
d Subject of the review
Road to Perdition is the latest film by Sam Mendes, director of the Oscar-winning film *American Beauty*. Adapted from a novel by Max Allan Collins and Richard Piers Rayner, *Road to Perdition* is extremely dark and atmospheric. Like a Greek tragedy, it follows the predestined fates of the main characters on their road to perdition (or hell).

e Summary of the plot
The film is set in a wintry 1930s Chicago and tells the story of a hitman called Mike Sullivan (Tom Hanks) and his mafia boss John Rooney (Paul Newman). Sullivan looks up to Rooney as a father figure. However, when Sullivan's son witnesses a gangland killing, Rooney turns against him, and both father and son are forced to go on the run.

b Positive points
Visually, the film is quite stunning. There are some impressive special effects, but what strikes you most are the dark images of rain and shadow. These create a heavy atmosphere of bleakness and fear. In many scenes brown and black are the dominant colours, which often makes the film look like a well-crafted oil painting. The acting too is first-rate, with both Hanks and Newman giving completely convincing performances.

c Negative points
However, although it is wonderfully directed and acted, *Road to Perdition* is not a gripping film. The plot is quite slow and the ending is totally predictable. But what the film really lacks is human warmth – the characters ultimately fail to move us.

a Recommendation
To sum up, *Road to Perdition* is a beautifully filmed gangster movie. It's well worth seeing, but it doesn't quite deliver the great film we expect.

3   Ask students to re-read the review, and answer the questions.

Answers
1   a thriller/gangster film
2   a Greek tragedy
3   an oil painting
4   • the visual imagery: *stunning, dark*
    • the atmosphere: *heavy, bleakness, fear*
    • the acting: *first-rate, convincing*
    • the plot: *quite slow*
    • the ending: *totally predictable*
5   the present tense.

4   Ask students to complete the sentences with a verb in the correct form.

Answers
1	is set	5	(to) create
2	is adapted	6	suspend
3	tells	7	strikes
4	is revealed	8	seeing

5   Ask students to choose a film, play or book, then follow the advice to prepare their review. Ask students to write the review for homework.

EXTENSION ACTIVITY
Get a scrapbook or a file, and paste or put the reviews inside. Label it 'Class reviews'. Encourage students to read other people's reviews when they have a quiet moment, and to add other reviews of books, films or plays whenever they can.

UNIT 9 Personal profile (SB p128)

Lead-in

Set the scene, and create interest, by asking students a few lead-in questions, e.g., *Have you ever needed a personal profile for a job or university application? What information did you include in it?*

1   Ask students to read the profile quickly, and match the paragraphs to the descriptions.

Answers
D   Summary of main skills and qualities
C   Leisure activities
A   Present responsibilities and skills
B   Experience and achievements

2   Ask students to answer the questions, and discuss them with a partner.

Answers
1   He contributes to university life through his involvement with the Student Union Executive Committee. The role requires leadership as well as organizational and negotiation skills.

2 He ran a student magazine.
3 He needed to be able to write well, work under pressure and meet tight deadlines.
4 His hobby is watching films and being a member of a film club. He has gained experience in organizing community events and working with young people.
5 His confidence and competitiveness, as well as his natural enthusiasm.

3 Ask students to complete the sentences with the correct verb.

Answers
1 Matt didn't want to *take* responsibility for the project. It was too much work.
2 Your education and experience *plays* a large part in the skills you have to offer.
3 It's not easy to *run* a newspaper. You often have to *meet* very tight deadlines.
4 People are sometimes most creative when they *work* under pressure.
5 Holly had to *coordinate* a lot of people for the fundraising event.
6 He's no good at *managing* budgets. He's hopeless at maths!

4 Ask students to write notes, following the paragraph plan, in preparation for writing their own personal profile. Ask them to write the profile for homework.

EXTENSION ACTIVITY
Once the students have written their profiles, write some jobs on the board: *tour guide, senior executive, teacher* etc.
Pass the profiles round the class, or put them on the wall for students to read, and ask students to decide which class member is best suited for each job and why. However, make sure your students don't mind other students reading their profiles before you start the activity.

UNIT 10 Entering a competition (SB p129)

Lead-in

Set the scene, and create interest, by asking students a few lead-in questions, e.g., *Have you ever entered a competition in a magazine? What was it for? What did you have to do to enter?*

1 Ask students to read the advert and answer the question.

Answers
They have to
• describe an adventure sport they do and how they started it
• explain why they enjoy it
• explain why these sports are becoming so popular

2 Ask students to read the competition entry, and answer the questions. Let them discuss their answers in pairs before discussing as a class.

Answers
1 It's mostly informal.
2 She engages the reader's interest by relating a personal anecdote. She sets the scene, describes how she felt before she started climbing, and her feelings after her first climb.
3 She says she is motivated by personal achievement, the idea of a challenge, and the desire to escape from everyday life.

3 Ask students to read the two versions, and say which they think is best at answering the question.

Answer
Paragraph B is the best because it clearly answers the final question in the competition entry.

4 Ask students to read the advert, and notice the three questions it asks.

5 Ask students to prepare their competition entry, following the paragraph plan. Ask students to write their entry for homework.

UNIT 11 Describing a journey (SB p130)

1 Ask students to read the three extracts and answer the questions.

Answers
1 He visited Argentina and Chile.
2 He travelled on a motorbike and slept in a tent.
3 • get on with the local people: extract A
   • experience bad weather: extract B
   • comment on the changing scenery: extracts A and C
   • feel anxious about his journey: extract A

2 Check that the students know the words, then ask them to improve the extract by adding them.

Possible answers
In the *desolate* Atacama desert, the *shimmering* road ahead was my only link with civilization. The *blazing* sun beat down on the *windswept* sand dunes and *derelict* ghost towns which lined the route. In the distance I could see *spectacular* volcanoes which marked the edge of the desert and the border with Bolivia.

3 Ask students to find adjectives in the extracts in exercise 1 to describe the places listed. Let students check their answers in pairs before discussing as a class.

Answers

- the beaches: *glorious, golden*
- towns and cities: *dreary, rain-drenched, bustling*
- the coastline: *storm-tossed, wild*
- people: *friendly, gloomy-looking*
- the mountains: *barren, snow-clad, desolate*

4   Ask students to match the sentence halves. Let students check their answers in pairs before discussing as a class.

Answers

1c   2b   3a   4f   5g   6e   7d   8h

5   Ask students to think of a memorable journey, and make notes to describe it, following the paragraph plan. Ask students to write the description for homework.

EXTENSION ACTIVITY

Ask students to choose four or five key phrases from their stories, and write them on a piece of paper. For example, *bus broke down, a violent thunderstorm, miles from the nearest town*

Divide the class into groups of four. Students in each group must look at the key phrases, then guess and tell the stories of each member of their group. At the end, they can read each other's stories.

UNIT 12 Bringing a biography to life (SB p131)

Lead-in

Write the following on the board:

Robert Capa   war photographer   Spanish Civil War
Normandy Invasion   land mine

Ask students: *What do you know of the historical events mentioned? What do you think is the connection between these things?*

1   Ask students to combine the sentences in each part into one sentence. Do the first as a class as an example.

Answers

(1) Robert Capa, the famous photojournalist and founder of Magnum Photos, was born in Budapest in 1913. (2) A talented self-taught photographer, he started working for a publishing house when he was just 18, as well as studying journalism at a Berlin university. (3) During the 1930s there was much political upheaval (and / in which) Capa, like many of his student companions, became very much involved. (4) Consequently he had to leave Hungary, then Berlin before finally going to live in Paris.

2   Ask students to read the rest of the biography, and match paragraphs to descriptions.

Answers

D   an evaluation of his achievements
C   the end of his career
B   his continuing success
A   how he built his reputation

3   Ask students to discuss the questions in pairs.

Answers

1   He got his big break through his assignment on the Spanish Civil War.
2   He probably wanted to educate people by showing them the horror of war. He felt ambiguous about recording the events rather than being a part of them.
3   Students' own answers.
4   The writer uses direct quotes to illustrate a point, in this case explain the risks Capa took and how he felt about his work. The effect is to make Capa more real and immediate.
5   Students' own answers.

4   Ask students to write the biography of Isabel Allende, using the notes, and following the paragraph plan. Alternatively, ask students to think of someone who interests them, research their lives and make notes, then use the notes and paragraph plan to write the biography.

Photocopiable material

Unit 1

Song An Englishman in New York

1 You are going to listen to a song called *An Englishman in New York*. Why might an Englishman feel 'alien' in New York?

2 Look at the words describing people who are different. What is the difference between them?

> a stranger   an alien worker   a foreigner
> an illegal immigrant   an asylum seeker
> an outsider   a misfit   a refugee

3 Listen to the song. Which of the words in 2 could be used to describe the person in the song? Match the summaries *a* to *e* to the five verses of the song.

a In a macho, aggressive society like that of New York, being gentle and polite makes you 'different'.

b Because I enjoy walking round the city, dressed ostentatiously, I'm very noticeable.

c It's important to be yourself and be polite, even if ignorant people are rude to you.

d I have different eating habits and speak differently from New Yorkers.

e Being a man means standing up for your principles and being yourself – not being aggressive and violent.

What do you think is the overall message of the song?

Vocabulary and Pronunciation

1 Look at the lists of words below, and decide which word has a different vowel sound from the others.

1 walk   talk   work   York
2 bone   one   gun   done
3 day   say   they   key
4 side   laid   lied   dyed
5 hear   dear   gear   pear
6 smile   I'll   meal   style

An Englishman in New York

I don't drink coffee I take tea my dear
I like my toast done on one side
You can hear it in my accent when I talk
I'm an Englishman in New York

See me walking down Fifth Avenue
A walking cane here at my side
I take it everywhere I walk
I'm an Englishman in New York

Chorus
I'm an alien, I'm a legal alien
I'm an Englishman in New York
I'm an alien, I'm a legal alien
I'm an Englishman in New York

If 'manners maketh man' as someone said
He's the hero of the day
It takes a man to suffer ignorance and smile
Be yourself no matter what they say

Chorus

Modesty, propriety can lead to notoriety
You could end up as the only one
Gentleness, sobriety are rare in this society
At night a candle's brighter than the sun

Takes more than combat gear to make a man
Takes more than a license for a gun
Confront your enemies, avoid them when you can
A gentleman will walk but never run

Repeat verse 3

Chorus

2 Mark the stress in the nouns from the song and check their meanings in a dictionary. Then write the adjectives and mark the stress in them.

<u>mo</u>desty   <u>mo</u>dest   sobriety _____
propriety _____   society _____
notoriety _____

3 Have you ever felt like a 'legal alien' in another country? Think of a country you have visited – or are visiting – and think of five or six cultural differences between you and that country. Discuss your ideas in groups.

Student B

MURDOCH, Iris Jean
(1919-1999)

She was born in (1) ___Dublin___ , the only child of Anglo-Irish parents. She read (2) _____ at Oxford University, then worked for four years in (3) UN refugee camps . She returned to Oxford to teach philosophy. Her first novel *Under the Net*, published in (4) _____ , was an immediate success. Other titles include *The Sandcastle, The Bell,* and *The Sea, The Sea*, for which she was awarded (5) the Booker prize . She said that in her novels she tried to convey (6) '_____ .'

In 1956 she married **John Bayley**, a professor of (7) English Literature at Oxford. They had a (8) _____ marriage, but no children.

Iris was still writing in her late 70s. Her 26th and last novel, *Jackson's Dilemma*, published in 1995, was written whilst she was suffering from the beginnings of (9) Alzheimer's Disease . She died in 1999.

The Oscar-winning film, *Iris*, (2002), starring (10) _____ , tells the story of her love affair with John Bayley and her tragic struggle with the disease.

--- ✂ ---

Student B

MURDOCH, Iris Jean
(1919-1999)

She was born in (1) ___Dublin___ , the only child of Anglo-Irish parents. She read (2) _____ at Oxford University, then worked for four years in (3) UN refugee camps . She returned to Oxford to teach philosophy. Her first novel *Under the Net*, published in (4) _____ , was an immediate success. Other titles include *The Sandcastle, The Bell,* and *The Sea, The Sea*, for which she was awarded (5) the Booker prize . She said that in her novels she tried to convey (6) '_____ .'

In 1956 she married **John Bayley**, a professor of (7) English Literature at Oxford. They had a (8) _____ marriage, but no children.

Iris was still writing in her late 70s. Her 26th and last novel, *Jackson's Dilemma*, published in 1995, was written whilst she was suffering from the beginnings of (9) Alzheimer's Disease . She died in 1999.

The Oscar-winning film, *Iris*, (2002), starring (10) _____ , tells the story of her love affair with John Bayley and her tragic struggle with the disease.

LADY B Do you smoke?

JACK Well, yes, I must admit I smoke.

LADY B I am glad to hear it. A man should always have an occupation of some kind. There are far too many idle men in London as it is. How old are you?

JACK Twenty-nine.

LADY B A very good age to be married at. I have always been of the opinion that a man who desires to get married should know either everything or nothing. Which do you know?

JACK [After some hesitation.] I know nothing, Lady Bracknell.

LADY B I am pleased to hear it. I do not approve of anything that tampers with natural ignorance. Ignorance is like a delicate exotic fruit; touch it and the bloom is gone. What is your income?

JACK Between seven and eight thousand a year.

LADY B [Makes a note in her book.] In land, or in investments?

JACK In investments, chiefly.

LADY B That is satisfactory.

JACK I have a country house with some land, of course, attached to it, about fifteen hundred acres, I believe; but I don't depend on that for my real income. In fact, as far as I can make out, the poachers are the only people who make anything out of it.

LADY B A country house! You have a town house, I hope? A girl with a simple, unspoiled nature, like Gwendolen could hardly be expected to reside in the country.

JACK Well, I own a house in Belgrave Square.

LADY B What number in Belgrave Square?

JACK 149.

LADY B [Shaking her head.] The unfashionable side. Now to minor matters. Are your parents living?

JACK I have lost both my parents.

LADY B To lose one parent, Mr Worthing, may be regarded as a misfortune; to lose both looks like carelessness. Who was your father? He was evidently a man of some wealth.

JACK I am afraid I really don't know. The fact is, Lady Bracknell, I said I had lost my parents. It would be nearer the truth to say that my parents seem to have lost me. I don't actually know who I am by birth. I was …, well, I was found.

LADY B Found!

JACK The late Mr. Thomas Cardew, an old gentleman of a very charitable and kindly disposition, found me, and gave me the name of Worthing, because he happened to have a first-class ticket for Worthing in his pocket at the time. Worthing is a place in Sussex. It is a seaside resort.

LADY B Where did the charitable gentleman who had a first-class ticket for this seaside resort find you?

JACK [Gravely.] In a handbag.

LADY B A handbag?

JACK [Very seriously.] Yes, Lady Bracknell. I was in a handbag – a somewhat large, black leather handbag, with handles to it – an ordinary handbag, in fact.

LADY B In what locality did this Mr. James, or Thomas, Cardew come across this ordinary handbag?

JACK In the cloakroom at Victoria Station. It was given to him in mistake for his own.

LADY B The cloakroom at Victoria Station?

JACK Yes. The Brighton line.

LADY B The line is immaterial. Mr. Worthing, I confess I feel somewhat bewildered by what you have just told me. To be born, or at any rate, bred in a handbag, whether it had handles or not, seems to me to display a contempt for the ordinary decencies of family life. As for the particular locality in which the handbag was found, a cloakroom at a railway station might serve to conceal a social indiscretion – has probably, indeed, been used for that purpose before now but it could hardly be regarded as an assured basis for a recognized position in good society.

JACK May I ask then what you would advise me to do? I need hardly say I will do anything in the world to ensure Gwendolen's happiness.

LADY B I would strongly advise you, Mr. Worthing, to try and acquire some relations as soon as possible, and to make a definite effort to produce at any rate one parent, of either sex.

JACK I don't see how I could possibly manage to do that. I can produce the handbag at any moment. It is in my dressing-room at home. I really think that should satisfy you, Lady Bracknell.

LADY B Me, sir! What has it to do with me? You can hardly imagine that I and Lord Bracknell would dream of allowing our only daughter – a girl brought up with the utmost care – to marry into a cloakroom, and form an alliance with a parcel! Good morning, Mr. Worthing!

Answers to 'What do you think?' 1-2 – SB p23.

How Jack Worthing came to be in the handbag.

As a baby, Jack had a rather scatterbrained nanny called Miss Prism. One day, Miss Prism was getting ready to take Jack for a walk, when she became distracted, and put the novel she was writing in the pram and the baby in her handbag. This handbag she then left, by mistake, in the cloakroom at Victoria Station. It turns out that Miss Prism had been the nanny for Lady Bracknell's sister, whose baby boy mysteriously disappeared 28 years ago. This baby was, of course, Jack, and he is therefore Lady Bracknell's nephew and Gwendolen's cousin. He had, in fact, been named Ernest, which is a wonderful coincidence, because Gwendolen has always wanted to marry someone called Ernest. Lady Bracknell is now delighted to approve the marriage.

Student A

You work for *Stay Well*. You are the Sales Manager for the *Sogood* drink. Explain that *Sogood* has been on sale for 60 years and was one of the first-ever health drinks. It has only ever been sold in pharmacies. It looks and tastes like cough medicine. The majority of *Sogood* buyers are older people. Seventy per cent of the sales are to people over 65. They are the generation who started drinking it as children and think it's so good that they have never stopped. Sales of the drink are declining as this older market dies, and are not being replaced by new buyers. You have the option to change the formula of the drink. You can add more vitamins so that *Sogood* would provide 100% of the vitamins that people need every day, and you could make it taste nicer. If you do this, the drink will be a different colour. It will become bright green.

Student B

You work for *Stay Well* in the packaging department. You are responsible for how the drink looks on the shelf. *Sogood* is currently sold in dark brown glass bottles. You cannot see what colour the drink is in these bottles. It looks old-fashioned but trustworthy. You have the option to keep this design or change the bottle to a modern-looking clear glass design, which would show off the new colour. Going for the new design risks alienating your present buyers, who might not recognize their trusted drink. Keeping the old one will make it difficult to attract new buyers.

Student C

You are responsible for distribution at *Stay Well*. You have been looking at alternative places to sell *Sogood*. You have identified two new opportunities. The first is in a popular national supermarket chain. They insist on low prices but could increase your sales dramatically. The other option is to sell it in a popular chain of bars and clubs. They have expressed an interest in healthy non-alcoholic drinks and would sell the drink at a high profit for them and you.

You don't have to change the distribution if you don't want to. You could just continue to sell *Sogood* through pharmacies. For the first year, you can only choose one form of distribution because you can only manufacture a limited quantity of the drink.

Student D

You are in charge of pricing at *Stay Well*. Improvements to the drink would make it more expensive to produce. You would need to cover these increased costs by increasing sales dramatically or by increasing the price. Families spend most of their disposable income on food and drink, but look for low prices. Teenagers and young adults spend the highest proportion of their income on soft drinks, and buy what is fashionable rather than cheap. Research has shown that your existing older market would pay more for the drink if they understood its new benefits

Student E

You work for a market research company and have been researching the health products and vitamins market sector. Overall sales in this sector have been increasing, alongside things such as gym membership, as young adults become more concerned with their health. Another growth area is parents. They buy the products for their children, who tend to eat too much fast food and not get enough vitamins. Your current most important market (pensioners) is also going to increase. People are beginning to retire earlier and live longer.

Student F

You are in charge of media for the advertising agency. Your recommendation is for the company to advertise on television, as you want to reach as many people as you can in as short a time as possible. Within your TV budget you can reach the older, retired people. They watch a lot of daytime TV, which is the cheapest airtime to advertise in. Unfortunately, you would reach the fewest parents. They are busy people – at work, out with friends, cooking, looking after children – and only watch television in the evening. As they have the highest income, other advertisers are trying to reach them at this time as well, which makes it expensive.

The younger market watches a lot of television at all times of the day, but as they see so much advertising it is harder to get your message through to them.

Unit 3　Comparing statistics

A

Interest rates during the first six months of the year

Jan	4.7%	Apr	2.1%
Feb	4.8%	May	2.1%
Mar	4.4%	Jun	5.2%

B

A comparison of crime figures (between this year and last year)

Number of reported crimes in the local area	Last year	This year
Street theft and muggings	100	203
Shoplifting	520	512
Burglary	326	339
Car theft	409	278
Armed robbery	27	27
Violent assaults	47	87

Unit 3　Word linking and intrusive sounds

Arriva Communications

Roberto Rossi
Company director

Via Monterotondo 12
20163 Milano
Tel: 64 35 034　Fax: 64 54 673

Wine & Dine International Magazines Inc.

James Taylor • Wine journalist

15 Honeywell St. London EC4 1DT
Tel: 0207 331 8579 Fax: 0207 331 2280

AMANDA LLEWELLYN
LANDSCAPE GARDENER
A & B LANDSCAPES

17A Meredith Close • Llanrug
Caernarfon LL5 2AD • Wales

Tel: (0286) 674498　Fax: (0286) 674499

Monique Bresson • Translator

Bresson translation services

26, rue Jules Ferry
75006 Paris
Tel: 1 – 43 45 22 49　Fax: 1 – 43 45 23 88

Brad Fleming
News Photographer
Newswide Report International

94 Madison Ave.
New York, NY 10016-4355
Tel: (800) 441-5232
Fax: (212) 726-7654

Reuter Chemicals

Heinz Muller
Research scientist

Engesserstrasse 46
79108 Freiburg
Germany
Tel: 49 761 559 64 60
Fax: 49 761 559 64 80

Stratikis Publications

Stavros Soutakis
Senior Sales Manager

9 Havriou St.
Athens 10562
Tel: 32 21 834
Fax: 32 34 768

Oxford University Press

Great Clarendon St.
Oxford OX2 6DP
Telephone 01865 556767
Fax 01865 267622

Sylvia Hancock
Commissioning Editor

Ravensburger International

Anna Navratilova
Marketing manager

Smetanova 66
46601 Jablonec nad nison
Czech Republic
Tel: 00 42- 0428443311
Fax:0042- 0428443323

Christina Allen
Aromatherapist

Touch of Health Therapy Clinic
363 Curie Ave. Abingdon
Tel: 01235 821259
Fax: 01235 821 266

English Institute

Lara van der Lingen
School director

50800 Musgrave, Durban 4062
South Africa
Tel: (+27 3) 261 9445
Fax: (+27 31) 261 9474

Opera Omaha

Karen Gardener
Opera director

1625 Farnam
Omaha Nevada 68102
USA
Tel: 346 7372
Fax: 346 7323

John M. Dove
Accountant
19 Dundonald Street
Warrington
WA4 7KJ
Tel: 01925 740655
Fax: 01925 740675

KING BRAITHWAITE & CO

PRODAJNA GALLERY

Sjenka Boban
Manager

Luscic 23
Karlovac
Croatia
Tel: 047/414 614
Fax: 047/600 880

Anna Karlsson
Record producer

Claus Frimanns gate 2A
5011 Bergen
Norway
Tel: 47 55 31 60 32
Fax: 47 55 31 60 33

ACOUSTIC Records

COMPANY PROFILE

Company:

Your position in the company:

Your job description:

What does your company do/make?

What is your company's market share? What is its turnover?

How does your company market itself? How does it advertise its products? What is its image?

How successful has your company been this year? What facts or figures do you know about your company?

What are your personal career ambitions for next year?

Unit 4

Speaking How to become an A-list celebrity (SB p44)

2

This is going to take a lot of careful party planning. Where would be the best place to go? You have thought of two ways of identifying the best clubs.

Just join the most exclusive, expensive, private club you can find. Major celebrities are bound to hang out there.

GO TO 3

Scour the glossy magazines to find out where the famous people are hanging out these days.

GO TO 4

6

They're more than happy to talk to you. In fact they won't stop talking. The trouble is they are extremely self-centred and dull. They must be lonely and ask you to accompany them to another bar.

You can't face listening to them any more – you didn't think stars would be so boring. Inventing a new identity would be a better way to fame than this.

GO TO 7

You decide to go with them. Maybe they'll lighten up, or you could meet someone else.

GO TO 15

3

You join the club. It's expensive but after a few visits you spot a major star. They don't look very approachable, in fact they look like they're here to avoid people like you. How are you going to start talking to them?

Spill your drink on them, then they won't be able to avoid starting a conversation.

GO TO 5

Just pluck up the courage and ask whether they mind you joining them for a drink.

GO TO 6

7

Who should you pretend to be? You think the best options for fame would be the 'love child' of some dead rock star or maybe someone from an old royal family.

You make up a story that you're royalty from an obscure principality.

GO TO 8

A love child seems to have more potential. You make up a story that you're the secret child of a dead pop star.

GO TO 9

4

You read the glossy magazines and go to some clubs that you saw the stars attend. However, such is the speed of fashion, these clubs are no longer 'in'. Instead, they're full of people like you trying to keep up with the latest trends.

Face up to it – you're going to have to join a private club to meet some stars.

GO TO 3

You meet someone who professes to be friends with a famous film star. In fact they're going to see them now and ask you along. They look a little suspicious but you decide to go.

GO TO 12

8

You have no success in getting any news organizations to pick up your story. Royalty just does not seem to interest them any more.

Better try the love child story and see whether you can get the media interested in that.

GO TO 9

5

It started a conversation, a very one-sided conversation. The celebrity shouted at you for five minutes and then demanded that you take their jacket to a specific dry cleaners that they use. Nowhere else cleans as well apparently, but it is also extremely expensive.

This cleaner is extortionate. You decide to take it to your local dry cleaner and hope that they don't notice the difference.

GO TO 16

If this is such a special dry cleaners, it may have a lot of famous people using it. You decide to ask for a part-time job and hope to meet some stars while you work.

GO TO 4

9

The story seems to work and some newspapers are interested. A couple of them want to interview you for an exclusive. You start to worry about the implications of the lie and whether it could get you in to some kind of trouble.

It's too risky. You'll come clean to the reporter and tell them you made it up to try and become famous.

GO TO 10

What trouble could you get into? Newspapers make things up all the time. You carry on with the lie.

GO TO 11

10

You own up to the lie. The reporter thinks it's quite a unique story and writes a piece about you as 'famous for trying to become famous'! A late night talk show gets wind of this and you're invited on to join an interview with other celebrity wannabees to show the lengths people will go to.

You decide to do the show, but to try and be noticed more than the other guests you dress up in the most outrageous clothes you can find.

GO TO 14

It's true you are going to great lengths to try and hang out with celebrities, so you decide to just go and be yourself.

GO TO 24

14

The show goes well and your clothing really gets you noticed. Later, a minor pop star contacts you for clothing advice and asks you to develop a new look for them.

Being a fashion consultant for a pop star should help you achieve fame. Even though you do not really know much about fashion, you accept.

GO TO 22

It gives you another idea. You could design for a living. Top designers live very glamorous lifestyles and you have some great ideas for outfits.

GO TO 19

11

You've been featured in a tabloid, and everyone has fallen for it, including the pop star's legitimate offspring. They contact you and ask that you come and meet the rest of the family.

It could ruin everything if you actually meet them. You stall them with an excuse about being too ill to travel.

GO TO 25

It seems this rock star had quite a few children. You could easily get away with this, so you go and visit your new 'family'.

GO TO 13

15

Your new friend takes you to a secret bar crawling with celebrities. During the night you see someone drop a slip of paper. You pick it up and see that it's an invite to a major awards ceremony. This could be just the chance you're looking for to meet lots of celebrities.

It's looks like an invite to a very important event. You give it back.

GO TO 18

You keep the ticket. They won't really miss it as they probably go to events like this all the time.

GO TO 28

12

Rather than being friends with the actor, this person stalks them. You secretly follow the actor back to their house. The person you're with decides that they're going to stay hidden there and try and see them again when they come out.

You're here now and decide to hang around and wait for the actor to emerge again.

GO TO 17

You want to be with the stars, not spying on them. It looks like you will have to join that expensive club if only to get away from strange people like this.

GO TO 3

16

You use your normal cleaners and save yourself a lot of money. The problem is that they ruin the jacket beyond repair and you're supposed to take it back to the star today!

Buy a fake copy of the jacket and hope they don't notice until you've got away.

GO TO 20

Own up and tell them that the jacket is wrecked.

GO TO 21

13

The lifestyle of this rock star was so outrageous that the family always suspected there might be more siblings out there. They fully believe your story and welcome you in to the family. It turns out there will be money left in the will and they want you to have a share of it.

You accept their offer. It cost you a lot of money to come out here and see them.

GO TO 33

You can't accept their generosity but decide to see whether there is a real love child out there who should receive the money.

GO TO 34

17

When they come out they are with someone they shouldn't be with! You have a camera and decide to take a few snaps of the secret couple. They see you and plead with you not to take the pictures to the press.

Respect their privacy and throw the photos away.

GO TO 18

Ignore their pleas and take the pictures to the newspapers. They should be valuable.

GO TO 31

18

Good deeds are rewarded. They are grateful, and to prove it they ask you to a big showbiz party next week. It sounds great, but it's on the same night as you're mother-in-law's birthday dinner. Where are you going to go?

Go to the party – your mother-in-law will understand.

GO TO 26

You decline the invitation – you haven't seen your mother-in-law for a long time.

GO TO 27

19

You've done some designs and friends think they're pretty good. However to make and display them is going to cost a lot of money. You can just about raise the money to make the range but to put on a fashion show as well will mean selling your home to raise the money. It's a big risk.

Nothing ventured, nothing gained. You sell your home to raise the money for the show.

GO TO 46

Just make the clothes and worry about showing them once they are ready.

GO TO 47

20

They didn't notice that it was fake at all, and you seem to have got away with it. When the star wears it to an important event, someone in the press notices the fake jacket. The star is mocked in the press for wearing one and then to make matters worse, is investigated by police looking into counterfeit designer clothing.

You decide you should go to the police and the press to clear the name of this star by telling them that you supplied the fake clothing.

GO TO 29

The star does not know where you live and you don't want to be in trouble with the police. You decide to keep quiet.

GO TO 30

21

You confess to having ruined the jacket. They are not pleased to say the least, and insist that you replace it. The problem is that it is so valuable you cannot possible afford to buy another.

You offer to work for them for free until the debt is repaid. You'll do any work they like.

GO TO 36

You sell all your possessions to get the money. You don't want to have anything more to do with this person.

GO TO 37

22

This pop star hates every idea you come up with. You can't stand working with the pop star any longer. However, all this experience has given you more confidence about becoming a designer.

You decide to try designing and work for yourself instead of this pop star idiot.

GO TO 19

23

You're working in the dry cleaners after your normal job and a lot of famous people do use it. You haven't got to know them personally, but you do know quite a bit about their lives. You could really use what you now know about these people.

Keep it to yourself and just try to get to know them better. Maybe you'll strike up a friendship with someone famous.

GO TO 38

You use your knowledge to write a monthly gossip column for a magazine, dishing the dirt on the stars that you know from the shop.

GO TO 39

24

The TV show goes well. You are actually creating quite a name for yourself as a pathetic loser. It's not the greatest thing to be known for, but it's still fame. Should you capitalize on this 'loser' image or try and take a new direction?

It's time to change direction before it's too late. You decide to try and become a pop singer. You've always had quite a good voice.

GO TO 48

Being a famous loser is better than being an unknown. You decide to make a go of it.

GO TO 51

25

Although you still have not met them, you hear that they are considering giving you some of the proceeds of the will. It could solve your dreams in one go. You could be instantly rich and famous.

You ask that any money they were thinking of giving to you goes to a special charity for celebrities who have fallen on hard times.

GO TO 32

Riches and fame sounds too tempting. You travel off to see them and accept the money.

GO TO 33

26

You're at the party and see plenty of famous people and reporters. The problem is that no one is interested in talking to you. You're going to have to do something to get yourself noticed at this party.

Streak in front of the most important guests when they arrive. Running in front of the cameras with no clothes on must get you on the TV news and hopefully some fame.

GO TO 43

Just walk up on stage, grab the microphone and speak to the audience. They'll have to notice you then.

GO TO 44

30

The police and the famous star never catch you. However, it means that you have to keep such a low profile that you cannot even go out with your friends, let alone go to glamorous parties and mingle with the rich and famous. You have failed in your quest.

BAD LUCK!

You have reached the end of the exercise.

27

You've got to be tougher than this to make it in the showbiz world. That was your best opportunity to meet and associate with the stars. You obviously don't have what it takes and should give up now. Your mother-in-law was pleased to see you though.

BAD LUCK!

You have reached the end of the exercise.

31

The newspapers are very impressed with your paparazzi skills and offer you full time work to take 'juicy' pictures of the stars.

You'd rather not be a part of this kind of work. It's not too late to do the decent thing and take the pictures back to the actor.

GO TO 18

Make a career of it. You like photography and it would be one way of hanging out with the stars.

GO TO 45

28

You're sitting at a table and getting a few odd looks from people. Halfway through the show a camera zooms in on you. Apparently the person whose ticket you have has won best new director of a short film. Are you going to go up and accept the award?

You'd better go on stage and get it. The camera is focused on you and the show must go on.

GO TO 41

They'll find out that you're not supposed to be here the moment you set foot on stage. You decide to make a run for the exit!

GO TO 42

32

It's the biggest donation the charity has ever received and they are very grateful to you. You are offered a director's position at the charity as head of fund raising for destitute stars. It would mean ending your pursuit of fame, but you would be involved with people who were once famous.

Take the position, it sounds interesting.

GO TO 52

You want to be with the real stars not the failed ones, so you decline the offer.

GO TO 53

29

You're helping the police with their enquiries and the famous star bitterly regrets ever meeting you. However, you do get written about in the press, as the star tells his nightmare story of how you met in a club. You are actually quite famous for a short time and it cures you of your fascination with celebrities. They're far too much trouble.

WELL DONE!

You have reached the end of the exercise.

33

You become a trusted member of this famous family and are starting to enjoy this new life. However, the family get sued for royalties by another member of the old group. Bankruptcy looks inevitable. You got involved with them for fame and fortune, not this.

Stick with them and try and help the family through the tough times to come.

GO TO 54

You don't want to be bankrupt as well. Time to sneak back to your old safer lifestyle.

GO TO 63

34

Your previous research into the life of this rock star helps you track down their real offspring. They look quite happy in their life, unaware of their real fame. Should you tell them their true background or just leave them alone?

You convince yourself that they would rather not know, and go back to pretending to be that person yourself.
GO TO 35

Tell them. They would surely love to know they are family of the rich and famous.
GO TO 40

38

No matter how nice you are when serving these people in the shop, you never see the slightest bit of friendship. They treat you very badly indeed. You get quite angry and decide that you'd like to dish the dirt on these people after all.

You write the gossip column to get a little bit of revenge.
GO TO 39

35

You go back to your false lifestyle of fame. After some years an investigator finds out that someone else is the real love child and you're a phoney. You're exposed for your actions, all in the pursuit of fame. You become disliked around the world for your manipulating ways and live out a miserable life of shame.

BAD LUCK!

You have reached the end of the exercise.

39

Your gossip column is a big hit in the newspaper. Through your dry cleaning contacts with famous people you're able to tell the public very different details about their lives. To protect your identity you've been writing under a pseudonym, but the newspaper needs you to come out into the open. You're frightened that you'll get harassed by the stars you write about.

Come out into the open, use your own name, and keep writing the column.
GO TO 49

Refuse to reveal your name and keep writing under a false name.
GO TO 50

36

It's such an expensive jacket that you end up working with this star for a long time. You're with them through the good and bad times and end up becoming an indispensable guide and PA to them. This means that you go where they do and become a part of the celebrity circuit. You have made it!

WELL DONE!

You have reached the end of the exercise.

40

You arrange an introduction between the real siblings and sneak quietly away from the family. Properly reunited, the family goes from strength to strength and you just become a memory of someone who helped them all get together. You had your taste of fame and are much happier in your own normal life, now comfortable in the knowledge of your good deed.

WELL DONE!

You have reached the end of the exercise.

37

Your pursuit of celebrity status has cost you everything you own. You're left without any possessions or friends. It was a futile quest to satisfy your ego and it has left you ruined.

BAD LUCK!

You have reached the end of the exercise.

41

You collect the reward on behalf of the director and actually make quite an amusing speech. The event gets reported the next day and you have your name in every newspaper. It is only 15 minutes of fame but it was enough for you. You give up the pursuit of stardom and settle down, happy with your press clippings.

WELL DONE!

You have reached the end of the exercise.

42

You turn and run for the exit, the spotlight following you all the way. The whole experience was terrifying and you don't dare show your face for months in case you're recognized. You're not made for this lifestyle at all and give up the pursuit of fame.

BAD LUCK!

You have reached the end of the exercise.

43

There are a few screams and some shocked faces as you run out naked. You're hauled off to the police station and have to answer questions all night. The next day you watch television, waiting for your grand entrance and expecting the press to be in touch any minute. Unfortunately your face isn't visible at all on film, just your backside. No one will know who it was and you've now got a criminal record too. You have failed.

BAD LUCK!

You have reached the end of the exercise.

44

You arrive on stage and tell a few of your favourite jokes. You don't receive as much as a giggle from the audience before being dragged off by security. However, the event is the highlight of an otherwise dull show. The clip makes very good television and is shown around the world, giving you fame as a comedian who was so bad they were dragged off stage.

WELL DONE!

You have reached the end of the exercise.

45

You need to make a name for yourself in this new job. You have an idea to clean up the image of the paparazzi. You could have good relationships and be friendly with the stars so that they let you take their pictures. Either that or you become the ultimate spying photographer and take shots no one has dared take before.

Clean up the profession and ask permission from the stars first.

GO TO 59

Become even more devious in search of scandalous pictures.

GO TO 60

46

It was a gamble that paid off. Your first fashion show is a huge success and your unique style is a big hit with famous people who need to stand out in a crowd of other celebrities. Your clothes, and you, are seen at all of the top functions and events around the world, and you become a celebrity in your own right.

WELL DONE!

You have reached the end of the exercise.

47

You have a great range of clothing but no way of getting it seen by the right people. You end up having to sell it to a downmarket department store. You become their chief designer but never make it in the celebrity world.

BAD LUCK!

You have reached the end of the exercise.

48

You've made a CD but it's very hard promoting it. You're offered the chance to sing it and represent your country at the Eurovision Song Contest. It will get some air time for your single, but will it compromise your musical integrity?

You decide to do the contest, otherwise no one is ever going to hear your music.

GO TO 55

Doing the contest will tarnish your singing career before it has begun. You decide not to do it.

GO TO 56

49

Once the famous people find out it's you dishing the dirt on them, they become far more interested in you. Rather than hate you for it, they use you to release information about them when they want it to be revealed. You become their trusted media contact, a legendary gossip column writer, and secret friend to the stars. You are a celebrity!

WELL DONE!

You have reached the end of the exercise.

50

You carry on under the false name for a short time. When one of the stars finds out that it's you telling their secrets to the media, they are furious. They organize a boycott of your dry cleaners, which soon puts you out of a job. Without a means of getting material for your column you are also out of a writing job too. You're ruined!

BAD LUCK!

You have reached the end of the exercise.

54

The family lose the legal battle and you all end up bankrupt. When the truth of your background comes out, they don't care, as you stayed with them through the tough times. You had fame and fortune and lost it all, but at least you had fun and made a lot of new friends.

WELL DONE!

You have reached the end of the exercise.

51

It is definitely starting to pay dividends being this famous loser. You are invited to lots of events and have just been offered the chance to star in a film called 'Return of the Geeks', a sequel to the successful film 'Geeks Away', which was about a group of spotty computer programmers who saved the world.

Take the film opportunity and establish yourself as a famous nerd.
GO TO 57

You ask for a 'serious' role in the film to try and create a new image for yourself.
GO TO 58

55

You win the Eurovision song contest and your song goes straight to the top of the charts. You have a successful and satisfying career being the warm-up act for some major bands. You tour with the stars and have a similar life as theirs, but without a lot of the pressures – pure bliss!

WELL DONE!

You have reached the end of the exercise.

52

As the director of fund raising you are in constant contact with the successful celebrities of the moment, and attend many functions to get donations. Congratulations! You have made it into the world of show business and even work for a worthy cause.

WELL DONE!

You have reached the end of the exercise.

56

You don't do the contest, but the auditions have attracted an agent to represent you. They want you to try and appeal to teenagers and young kids, as that's where the real money is. You were hoping to be a more respected artist, but the thought of all that money is tempting.

Time to become a teen sensation. It sounds like fun.
GO TO 61

You attempt to be a more serious musician.
GO TO 62

53

You didn't take the charity position and you have no further contacts with the famous family. You've tried your best but you're at a dead end in your pursuit of becoming a celebrity. You haven't made it.

BAD LUCK!

You have reached the end of the exercise.

57

You play the part of a geek to perfection. You star in two further sequels and become famous for your portrayal of losers. It's the start of a successful acting career, making you famous, wealthy and on the Celebrity A List.

WELL DONE!

You have reached the end of the exercise.

58

You get a serious role, but as the film is all about the geeks, you only get few lines and little exposure. You should have swallowed your pride this time. Your film career ends as quickly as it began.

BAD LUCK!
You have reached the end of the exercise.

59

Boring! The stars demand that all the pictures are carefully set up and controlled. You might as well be working for their fan club. Instead of becoming part of the scene, you are treated like a servant. This was not what you had in mind.

BAD LUCK!
You have reached the end of the exercise.

60

The sordid images of celebrities' true lifestyles is exactly what the public wants. It's a very lucrative business and it keeps you travelling with the stars, even if they're never going to like you.

WELL DONE!
You have reached the end of the exercise.

61

Wow! Who would have thought you could have thousands of young screaming fans? Amazingly, you become a teenage pop idol, and have a string of successful but pretty awful hits. The singing fame only lasts for two years, but your public profile, party invitations, and happiness continue when you get an acting part in a soap opera.

WELL DONE!
You have reached the end of the exercise.

62

Your serious music becomes very popular with the older generation but no one else. It isn't really the type of fame you were looking for.

BAD LUCK!
You have reached the end of the exercise.

63

You pick up your old life, having achieved a certain level of fame. The guilt of what you did to that family is something that you just can't forget. It makes you very unhappy and ashamed of yourself for years to come.

BAD LUCK!
You have reached the end of the exercise.

Unit 4

Song Mary C. Brown and the Hollywood sign

1 Discuss in pairs what you think the Hollywood sign represents.

2 Listen to the song. It is about a Hollywood starlet called Mary Cecilia Brown. What happens to Mary?

3 Read the song. Work in pairs to replace the words in italics with near synonyms from the song (the two corrected words in each verse should rhyme). Listen again and check your answers.

4 The chorus of the song describes the sort of people who are attracted to Hollywood.

Match the words from the song in **A** to the definitions in **B**.

A		B	
1	black-listed	a	used to be stars, but too old now
2	busted	b	not allowed to work because of their political views
3	carhops	c	prostitutes
4	cripples	d	young women who want to be famous
5	flunkies	e	abnormally short people
		f	people who can't walk
6	freaks	g	people who take drugs
7	has-beens	h	people who have an unusual physical appearance
8	junkies	i	people who park cars at big hotels
9	midgets	j	arrested by the police, probably for drug use
10	starlets	k	people who work for and obey more important people, (an insulting word)
11	whores		

5 Discuss the questions in pairs or groups.

  1 How does the singer feel about the death of Mary C. Brown?
  2 What is the message of the song?
  3 What is the tone of the song?
  4 Do you agree with the singer's very negative view of Hollywood and the pursuit of fame?

---

mary c. brown and the hollywood sign

you know the hollywood sign
that stands in the hollywood *mountains*
i don't think the christ of the andes
ever blessed so many *problems*

the hollywood sign seems to smile
like it's constantly saying *smile*
i doubt if the statue of liberty
ever welcomed more *emigrants*

give me your poor, your tired, your pimps
your carhops, your cowboys, your midgets, your chimps
give me your freaks, give me your flunkies
your starlets, your whores
give me your junkies

mary cecilia brown rode to town
on a malibu *coach*
she climbed to the top of the hollywood sign
and with the smallest possible *drama*

she jumped off the letter 'h'
'cause she did not become a *celebrity*
she died in less than a minute and a half
she looked a bit like *marlene dietrich*

sometimes i have this dream
when the time comes for me to *leave*
i will climb that hill and i'll hang myself
from the second or third letter '*w*'

when mary cecilia jumped
she finally made the *success*
her name was in the obituary column
of both the daily *newspapers*

i hope the hollywood sign
cries for the town it *affects*
the lady of lourdes in her grotto
saw fewer cripples and *sticks*

give me your poor, your maladjusted
your sick and your beat
your sad and your busted
give me your has-beens, give me your twisted
your loners, your losers
give me your black-listed

you know the hollywood sign
witness to our *perplexity*
a symbol of dreams
turns out to be a sign of *disappointment*

Unit 4

Celebrity questionnaire

Celebrity

QUESTIONNAIRE

★ Name:

★ Reason for celebrity status:

★ What are you like?

★ What is your best or most famous attribute?

★ What are your hobbies or leisure interests?

★ Where do you live?

★ Who is important to you in your life?

★ What is your greatest fear?

★ What was your big break?

★ Who or what was your inspiration?

★ What are the highlights of your career?

★ What is your most significant achievement?

★ What have you been doing recently?

★ What are your plans for the coming year?

★ How would you like to be remembered?

Unit 5

Song When You Are Old And Grey

1 Listen to a song by Tom Lehrer, an American writer of humorous songs. What is his view of long-term relationships?

2 Work in groups. How many nouns can you remember from the song that ended in *-ility*?

   Read through the song and try to complete the gaps.

3 Listen again and check.

4 Complete the sentences below with some of the *-ility* words from the song.

   a If you feel physically weak, you suffer from
      _____debility_____ .

   b The ability to learn or do things easily is called
      _____ .

   c Becoming forgetful when you're old is a feature of
      _____ .

   d If you can move easily, then you have good
      _____ .

   e A woman's ability to produce babies is called
      _____ .

   f If something causes more problems than it is worth then it
      is a _____ .

   g A man's sexual potency is called _____ .

   h If something is completely hopeless or pointless then it is an
      example of _____ .

   i If you show strong dislike or anger towards something then
      you show _____ .

   j If you can't have children then you suffer from
      _____ .

5 Match the adjectives below with the *-ility* words from the song
   that have a similar root.

   a useful   b agile   c desirable

debility virility liability utility futility facility

When You Are Old And Grey

by Tom Lehrer

Since I still appreciate you,
Let's find love while we may.
Because I know I'll _____ you
When you are old and grey.
So say you love me here and now,
I'll make the most of that.
Say you love and trust me,
For I know you'll _____ me
When you're old and getting _____ .
An awful debility,
A lessened utility,
A loss of m_____ility
Is a strong p_____ility.
In all p_____ility
I'll lose my virility
And you your f_____ility
And d_____ility,
And this liability
Of total s_____ility
Will lead to h_____ility
And a sense of futility,
So let's act with a_____ility
While we still have facility,
For we'll soon reach s_____ility
And lose the a_____ility.
Your teeth will start to go, dear,
Your waist will start to _____ .
In twenty years or so, dear,
I'll wish that you were _____ .
I'll never love you then at all
The way I do today.
So please remember,
When I leave in December,
I told you so in May.

SITUATION 1

You have been to a party with a friend, who is supposed to be driving you home. It is late at night and time to go home, but you think your friend has had too much to drink, even though he / she insists that he / she can drive all right.

What would you do?

SITUATION 2

You are in a hotel lobby. You see someone approaching the door with heavy bags, so you open the door. The person gives you £5, obviously mistaking you for the hotel doorman.

What would you do?

SITUATION 3

You are looking for a house to buy. You find a beautiful one which is really quite cheap. Then you learn that it is supposed to be haunted.

What would you do?

SITUATION 4

Your neighbour, Henry, is having a row with his wife. Henry asks you a favour. 'If my wife asks where I was last night, say I was with you, OK?'

What would you do?

SITUATION 5

You are having a dinner party at your house. A husband and wife that you have invited suddenly begin to have a violent argument.

What would you do?

SITUATION 6

You have booked a much-needed holiday with your family on a remote exotic island. The children are very excited about it. Just before you are about to go, you read in a newspaper that the government of the island have evicted local people from their homes in order to make way for more tourist development.

What would you do?

SITUATION 7

You are at a party. You meet a man / woman who you fall instantly in love with. At the end of the party, the man / woman proposes that you get married immediately.

What would you do?

SITUATION 8

You have invited several people to your house for a meal. One of them, you know, is a strict vegetarian. You prepare some soup, then realize you used a chicken stock cube in its preparation. It is too late to do anything about it.

What would you do?

SITUATION 9

You are in the street. You see a mother beating her four-year-old child.

What would you do?

SITUATION 10

You have been invited to a very posh dinner party. You are eating your meal when you discover a dead beetle in it.

What would you do?

SITUATION 11

You have arranged to meet a friend to go out for the evening. You wait at the pre-arranged spot. He / she finally turns up three-quarters of an hour late.

What would you say?

SITUATION 12

You are in an exotic restaurant. Not knowing what to order, you ask for the same as what someone at the next table is having. It looks delicious. When yours arrives, you ask the waiter what it is. 'Fried worms' comes the answer.

What would you do?

SITUATION 13

You are on a bus. Someone is listening to music on a personal stereo system, and without knowing it, singing out very loud.

What would you do?

SITUATION 14

At a formal social gathering, a friend introduces you to some guests. In the introduction, he / she exaggerates the facts and says many things about you which aren't true, but it sounds very impressive.

What would you do?

SITUATION 15

You have just had a meal in an expensive restaurant. The bill comes, and you realize you have no money and no credit cards on you.

What would you do?

SITUATION 16

You get on a train, anxious to find a seat as you feel weary. There is only one seat free, next to a drunk who is singing and shouting abuse at the other passengers.

What would you do?

SITUATION 21

You are having a short taxi ride. The driver insists on telling you his political views, which are of an extreme nature and totally the opposite to your own.

What would you do?

SITUATION 26

You have invited some friends to your house for a meal. You go to quite a lot of trouble to prepare something special. When the friends arrive, they ask if they could have their meal in front of the television, as their favourite programme is on.

What would you say?

SITUATION 17

You are at an airport. Suddenly a well-dressed stranger approaches you. He / she explains that his / her money has been stolen, and asks to borrow £20 to get home, with a promise of repayment.

What would you do?

SITUATION 22

You arrive home one afternoon, open your front door and come face-to-face with a burglar

What would you do?

SITUATION 27

Your boyfriend / girlfriend / husband / wife has just bought some new clothes, which he / she thinks are wonderful. You think they look ridiculous. You are asked for your opinion.

What would you say?

SITUATION 18

You have been playing roulette at a casino, and have won over £5,000. If you bet it all and win, you will never have to do another day's work in your whole life.

What would you do?

SITUATION 23

A friend of yours has a small baby. You are at her house. She is very busy and asks you to change the baby's nappy. You have never done this before.

What would you do?

SITUATION 28

You are an employer. You recently took on a new employee, who is doing very well. Then you discover that he / she has a criminal record for deceit which wasn't revealed on his / her application for the job.

What would you do?

SITUATION 19

You are going round a supermarket when you see an old man, who is obviously not well off, stealing a tin of peas.

What would you do?

SITUATION 24

You have been standing in a queue, patiently, along with several other people, when an old lady elbows her way in front of you.

What would you do?

SITUATION 29

You are driving at night. It is very cold and wet. Suddenly you see a hitchhiker, looking shabbily-dressed and staggering slightly.

What would you do?

SITUATION 20

You have had a serious row with your boyfriend / girlfriend / husband / wife. It is his / her birthday today.

What would you do?

SITUATION 25

You have fallen out with your neighbour, and are not on speaking terms any more. One day, you are going out when see your neighbour's front door open. You know no-one is in – he / she must have forgotten to close the door.

What would you do?

SITUATION 30

You are at a friend's house. His / her six-year-old son sticks his tongue out at you.

What would you do?

SITUATION 31

Your sixteen-year-old son / daughter has expressed his / her intention to hitchhike around the world next year.

What would you do?

SITUATION 32

You have been invited to a fancy-dress party. You arrive, looking outrageous, to find that it isn't a fancy dress party at all. Every one is very smart and elegant.

What would you do?

SITUATION 33

You are in a restaurant in a non-smoking area. The person at the next table has just lit up a cigarette.

What would you do?

SITUATION 34

You are in a restaurant. You have been kept waiting for some time, when the waiter appears and goes to the table of someone who arrived after you.

What would you do?

SITUATION 35

Your ten-year-old child is being bullied at school.

What would you do?

SITUATION 36

You are just setting down to a long, peaceful train ride with a good book, when a stranger comes up and says, 'Hi! I'm Pat. Mind if I join you?'

What would you do?

SITUATION 37

You have enrolled at a new language school. At the very beginning of the first lesson, your teacher comes in and says, 'I want you all to take off your shoes, lie on the floor, close your eyes and relax.'

What would you do?

SITUATION 38

You enjoy painting as a hobby, but have never been very good at it. You have just finished a landscape when a stranger approaches and says, 'What a beautiful painting! How much do you want for it?'

What would you do?

SITUATION 39

You are offered a prestigious new job with an excellent salary. However, it entails spending six months a year out of the country, away from your family.

What would you do?

SITUATION 40

You open the morning post. The first letter contains an unexpected cheque for £500. The second letter is a charity appeal for a famine that is killing hundreds of people every day.

What would you do?

SITUATION 41

A colleague at work is drinking too much.

What would you do?

SITUATION 42

You go to work wearing brand-new clothes that you are very proud of. Your boss says, 'It's about time you got some new clothes. We need to create a good impression on our customers.'

What would you do?

SITUATION 43

Someone begins telling you a joke that you've heard before.

What would you do?

SITUATION 44

An eighteen-year-old friend of yours wants some advice. 'I am passionately in love. Do you think I should get married?'

What would you say?

SITUATION 45

You are in the street. Some people in front of you are dropping all the litter from their take-away hamburgers.

What would you do?

SITUATION 46

You have been round a wonderful museum. Entrance is free, but on the way out there is a sign asking for voluntary contributions.

What would you do?

SITUATION 47

A five-year-old child asks you, 'Does Father Christmas really exist?'

What would you say?

SITUATION 48

A five-year-old child asks you, 'Where was I ten years ago?'

What would you say?

SITUATION 49

Yesterday evening you ate at a friend's house. During the night you were violently ill. You are sure it was food poisoning and you think it was something you ate at your friend's house.

What would you do?

SITUATION 50

In your attempt to impress a boy / girl who you want to get to know, you have said that you are a very good tennis player, which is not true. He / she later invites you to spend the weekend with some friends. You are over the moon. Then he / she says, 'Bring your tennis racket. They've got a tennis court.'

What would you do?

SITUATION 51

You have played tennis with the same friend many times, and never succeed in beating him / her, much to your frustration. Finally, after a long game, you have match point. Your opponent hits the ball and it lands just on the line. If you call it out, you will win the match.

What would you do?

SITUATION 52

You have just come out of a supermarket. You suddenly realize that by mistake you put into your shopping bag an item to the value of £1.50 whilst going round the shop, and so you weren't charged for it.

What would you do?

SITUATION 53

When your bank statement arrives, you see that you have been credited with an extra £300 that you know is not yours.

What would you do?

SITUATION 54

There is a General Election in your country. One of the candidates is speaking on television about his / her childhood. You in fact went to the same school, and know that a lot of what he / she is saying is a lie.

What would you do?

SITUATION 55

The police are about to tow your car away because it was parked illegally. One of the policemen seems to suggest that if you offered him a bribe of £40, he would let you off.

What would you do?

SITUATION 56

You are desperate for work. You see an advertisement that asks for previous experience that you don't have, but you think you could do the job anyway. If you pretended you had previous experience, you feel pretty sure you would get the job.

What would you do?

SITUATION 57

Your boss praises you for an enterprising idea, and gives you a pay rise. In fact the idea came from your deputy.

What would you do?

SITUATION 58

You are due to sit an important exam. You are waiting in a tutor's office when you happen to see a copy of the exam paper.

What would you do?

SITUATION 59

You see a fight in the street. There is nobody else about.

What would you do?

SITUATION 60

Your boyfriend / girlfriend / husband / wife keeps a diary that you are never allowed to see. Usually it is kept hidden, but one day you find it on the table.

What would you do?

Unit 7

Song Father and Son

1 Why do teenagers often feel misunderstood by their parents and dream of leaving home to start a life of their own?

What advice would you give to a young person feeling this way?

2 Decide if the sentences below are **A:** *The conservative advice of a parent* or **B:** *The radical advice of a friend.* Write **A** or **B**.

> You should settle down and get married. ___
> You only live once. ___
> You've just got to get away and live a little. ___
> Just take it easy – don't rush into things. ___
> You ought to take your time and think things through. ___
> You're vegetating at home – get a life. ___

Which of these pieces of advice would you give to a young person?

3 Listen to the song. What does the father advise? How does the son feel?

4 Work in pairs. Student A should complete verses 1 and 2 in which the father gives advice. Student B should complete verses 3 and 5 in which the son says how he feels.

Listen again. Check your answers and help your partner complete the rest of the song.

5 Look at these phrases from the song. What do you think they mean?

1 *you're still young, that's your fault*
2 *you will still be here tomorrow but your dreams may not*
3 *it's them they know not me*

6 What were you like when you were a teenager? Were you rebellious and eager to escape the restrictions of home? What words of wisdom influenced you at that time? Who did you listen to?

If you're still in your teens, who do you listen to, and what words of wisdom influence you?

7 Imagine that you are the young person in the song, and that you have already run away from home to find a new life. Write a letter to your father explaining why you have left.

Father and Son

1 It's not time to make a change
Just relax, _____
_____ , that's your fault
There's _____ know
Find a girl, settle down
_____, you can marry
Look at me, I am old but I'm happy

2 I was _____ are now
And I know that it's not easy
To _____ you've found
Something's going on
But _____, think a lot
Think of everything you've got
For you _____ tomorrow
But your dreams may not

3 How _____ explain
When I do he _____ again
It's always been the same, _____
From the moment I could talk
I was ordered to listen
Now _____ and I know
That I have to go away
I know I have to go ...

4 *It's not time to make a change*
Just sit down and take it slowly
You're still young that's your fault
There's so much you have to go through
Find a girl, settle down
If you want, you can marry
Look at me, I am old but I'm happy

5 _____ that I've cried
Keeping _____ inside
It's hard, but _____ it
If they were right, I'd agree
But _____ not me
Now there's a way and I know
That I have to go away
I know I have to go ...

listen stay settle go marry away change relax agree explain

HOW TO MAKE A PRESENTATION

How do I start?

- You could introduce your talk or presentation formally.

  Today I'm going to talk about …

  In this presentation, I'd like to tell you a little bit about …

- Alternatively, you could grab your audience's attention by starting with a question or a challenging statement. Use pictures or objects.

  So, how much do you know about _____ ?

  Have you ever asked yourself why … ?

  What I'm going to tell you about today will change the way you think about …

  Pass around the picture/object. What do you think it is?

How do I organize the presentation?

- Make it short. Write down the points you want to make, edit them down to, say, four, then decide which order you are going to make them in.

- Introduce each point with an expression from the list below.

  The first/key thing to say about _____ is …

  The main point to make about _____ is …

  What you really need to know about _____ is …

  Now let's look at …

  Let's turn to/move on to …

  Another interesting thing to say about _____ is …

  Finally, I'd like to say a few words about …

What do I say?

- After introducing the point, add information briefly in two, three, or, at the most, four sentences. Use markers like the ones below to construct long, well-balanced sentences.

  Anyway, … ; Naturally, … ; Of course, …

  Similarly, … ; Surprisingly, … ; Remarkably, …

  Despite, … ; However, … ; Although, … ; Whereas …

  Consequently, … ; In addition, … ; Moreover, … ; Furthermore, …

  Incidentally, … ; By the way, … ; It's worth noting that …

How do I finish?

- Conclude the presentation by briefly summarizing what you have said, or the points you have made. You could end by asking for comments or questions.

  In conclusion, … ; To sum up, …

  So, remember that _____ is all about _____ , _____ , and _____ .

  So, there are three things to remember about _____ …

  Does anybody have any questions?

Unit 9 Verb patterns

Verb + -ing	
admit	
adore	
appreciate	
avoid	
can't help	
can't stand/bear	
consider	
deny	
enjoy	
hate	
finish	
imagine	
involve	
justify	
like	doing
look forward to	coming
love	going
mention	
mind/don't mind	
miss	
practise	
prefer	
resent	
resist	
risk	
spend/waste time	
suggest	
it's (not) worth	
it's no use	
it's no good	
there's no point (in)	

Verb + infinitive	
afford	
agree	
ask	
attempt	
beg	
dare	
decide	
expect	
forget	
help	
hope	
learn	to do
long	to come
manage	to go
need	
offer	
promise	
refuse	
seem	
want	
would like	
would love	
would prefer	
would hate	

Verb + somebody + infinitive		
advise		
allow		
ask		
beg		
cause		
dare		
enable		
encourage		
expect		
forbid		
force		
help		
inspire	me	to do
invite	him	to come
need	them	to go
order	someone	
permit		
persuade		
remind		
teach		
tell		
trust		
want		
warn		
would like		
would love		
would prefer		
would hate		

Verb + infinitive without *to*	
dare	
had better	do
help	come
would rather	go

Verb + somebody + infinitive without *to*		
help	him	do
let	them	come
make	someone	go

Verb + -ing or infinitive (with no change in meaning)	
begin	
continue	doing
love	to do
start	

Verb + -ing or infinitive (with a change in meaning)	
forget	
like	
remember	doing
regret	to do
stop	
try	

Stop and check 1

Avoiding repetition – missing words out

Read the interview with successful businesswoman, Sally Marsden. Complete the interview with the correct auxiliary or modal verb, positive or negative.

Interviewer   Business World once described you as the nation's favourite businesswoman, as (1)_____ many other publications recently. Are you happy with that description?

Sally   Well, yes, I suppose I (2)_____ . Who (3)_____ be? I quite like the description. But even if I (4)_____ , there wouldn't be much I could do about it, anyway.

Interviewer   Many businesswomen claim to suffer from discrimination when it comes to promotion, but you clearly (5)_____ . What do you put your success down to?

Sally   That's the million-dollar question everybody would like to answer, but in truth nobody (6)_____ . If I had a magic answer to give you, I (7)_____ . But I suppose it's really down to very ordinary things like hard work, being in the right place at the right time, taking risks when I (8)_____ , that sort of thing. Most business people won't take risks, but I (9)_____ .

Interviewer   It all started for you with a stroke of luck, didn't it?

Sally   Well, yes. I applied for a job with ITG, and got it when I didn't think I (10)_____ . Then, when most of the senior management left, I was asked whether I wanted to take over the marketing division of the company. Frankly, I (11)_____ , but I told them that I (12)_____ . I'd just had my first baby and I didn't need the extra work, and neither (13)_____ my husband! But we managed, as you always (14)_____ when you really (15)_____ . My work was appreciated, and I was soon promoted to senior executive.

Interviewer   Have you ever considered working in the States?

Sally   Yes, I (16)_____ , and one day I (17)_____ . I was actually offered a senior position four years ago.

Interviewer   (18)_____ you?

Sally   Yes, and I wanted to go, but because of my family, I (19)_____ . But if I were given another chance to go, I (20)_____ .

`20`

Avoiding repetition – reduced infinitives

Complete the sentences with the verb in brackets, and a reduced infinitive where appropriate.

1   He apologizes for offending you, and says that he really _____ (intend).
2   Why didn't you bring me a present back? You _____ (promise).
3   She isn't famous yet, but she _____ (hope) in the future.
4   I think she should emigrate if she really _____ (want).
5   I don't know why I ended the novel in that way. I certainly didn't _____ (plan).

`5`

Correct the mistake

Correct the mistake in each sentence.

1 I've been burning my hand.

   _____

2 What are you thinking of my suggestion?

   _____

3 The project will supervise by Suzanne.

   _____

4 When she was calling round to see me, I was working in the garden.

   _____

5 Happy anniversary! I can't believe you were married for ten years!

   _____

5

Adverbs

Complete the sentences with adverbs. The first letter of each adverb is given.

1 She gazed l_____ at the dress in the window – it was just perfect.

2 The headmaster's speech went on i_____ . Everyone was asleep by the end.

3 What have you been up to l_____ ? I haven't seen you for a while.

4 I'm d_____ worried about Frank. He seems so depressed.

5 If you'd j_____ try to get here on time, I wouldn't get so angry.

6 The priest apologized p_____ for arriving late at the wedding.

7 Take it e_____ ! You'll have a heart attack if you go on like this.

8 I d_____ remember telling you this yesterday.

9 Claire will be s_____ missed, but we wish her all the best in her new job.

10 The film was j_____ as exciting the second time I watched it.

10

Phrasal verbs

Complete the sentences with phrasal verbs. All the missing phrasal verbs contain the particle *up*.

1 Bonnie and Clyde refused to _____ themselves _____ , and were shot by the police.

2 I don't know what the children _____ when we're not here. I hope they aren't causing any trouble.

3 Calm down! You shouldn't _____ yourself _____ into such a state.

4 You'll need to think of an excuse. Just _____ one _____ , she won't know whether it's true or not.

5 Can you _____ me _____ for a night or two? I'll be no trouble.

6 I haven't seen any suitable jobs yet, but I'm sure something will _____ .

7 I didn't expect to _____ so many problems in this research.

8 If the government _____ taxes again, they'll be very unpopular.

9 I didn't finish the test. I only _____ question 16.

10 I can't do any more of this crossword. I think it's time to _____ .

10

TOTAL   50

Stop and check 2

Discourse markers

Read part of an email from a teenager to her friend. Choose the correct discourse marker.

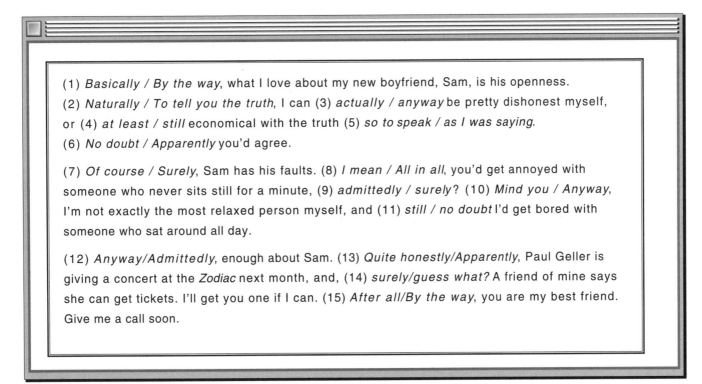

(1) *Basically / By the way*, what I love about my new boyfriend, Sam, is his openness.
(2) *Naturally / To tell you the truth*, I can (3) *actually / anyway* be pretty dishonest myself,
or (4) *at least / still* economical with the truth (5) *so to speak / as I was saying*.
(6) *No doubt / Apparently* you'd agree.

(7) *Of course / Surely*, Sam has his faults. (8) *I mean / All in all*, you'd get annoyed with
someone who never sits still for a minute, (9) *admittedly / surely*? (10) *Mind you / Anyway*,
I'm not exactly the most relaxed person myself, and (11) *still / no doubt* I'd get bored with
someone who sat around all day.

(12) *Anyway/Admittedly*, enough about Sam. (13) *Quite honestly/Apparently*, Paul Geller is
giving a concert at the *Zodiac* next month, and, (14) *surely/guess what?* A friend of mine says
she can get tickets. I'll get you one if I can. (15) *After all/By the way*, you are my best friend.
Give me a call soon.

15

Passive constructions

Rewrite the radio news reports using passive constructions.

1 We've had reports that a leading politician has been arrested.
A leading politician _____ .

2 We think he's a senior government figure.
He _____ .

3 We understand that he is in police custody.
He _____ .

4 There are allegations that he has been taking bribes.
He _____ .

5 It would appear that he's denied all the charges.
He _____ .

10

Adding emphasis

Rewrite the sentences using the ways of adding emphasis.

1 I'm looking forward to the dessert.
It _____ .

2 I'll never trust her again.
Never _____ .

3 I admire the way you stay so calm.
What _____ .

4 I hate the endless adverts.
The thing _____ .

5 You rarely find an honest politician.
Rarely _____ .

5

Tags and replies

Complete the conversation with auxiliary or modal verbs, positive or negative.

Alan You ____*don't*____ go out much, (1)_____ you?

Jim These days I (2)_____ , no. Carolyn (3)_____ , though. She (4)_____ a real socializer, she (5)_____ .

Alan (6)_____ she? I didn't know that.

Jim Well, you (7)_____ , (8)_____ you. You hardly know her.

Alan So she likes going out, (9)_____ she? Tell her to give me a call, (10)_____ you?

> 10

Vocabulary

Write the antonym of these words. The first and last letter is given.

1 real   b_____s
2 admiration c_____t
3 wild   t_____e
4 love   l_____e
5 accidental d_____e

> 5

Nouns from phrasal verbs

Complete the sentences with a noun formed from the verbs and particles in the box.

| build   burst   fall | back   down   out |
| set   take | over   up |

1 She's usually so calm, so her angry _____ really took me by surprise.

2 Losing this contract is a real _____ to our plans to expand this department.

3 Trying to work in Hollywood proved to be his _____ , and his acting career never recovered.

4 The _____ to this premiere has been so massive. I hope the critics won't be disappointed.

5 Halico shares rose sharply after rumours of a foreign _____ bid.

> 5

> TOTAL 50

Stop and check 3

Tense review

Complete the text with verbs from the box in the correct tense, active or passive.

> be (x 3)　believe　borrow　bury　conduct　make　go on　happen　help
> join in　last　meet　sing (x2)　strengthen　take place　visit　wake

The Christmas truce

The war (1) __had been going on__ for only a few months when on Christmas Eve 1914, an extraordinary

event (2)_____ . At midnight the sleeping British (3)_____ by the sound

of carols (4)_____ in the German trenches. They immediately (5)_____

with English carols and soon both sides (6)_____ together. The next morning they all

(7)_____ in no-man's land and in a very short time many friendships

(8)_____ . Not only (9)_____ they _____ to bury each

other's dead, but often German and British soldiers (10)_____ together in the same

grave. Tools (11)_____ also _____ from each other and defences

(12)_____ . There was no fear or suspicion on either side. If there

(13)_____ fear, such a truce (14)_____ never _____ .

Incredibly some friendships (15) _____ a lifetime. Harold Startin, who

(16)_____ dead for many years now, (17)_____ regularly during his life

by his friend Otto from Stuttgart.

Nowadays it (18)_____ generally _____ that such a truce

(19)_____ impossible. Most modern warfare (20)_____ from the air.

☐ 20

Verb patterns

Rewrite the sentences to report what was said.

1　'You really should see a specialist.'
　　My doctor persuaded _____
　　_____ .

2　'Why don't you look for another job?'
　　My best friend suggested _____
　　_____ .

3　'You look awful. Go back to bed.'
　　My mother made _____
　　_____ .

4　'I wasn't even in the shopping centre when the theft took place.'
　　The defendant denied _____
　　_____ .

5　'Life here in Acapulco just doesn't suit me.'
　　Uncle Frank couldn't get used _____
　　_____ .

☐ 5

Modals

Match a sentence in A with a sentence in B that illustrates the meaning of the modal verb.

A	
1	☐ Gary must have worked very hard this term.
2	☐ Gary would have worked very hard this term.
3	☐ Gary can't have worked very hard this term.
4	☐ Gary should have worked very hard this term.
5	☐ Gary might have worked very hard this term.

B	
a	But he didn't. I'm very disappointed with him.
b	He failed all his exams, and had clearly learnt nothing.
c	His grades have improved considerably.
d	On the other hand, perhaps he did very little. It's hard to tell with him.
e	But he didn't get the chance because of personal problems.

5

Tense usage for non-fact

Complete the sentences with the correct form of the verb in brackets.

1 I wish it _____ (be) Friday. It's only Tuesday.
2 If I _____ (know) you were going to arrive so early, I _____ (take) half a day off work.
3 If only we _____ (book) earlier. The flight costs twice as much now.
4 I wish you _____ (not drink) so much when we go out. You get so aggressive.
5 It's time we _____ (get) back to the hotel. We're going to miss dinner.
6 If I _____ (not listen) to your advice then, where _____ I _____ (be) now?
7 Stop acting as if you _____ (be) some sort of celebrity.
8 I'd rather you _____ (not tell) everybody about my problems. Now everyone is talking about me.

10

Metaphors and idioms

Complete the sentences.

1 Don't point the _____ at me! It's not my fault.
2 When they told me I had passed the test, I was over the _____ .
3 I'm really sorry if I've put my _____ in it. I didn't know that was your boss when I said you were looking for another job.
4 My brother just turned up out of the _____ . I hadn't seem him for years.
5 It gradually _____ on me that it was my friend she fancied, not me.

5

Softening the message

Express the following statements in a tactful, polite way. Use the words in brackets.

1 Lend me £100. (possibly)

_____ .

2 You shouldn't tell him. (better)

_____ .

3 Don't wear that dress. (If I … you)

_____ .

4 It won't work. (surprised)

_____ .

5 Samantha is over forty years old. (thought)

_____ .

5

TOTAL 50

Stop and check 4

Linking devices

Complete the text with linking devices – conjunctions, adverbs, infinitives, participles, and relative pronouns.

(1)_____ having a demanding full-time job, Terry Ambler is training hard (2)_____ compete in his second Olympics. (3)_____ the weather, rain or shine, and (4)_____ most of us are still fast asleep, Terry is power-walking the streets of Bristol. (5)_____ he is selected again for the national team, he will be lining up in the 10,000-kilometre walk this summer, (6)_____ completed four years of rigorous training. Terry was disqualified in the preliminary heats of the last games (7)_____ a judges' ruling that he had been running rather than walking.

'(8)_____ I was a kid, I've always wanted to represent my country at sport, and it's this thought (9)_____ drives me on. (10)_____ , I must say that (11)_____ these Olympics are over, I don't think I'll be in any hurry to start training again. It's (12)_____ an exhausting training programme (13)_____ I will need to take a long break before considering future plans.'

In truth, it doesn't really matter (14)_____ he wins or not, (15)_____ Terry will have lived his dream even if he manages to take part in the finals.

| 15 |

Intensifying adverbs

Complete the interview with Terry Ambler using intensifying adverbs from the box. Use each intensifying adverb once only.

| very absolutely deeply strongly bitterly |
| perfectly thoroughly entirely totally sincerely |

Interviewer How is your Olympic training going, Terry?

Terry Well, so far training has been (1)_____ brilliant. I'm in great shape and I (2)_____ hope that my performance will live up to everyone's expectations. I've been (3)_____ dedicated to my training programme for the last eighteen months, and although it's been hard, I can also say that I've (4)_____ enjoyed myself during this period.

Interviewer What do you hope to achieve at the Games?

Terry Well, it's (5)_____ simple – I want to finish the race this time! I (6)_____ disagreed with the judges' decision to disqualify me in the last games, and I found all the media coverage (7)_____ embarrassing. It left me and all my fans feeling (8)_____ disappointed. So, this time, I'll just be (9)_____ pleased to finish. Of course, I would like to finish in the top three, too, but whether that happens depends (10)_____ on me.

| 10 |

Relative pronouns

Complete the sentences with relative pronouns. If no pronoun is necessary, put — . Add commas where necessary.

1 My father _____ died recently was the most amazing man _____ you could ever meet.
2 The time of year _____ I love the most is early Spring.
3 I was very concerned about _____ you said _____ you and your friends had been up to.
4 Jill lives in Brazil _____ the big carnival is held.
5 All the children _____ mums were there enjoyed the concert more.
6 Everyone _____ I asked was full of praise for him.
7 To _____ it may concern.
8 I'm not exactly sure _____ I'm asking you this.
9 I can't stand people _____ are always moaning about everything.
10 The clothes in _____ she was found were not the ones she was wearing when she left home.

10

Participles

Underline the correct participle in each sentence.

1 *Cycled* / *Cycling* home, I crashed straight into a lamp post.
2 I worked all morning in a market *selling* / *sold* shirts.
3 *Brought* / *Bringing* up on a tough housing estate, Gerry Hillman was to go on to great things.
4 I've had a terrible evening, first *losing* / *lost* my bag on the underground, then *missing* / *missed* the last train home.
5 Frankly, *had* / *having* seen it, I would give that film a miss.
6 *Breaking* / *Broken* up the journey by stopping for lunch would be a good plan.
7 *Given* / *Giving* that this was her first attempt, and *known* / *knowing* that she hadn't had any time to rehearse, I think that was a pretty decent performance.
8 I managed to ruin a perfectly good shirt *eating* / *eaten* spaghetti bolognese in a restaurant last night.

10

Vocabulary

Complete the sentences using one word from A and one word from B.

A
cost   foot   mind   safe   takes

B
bill   boggles   earth   sorry   sorts

1 I'm sure you'd like to invite all your friends to the wedding, but who's going to _____ the _____ ?
2 Can you imagine what it must be like having two sets of identical twins? The _____ !
3 You could have the whole house redecorated, but it would _____ the _____ .
4 I know it seems a lot to pay for insurance, but better _____ than _____ .
5 He does seem to have some pretty strange habits, I admit, but remember, it _____ all _____ .

5

TOTAL   50

Progress test 1

1 Avoiding repetition

Complete the sentences with an auxiliary or modal verb, positive or negative.

1 I hope John gets here soon. If he _____ , we'll have to go without him.
2 I thought I'd read the book before but I _____ , so I quite enjoyed it.
3 **A** We're thinking of going to Spain for our holidays.
  B You _____ . It's a beautiful country.
4 **A** Do you think Jack will have got home by now?
  B He _____ , but I doubt it.
5 **A** I'm not sure whether to invite Anna.
  B I _____ . She'll only cause trouble.

☐ 5

2 Adverbs

Underline the correct adverb in each sentence.

1 He's worked very *deliberately* / *conscientiously* all year.
2 I don't know why she always arrives *late* / *lately*.
3 He was *deeply* / *severely* injured in the crash.
4 Both my parents travelled *remotely* / *widely* in Africa.
5 The pop star's arrival is *eagerly* / *highly* awaited.

☐ 5

3 Discourse markers

Complete the sentences with *actually*, *anyway*, *just*, *mind you*, or *naturally*.

1 She seemed very upset, and _____ , I tried to comfort her as much as I could.
2 There's no way she'll listen to you. _____ , what was I talking about? Yes, about the holiday…
3 _____ stop talking and concentrate!
4 She thinks it's one of the best things she's done, but _____ , it's probably one of the worst.
5 He did a good job redecorating the bedroom. _____ , he spent a month doing it.

☐ 5

4 Ways of adding emphasis

Rewrite the sentences to add emphasis. Start each sentence with the word given.

1 I like Bob's big blue eyes.
  What _____ .
2 My father worked very long hours.
  Something _____ .
3 I really hate working late.
  It's _____ .
4 I'll never forget the loyalty you have all shown to me.
  Never _____ .
5 This company must change and move forward.
  What _____ .

☐ 5

5 Passive constructions

Rewrite the sentences, beginning with the words in italics.

1 It is expected that *Brad Fitt and Jemima Aspin* will attend tonight's film première.

  _____ .

2 It is assumed that *all applicants* are over 18.

  _____ .

3 They say *John Lennon* lived here in the early sixties.

  _____ .

4 It is thought that *women today* are smoking more.

  _____ .

5 Many believe that *a number of people* survived the initial impact.

  _____ .

☐ 5

6 Phrasal verbs

Complete the sentences with phrasal verbs.

1 I have nowhere to stay tonight. Can you _____ me _____ ?
2 She's terrible at lying. Her face always _____ her _____ .
3 Nobody can _____ how the prisoners managed to escape from a heavily guarded room.
4 When we were kids, my sister and I didn't _____ each other, but now we're great friends.
5 I've no idea what the answer is. I _____ . Just tell me.

| | 5 |

7 Nouns from phrasal verbs

Complete the sentences with a compound noun formed from the verb given.

1 **break**
The discovery of penicillin was a major _____ in medicine.
2 **slip**
There's been a big _____ in the accounts department. Apparently they've withdrawn money from employees' accounts instead of crediting them.
3 **come**
After ten years without a hit, Rory Flash has made a _____ . His new song is in the charts at number 3.
4 **draw**
Rising crime is the city's biggest _____ and may undermine its bid to host the next Olympics.
5 **show**
They've had a few rows in public, but I think this meeting is going to be the final _____ .

| | 5 |

8 Vocabulary – synonyms and antonyms

Complete the sentences with a synonym of the word in *italics*. The first letter is given.

1 A number of American presidents have been *murdered* while in office. Kennedy was a _____ in 1963.
2 It was very *surprising* to see him turn up for work as usual the next day – in fact it was a _____ .
3 These days we *examine* the behaviour of celebrities in great detail – we s_____ their lives much more than in the past.
4 There was a *sharp* rise in house prices last month. It was a d_____ increase.
5 In Britain, people ask for the *bill* in a restaurant, but in the United States, people ask for the c_____ .
6 My entire family are *skilled* musicians. My sister, is a very a_____ pianist.
7 It's very *important* that this parcel arrives tomorrow – v_____ , in fact, so send it by courier.
8 Most extreme sports are *dangerous* – but then, I like doing r_____ things.

Complete the sentences with an antonym of the word in *italics*. The first letter is given.

9 He thinks that everything he does is really *important*, and everything I do is t_____ .
10 The stock market price rose *sharply*, then began to fall g_____ .
11 I find cooking *relaxing*, but shopping for the ingredients can be s_____ .
12 John is very *modest* about his success, but Joe is really b_____ .
13 The road is *straight* for two miles, then there is a sharp b_____ to the right.
14 The passengers were only *slightly* hurt, but, sadly, the driver was f_____ injured.
15 Sam was Jack's oldest *friend*, but he was also a r_____ for the affections of Rebecca.

| | 15 |

| TOTAL | 50 |

Progress test 2

1 Verb forms

Complete the text with the correct form of the verb in brackets. When there is no verb in brackets, use a suitable modal verb, positive or negative.

Robert Mitchum's childhood

In his later years, Hollywood legend, Robert Mitchum, (1)_____ paint a rosy picture of his childhood, but this idealized picture (2)_____ be further from the truth.

As a skinny, wilful child, he (3)_____ pick fights with kids much older than himself, and nobody (4)_____ make him (5)_____ (attend) school if he didn't feel like (6)_____ (go) . In 1932, at the age of fourteen, young Bob decided (7)_____ (run) away from home. Nobody dared (8)_____ (stop) him from (9)_____ (leave) . He jumped aboard a freight train (10)_____ (head) south, and became a hobo.*

This experience (11)_____ very easily have been the end of Robert Mitchum. A number of his fellow hobos threatened (12)_____ (kill) him. One hobo, in particular, accused him of (13)_____ (steal) some bread from him, and pulled a knife on him. Young Bob managed (14)_____ (escape) , but decided that he had better (15)_____ (keep) his food hidden from then on.

It was these experiences that helped (16)_____ (make) Robert Mitchum the great actor he later became. He (17)_____ have been able to play the violent, menacing roles he did if he hadn't had such a difficult childhood.

'I (18)_____ act,' Mitchum used to enjoy (19)_____ (say) . 'I just play myself. And, by rights, I (20)_____ be dead by now, but it's been a great life.'

*a hobo = an American word for a tramp – a homeless person, travelling in search of work.

20

2 Verb patterns

Correct the sentences.

1 He persuaded to leave.
   _____.

2 They wanted that I tell them a joke.
   _____.

3 Both defendants denied to be there on the day of the crime.
   _____.

4 I would rather to be in here with you.
   _____.

5 Do you mind me open the window?
   _____.

5

3 Intensifying adverbs

Underline the correct adverb.

1 The whole office was *bitterly* / *highly* disappointed when we lost the contract.
2 Thank you for everything. We *completely* / *thoroughly* enjoyed the evening.
3 Do you *seriously* / *perfectly* believe in all that rubbish?
4 In the end, we were *hopelessly* / *deeply* lost, and had to call a taxi.
5 We were all *very* / *utterly* devastated when we heard what had happened.

5

4 Relative clauses

Express the ideas in one sentence, using relative clauses.

1 I have an only daughter. She lives in Edinburgh. She is doing very well at college.
   My _____ .
2 I went to school with Naomi. Her brother is now a senior judge.
   I _____ .
3 I don't understand it. He never seems to make friends at school.
   I _____ .
4 Cornwall is the most beautiful part of Britain. I was brought up there.
   Cornwall _____ .
5 History is becoming increasingly popular. I studied it at university.
   History _____ .

| | 5 |

5 Participles

Rewrite the sentences, starting each sentence with a present or past participle.

1 I work long hours, so I know what it's like to have little or no free time.
   _____ .
2 If you book them in advance, flights abroad can be very cheap.
   _____ .
3 Because I have spent part of my life living on the streets, I understand the problems of homeless people.
   _____ .
4 Carol White's first novel was written in only nine months. It soon became a best-seller.
   _____ .
5 Claire hid all the Christmas presents carefully because she knew her children would try to find them.
   _____ .

| | 5 |

6 Linking

Underline the correct linker.

1 It's easy to install *so that / so long* as you follow the instructions carefully.
2 We'll take this path, *no matter / unless* you have a better idea.
3 Alan got a job in the hospital, *although / despite* he did not really have the right sort of qualifications.
4 *Providing / Supposing* the weather had changed suddenly? You could have been stuck up on the mountain.
5 *So / As* I work at home, I have a lot of control over when and how much I work.

| | 5 |

7 Vocabulary

Rewrite the sentences, replacing the words in *italics* with a word or expression containing the word in brackets.

1 She's very *unreliable*. (count)
   _____ .
2 If you *work harder*, you'll pass the exam. (socks)
   _____ .
3 My father had to *pay* when my brother crashed his car. (foot)
   _____ .
4 John is in *terrible trouble* after sending that email. (deep)
   _____ .
5 Sara was *absolutely delighted* when I called. (moon)
   _____ .

| | 5 |

| TOTAL | 50 |

Answer keys

Unit 1

Song – An Englishman in New York

Note

This song was written by Sting in 1987. It is about Quentin Crisp, an eccentric English homosexual who lived in New York in his later years. Crisp was famous for writing *The Naked Civil Servant*, a novel about living as a homosexual in 1950s London.

Answers

2 *a stranger* = someone you don't know
   an alien worker = in American English, a worker from another country who has permission to work in the USA.
   a foreigner = someone from another country
   an illegal immigrant = someone who has come to live in a country without government permission
   an asylum seeker = somebody living in a country, looking for permission to stay and live in that country
   an outsider = somebody who does not belong to a group
   a misfit = someone who is not accepted by a group
   a refugee = someone who has escaped their country because of war or natural disaster

3 *an alien worker*, (a legal alien), *a foreigner*, (Englishman), and *an outsider* or *a misfit* could be used to describe the person in the song.

   1d, 2b, 3c, 4a, 5e

   The overall message of the song is be yourself, no matter what other people think of you.

Vocabulary and Pronunciation

1 1 work   4 laid
   2 one   5 pear
   3 key   6 meal

2 *propriety* = morally correct behaviour, *proper*
   notoriety = fame for being morally bad, *notorious*
   sobriety = serious behaviour/not being drunk, *sober*
   society / *social*

Tapescript

I don't drink coffee I take tea my dear
I like my toast done on one side
You can hear it in my accent when I talk
I'm an Englishman in New York

See me walking down Fifth Avenue
A walking cane here at my side
I take it everywhere I walk
I'm an Englishman in New York

I'm an alien, I'm a legal alien
I'm an Englishman in New York
I'm an alien, I'm a legal alien
I'm an Englishman in New York

If 'manners maketh man' as someone said
He's the hero of the day
It takes a man to suffer ignorance and
   smile
Be yourself no matter what they say

I'm an alien, I'm a legal alien
I'm an Englishman in New York
I'm an alien, I'm a legal alien
I'm an Englishman in New York

Modesty, propriety can lead to notoriety
You could end up as the only one
Gentleness, sobriety are rare in this
   society
At night a candle's brighter than the sun

Takes more than combat gear to make a
   man
Takes more than a license for a gun
Confront your enemies, avoid them when
   you can
A gentleman will walk but never run

If 'manners maketh man' as someone said
He's the hero of the day
It takes a man to suffer ignorance and
   smile
Be yourself no matter what they say

I'm an alien, I'm a legal alien
I'm an Englishman in New York
I'm an alien, I'm a legal alien
I'm an Englishman in New York

Unit 4

Song – Mary C. Brown and the Hollywood sign

Notes

Mary C. Brown and the Hollywood sign is from *ON MY WAY TO WHERE* by Dory Previn. The story of Mary C. Brown echoes the real-life tragedy of Peg Entwistle. She was a British actress who moved to Hollywood, and committed suicide by jumping from the letter 'H' in the Hollywood sign in 1932, after her acting career appeared to have failed.

You may need to explain the following references:
Malibu bus = Malibu (beach) is a town in California.
Hedy Lamarr = A very beautiful, Austrian-born Hollywood star of the thirties and forties.
Daily trades = trade newspapers – here, newspapers for Hollywood people, advertising jobs in the film industry

Answers

1 It is a symbol of the glamour of the entertainment industry.

2 Mary Cecelia Brown commits suicide by jumping from the 'H' in the Hollywood sign, because she had failed to find fame in Hollywood.

3 See tapescript.

4 1b, 2j, 3i, 4f, 5k, 6h, 7a, 8g, 9e, 10d, 11c

Note

You may wish to point out that many of these words are offensive, politically incorrect, and should not normally be used. *Cripples*, *freaks* and *midgets* are words that would cause offence to many people. *Whore* is also pejorative. The singer is using the words for effect – it helps make the tone of the song very angry and hard-hitting.

5 1 Arguably, the singer feels angry. Mary C. Brown died because she was exploited by Hollywood.

   2 That the pursuit of unrealistic dreams, as symbolised by Hollywood, leads to disillusionment and tragedy.

   3 The tone is bitter and cynical.

   4 Students' own ideas.

Tapescript

you know the hollywood sign
that stands in the hollywood hills
i don't think the christ of the andes
ever blessed so many ills

the hollywood sign seems to smile
like it's constantly saying cheese
i doubt if the statue of liberty
ever welcomed more refugees

give me your poor, your tired, your pimps
your carhops, your cowboys, your
    midgets, your chimps
give me your freaks, give me your flunkies
your starlets, your whores
give me your junkies

mary cecelia brown rode to town
on a malibu bus
she climbed to the top of the hollywood
    sign
and with the smallest possible fuss

she jumped off the letter 'h'
'cause she did not become a star
she died in less than a minute and a half
she looked a bit like hedy lamarr

sometimes i have this dream
when the time comes for me to go
i will climb that hill and i'll hang myself
from the second or third letter 'o'

when mary cecelia jumped
she finally made the grade
her name was in the obituary column
of both the daily trades

i hope the hollywood sign
cries for the town it touches
the lady of lourdes in her grotto
saw fewer cripples and crutches

give me your poor, your maladjusted
your sick and your beat
your sad
and your busted
give me your has-beens, give me your
    twisted
your loners, your losers
give me your black-listed

you know the hollywood sign
witness to our confusion
a symbol of dreams
turns out to be a sign of disillusion

Unit 5
Song – When you are old and grey

Notes

This song presents a cynical, amusing view of love and marriage. Tom Lehrer (1928 –) is a famous American songwriter, well-known for his satirical songs and parodies of other songs. For many years, he also taught mathematics at Harvard University.

1 Tom Lehrer thinks that, although we promise to love each other forever when we are young and beautiful, when we are old and ugly, we will find each other very unloveable. He thinks we should enjoy love now because when we are old we won't love each other anymore.

2 and 3   See tapescript

4 a debility   f liability
   b facility   g virility
   c senility   h futility
   d mobility   i hostility
   e fertility   j sterility

   Point out that in each word the first syllable of -ility is stressed.

   For example, *senílity*.

5 a utility
   b agility
   c desirability

   Other adjectives from the –ility words in the song: *mobile, possible, probable, virile, fertile, liable, sterile, hostile, futile, senile, able.*
   Debility and *facility* don't have adjectives.

Tapescript

Since I still appreciate you,
Let's find love while we may.
Because I know I'll hate you
When you are old and grey.

So say you love me here and now,
I'll make the most of that.
Say you love and trust me,
For I know you'll disgust me
When you're old and getting fat.

An awful debility,
A lessened utility,
A loss of mobility
Is a strong possibility.
In all probability
I'll lose my virility
And you your fertility
And desirability,
And this liability

Of total sterility
Will lead to hostility
And a sense of futility,
So let's act with agility
While we still have facility,
For we'll soon reach senility
And lose the ability.

Your teeth will start to go, dear,
Your waist will start to spread.
In twenty years or so, dear,
I'll wish that you were dead.

I'll never love you then at all
The way I do today.
So please remember,
When I leave in December,
I told you so in May.

Unit 7
Song – Father and Son

Notes

Father and Son was written by Cat Stevens. It was released on his *Tea for the Tillerman* album in 1970.

Answers

2 **A:** *The conservative advice of a parent*: You should settle down and get married, Just take it easy – don't rush into things, You ought to take your time and think things through.
   B: *The radical advice of a friend*: You only live once, You've just got to get away and live a little, You're vegetating at home – get a life.

Vocabulary

settle down = begin to live a quieter life by getting married, buying a house, etc.
You only live once = an expression meaning you only have one life, so live every minute of it.
live a little = enjoy yourself/have a good time
take it easy – don't rush into things = relax – don't make decisions too quickly
think things through = think about your plans carefully, over a period of time
You're vegetating = you're becoming like a vegetable, leading a dull, inactive life
get a life = an expression that means start living/start having fun

3 The father advises his son to take it easy, not rush into a decision to leave, settle down, get married. The son feels that nobody has ever listened to him, he is not prepared to listen to his father now, and he has to go.

4 See tapescript

5 1 The 'fault' is that you are too young to make sensible decisions.
   2 Your dreams may come to nothing in the future, but you will still have to find a way to make a life for yourself.
   3 My parents know what they are like, but they don't know what I am like.

Tapescript

It's not time to make a change
Just relax, take it easy
You're still young, that's your fault
There's so much you have to know
Find a girl, settle down
If you want, you can marry
Look at me, I am old but I'm happy

I was once like you are now
And I know that it's not easy
To be calm when you've found
Something's going on
But take your time, think a lot
Think of everything you've got
For you will still be here tomorrow
But your dreams may not

How can I try to explain
When I do he turns away again
It's always been the same, same old story
From the moment I could talk
I was ordered to listen
Now there's a way and I know
That I have to go away
I know I have to go ...

It's not time to make a change
Just sit down and take it slowly
You're still young that's your fault
There's so much you have to go through
Find a girl, settle down
If you want, you can marry
Look at me, I am old but I'm happy

All the times that I've cried
Keeping all the things I knew inside
It's hard, but it's harder to ignore it
If they were right, I'd agree
But it's them they know not me
Now there's a way and I know
That I have to go away
I know I have to go ...

Stop and check 1

Avoiding repetition – missing words out

1	have	11	didn't
2	am	12	did / would
3	wouldn't	13	did
4	didn't	14	do
5	haven't	15	have to
6	can	16	have
7	would	17	will / hope to
8	have to	18	Were
9	will / do	19	couldn't / didn't
10	would	20	would

Avoiding repetition – reduced infinitives

1 didn't intend to
2 promised to
3 hopes to be
4 wants to
5 plan to

Correct the mistake

1 I've **burnt** ...
2 What **do you think** ...
3 The project **will be supervised** ...
4 When she **called** ...
5 ... you**'ve been married** ...

Adverbs

1 longingly
2 interminably
3 lately
4 deeply / desperately
5 just
6 profusely
7 easy
8 distinctly
9 sorely
10 just

Phrasal verbs

1 give ... up
2 get up to
3 work ... up
4 make ... up
5 put ... up
6 turn up
7 come up against
8 puts up
9 got up to
10 give up

Stop and check 2

Discourse markers

1	Basically	9	surely
2	To tell you the truth	10	Mind you
3	actually	11	no doubt
4	at least	12	Anyway
5	so to speak	13	Apparently
6	No doubt	14	guess what?
7	Of course	15	After all
8	I mean		

Passive constructions

1 A leading politician is reported to have been arrested.
2 He is thought to be a senior government figure.
3 He is understood to be in police custody.
4 He is alleged to have been taking bribes.
5 He would appear to have denied all the charges.

Adding emphasis

1 It's the dessert I'm looking forward to.
2 Never again will I trust her.
3 What I admire is the way you stay so calm.
4 The thing I hate is the endless adverts.
5 Rarely do you find an honest politician.

Tags and replies

1 do
2 don't
3 does
4 's
5 is
6 Is
7 wouldn't
8 would
9 does
10 will / would

Vocabulary

1 bogus
2 contempt
3 tame
4 loathe
5 deliberate

Nouns from phrasal verbs

1 outburst
2 setback
3 downfall
4 build-up
5 takeover

Stop and check 3

Tense review

2 took place
3 were woken
4 being sung
5 joined in
6 were singing
7 met
8 were made
9 did … help
10 were buried
11 were … borrowed
12 were strengthened
13 had been
14 would / could… have happened
15 lasted / were to last
16 has been
17 was visited
18 is … believed
19 would be
20 is conducted

Verb patterns

1 My doctor persuaded me to see a specialist.
2 My best friend suggested (that) I (should) look for another job.
3 My mother made me go back to bed.
4 The defendant denied (even) being in the shopping centre when the theft took place.
5 Uncle Frank couldn't get used to living in Acapulco.

Modals

1 c   2 e   3 b   4 a   5 d

Tense usage for non-fact

1 were / was
2 'd known, 'd have taken
3 'd booked
4 wouldn't drink / didn't drink
5 got
6 hadn't listened, would … be
7 were
8 hadn't told

Metaphors and idioms

1 finger
2 moon
3 foot
4 blue
5 dawned

Softening the message

1 Could you possibly lend me £100?
2 It would be better not to tell him.
3 If I were you, I wouldn't wear that dress.
4 I wouldn't be surprised if it didn't work. / I'd be surprised if it worked.
5 I'd have thought Samantha was over forty years old.

Stop and check 4

Linking devices

1 Despite
2 to
3 Whatever
4 while / when
5 Provided / If
6 having
7 due to / following / after / owing to / as a result of
8 Since
9 that / which
10 However / Nevertheless / All the same / Still
11 when / once
12 such
13 that
14 whether/if
15 as / since / because

Intensifying adverbs

1 absolutely
2 sincerely
3 totally
4 thoroughly
5 perfectly
6 strongly
7 deeply
8 bitterly
9 very
10 entirely

Relative pronouns

1 My father, **who** died recently, was the most amazing man you could ever meet.
2 The time of year I love the most is early Spring.
3 I was very concerned about **what** you said you and your friends had been up to.
4 Jill lives in Brazil, **where** the big carnival is held.
5 All the children **whose** mums were there enjoyed the concert more.
6 Everyone I asked was full of praise for him.
7 To **whom** it may concern.
8 I'm not exactly sure **why** I'm asking you this.
9 I can't stand people **who** are always moaning about everything.
10 The clothes in **which** she was found were not the ones she was wearing when she left home.

Participles

1 Cycling
2 selling
3 Brought
4 losing, missing
5 having
6 Breaking
7 Given, knowing
8 eating

Vocabulary

1 foot … bill
2 mind boggles
3 cost … earth
4 safe … sorry
5 takes … sorts

Progress test 1

1
1 doesn't
2 hadn't
3 must / should
4 might have / may have / could have
5 wouldn't

2
1 conscientiously
2 late
3 severely
4 widely
5 eagerly

3
1 naturally
2 Anyway
3 Just
4 actually
5 Mind you

4
1 What I like about Bob is his big blue eyes.
2 Something my father did was work very long hours.
3 It's working late that I really hate.
4 Never will I forget the loyalty you have all shown to me.
5 What this company must do is change and move forward.

5
1 Brad Fitt and Jemima Aspin are expected to attend tonight's film première.
2 All applicants are assumed to be over 18.
3 John Lennon is said to have lived here in the early sixties.
4 Women today are thought to be smoking more.
5 A number of people are believed to have survived the initial impact.

6
1 put … up
2 gives … away
3 work out
4 get on with
5 give up

7
1 breakthrough
2 slip-up
3 comeback
4 drawback
5 showdown

8
1 assassinated
2 astonishing / amazing / astounding
3 scrutinize
4 dramatic
5 check
6 accomplished
7 vital
8 risky
9 trivial
10 gradually
11 stressful
12 boastful
13 bend
14 fatally
15 rival

Progress test 2

1
1 would
2 couldn't
3 would
4 could
5 attend
6 going
7 to run
8 (to) stop
9 leaving
10 heading
11 might / could
12 to kill
13 stealing
14 to escape
15 keep
16 (to) make
17 wouldn't
18 can't
19 saying
20 should

2
1 He persuaded me / you / him / her / us / them to leave. / He was persuaded to leave.
2 They wanted me to tell them a joke.
3 Both defendants denied being there on the day of the crime.
4 I would rather be in here with you.
5 Do you mind me opening the window? / Do you mind if I open the window?

3
1 bitterly
2 thoroughly
3 seriously
4 hopelessly
5 utterly

4
1 My only daughter, who lives in Edinburgh, is doing very well at college.
2 I went to school with Naomi, whose brother is now a senior judge.
3 I don't understand why he never seems to make friends at school.
4 Cornwall, where I was brought up, is the most beautiful part of Britain.
5 History, which I studied at university, is becoming increasingly popular.

5
1 Working long hours, I know what it's like to have little or no free time.
2 Booked in advance, flights abroad can be very cheap.
3 Having spent part of my life living on the streets, I understand the problems of homeless people.
4 Written in only nine months, Carol White's first novel soon became a best-seller.
5 Knowing her children would try to find them, Claire hid all the Christmas presents carefully.

6
1 so long as
2 unless
3 although
4 Supposing
5 As

7
1 You *can't count on* her.
2 If you *pull your socks up*, you'll pass the exam.
3 My father had to *foot the bill* when my brother crashed his car.
4 John is in *deep water* after sending that email.
5 Sara was *over the moon* when I called.